# THE LEGISLATIVE CONNECTION:
# THE POLITICS OF
# REPRESENTATION IN
# KENYA, KOREA,
# AND TURKEY

Chong Lim Kim

Joel D. Barkan

Ilter Turan

Malcolm E. Jewell

Duke University Press   Durham, North Carolina   1984

*To G. L.*
*Magnanimous colleague,*
*pioneer in comparative legislative research*

Library of Congress Cataloging in Publication Data
Main entry under title:

The Legislative connection.

  Includes bibliographical references and index.
  I. Legislative bodies—Developing countries—Case
studies.  2. Legislative bodies—Kenya.  3. Legislative
bodies—Korea (South)  4. Legislative bodies—Turkey.
I. Kim, Chong Lim.
JF60.L43  1984    328'.3'091724    83-20725
ISBN 0-8223-0534-8

# THE LEGISLATIVE CONNECTION

This book examines the key functions of parliamentary institutions in the representative developing nations of Kenya, Korea, and Turkey. Using a crossnational comparative survey designed on the basis of the differences among the three countries involved, the authors focus on the nature of political representation, the allocative role of parliaments, and the level of support given by the citizens of each nation to their parliamentary institutions.

## PUBLICATIONS OF THE CONSORTIUM
## FOR COMPARATIVE LEGISLATIVE STUDIES

### Lloyd D. Musolf
*General Editor*

G. R. Boynton and Chong Lim Kim, editors, *Legislative Systems in Developing Countries*

Abdo I. Baaklini, *Legislative and Political Development: Lebanon, 1842–1972*

Allan Kornberg and William Mishler, *Influence in Parliament: Canada*

Peter Vanneman, *The Supreme Soviet: Politics and the Legislative Process in the Soviet Political System*

Albert F. Eldridge, editor, *Legislatures in Plural Societies: The Search for Cohesion in National Development*

Michael L. Mezey, *Comparative Legislatures*

John D. Lees and Malcolm Shaw, editors, *Committees in Legislatures: A Comparative Analysis*

Joel Smith and Lloyd D. Musolf, editors, *Legislatures in Development: Dynamics of Change in New and Old States*

Chong Lim Kim, Joel D. Barkan, Ilter Turan, and Malcolm E. Jewell, *The Legislative Connection: The Politics of Representation in Kenya, Korea, and Turkey*

# CONTENTS

# TABLES AND FIGURES

## Tables

**Figures**

# FOREWORD

The study reported here occupies a distinctive place in the development of our ability to amass knowledge about the political world.

Methodologically it represents the latest (but probably not the last) step in a generation-long development of the application of survey research techniques to the study of institutional bodies, and of legislative bodies in particular. At the same time, it draws on knowledge accumulated from similar prior studies and from a wide range of theoretical and methodological literature, especially as concerns problems of conceptual equivalence, to make the data elicited by the surveys relevant to the substantive research concerns. And it casts the comparative net more widely than have any previous studies of similar scope and kind, producing the broadest possible generalizations. In all these respects it constitutes a substantial step down the road of methodological development begun over twenty years ago.

The precursor of this study was, of course, V. O. Key's pioneering examination of politics in the American south, made through interviews with the politicians of the region. Most custodians of the then-prevailing paradigms of political research advised against the study, assuring Key that most prospective respondents would make themselves inaccessible for interviewing, and that the rest would be far less than candid in their responses. That *Southern Politics*, based heavily on numerous such interviews successfully completed by Key and Alexander Heard, made a landmark contribution to our political knowledge did not, however, immediately establish the respectability of this mode of research.[1] Early legislative studies of Vermont legislators by Garceau and Silverman, of United States senators by Donald R. Matthews, and of legislators in four states by Wahlke, Eulau, Buchanan, and Ferguson as well as others, encountered similar warnings while in progress. These warnings were couched partly in terms of fears that higher level public officials might be less accessible than Key's southern politicians, and partly on rejection of the "behavioralist" notion of interviewing to obtain systematic and quantitative data about respondents' attitudes and behavior in the systems where they operated.[2] Later proposals for similar study of European- and Western-style parliaments and politicians—for example, Hunt's concerning French parliamentarians—encountered the objection that systematic interview research might perhaps work with American representatives, whose culture socialized them to accept such procedures, but would surely be rejected by MPs and public officials brought up in cultures where those procedures were supposedly alien.[3] Nevertheless, over the almost thirty years following the earliest interview-based studies of representative bodies, increasing numbers of systems have been subjected to such examination—for example, Argentina, Italy, Austria, Belgium, Finland, France, and Japan, to name the most prominent.[4]

A perhaps surprising feature of the developments sketched above is the relative paucity of genuinely comparative studies, as distinguished from discrete studies of particular systems. For, as students of methodology are repeatedly told, generalizations and cumulation of knowledge are promoted hardly at all by unrelated idiosyncratic case studies, and proportionately little even by series of case studies addressing common questions of theoretical importance. Where the object is generalization about political systems and where the unit of analysis is the political system itself, comparison of at least several systems is essential. Yet the genuinely comparative studies of legislative bodies or of legislators—e.g., Eulau and Prewitt, Putnam—are still far outnumbered by studies of single representative bodies in single political systems.[5]

In addition to the obvious logistical and financial difficulties of mounting such studies across more than one political system, comparative studies have encountered the major obstacle of ensuring conceptual equivalence in the design and analysis of the research. This problem confronts all crosscultural research, but none more squarely than survey-based crosscultural studies, where the problem must be dealt with on at least two levels.

At the lowest level, which might be called empirical conceptual equivalence, the problem is translating words and concepts in one given culture into words and concepts of any other, in use as well as in the grammatical and semantic sense. At a higher level, which might be called analytical conceptual equivalence, the problem involves the researchers' definition and theoretical understanding of the analytic concepts which they themselves relate to observed political behavior, events, and institutions in the culturally diverse systems under study.

The choice of political systems as geographically, historically, and culturally diverse as Kenya, Korea, and Turkey confronted the authors of this study with problems of conceptual equivalence as formidable as any yet tackled in this type of research. Social scientists will find it especially rewarding in reading the chapters that follow to see the forms these problems took in each country, and to see the ways in which the authors have operationalized their key concepts and translated these operationalizations into question-and-response terms in the various survey instruments that have been developed. It is especially in these respects that the present study constitutes a methodological culmination of preceding survey studies of representative bodies.

One other aspect of this study is noteworthy with respect to the study's place in the annals of representation-research development, namely, its generation of systematic data on important classes of political actors in addition to the data generated on the main targets, the legislators themselves. Hunt earlier interviewed political party counterparts of the French MPs questioned in his study.[6] And the path-breaking study of representation by Miller and Stokes utilized survey data from citizens in a sample of U.S. Congressional districts, roll-call records of congressmen and survey-based data about congressmen's policy preferences.[7] Patterson, Hedlund, and Boynton combined the kinds of data used in the Miller-Stokes study with survey data about individuals in selected local political elites in their study of representation in Iowa.[8] In this study the authors go beyond these and earlier analyses of multiple subpopulations by increasing the number of parliamentarians sampled, expanding the scope of constituent-population and local notable samples, and refining the techniques for identifying these samples.

While this glimpse of the study's methodology from a historical perspective may be helpful in providing a framework for better understanding the substantive information presented in the following chapters and may be of interest to specialists in problems of research methodology or in the sociology of social science disciplines, it is, nevertheless, the substance of the subject matter, and not the method of studying it, which will be of primary interest to the nonspecialist reader. Here again, awareness of where this study and its objectives stand in relation to the line of comparative representation studies preceding it should prove helpful.

The earliest of these studies, and many of the later ones, were primarily descriptive mappings of particular portions of hitherto unexplored legislative terrain. Garceau and Silverman, for example, were concerned with pressure groups in the legislative process; Matthews concentrated on senators' conceptions of unwritten rules of the legislative game; Wahlke, Eulau, Buchanan, and Ferguson explored legislators' role orientations in several key dimensions, including those orientations involved in what Matthews had studied under the heading of informal rules.[9] This is not to say that such works were journalistic or historical accounts, but only that their theoretical reach was relatively limited, both in terms of the legislative and representational domain on which they focused and in terms of their attempts to relate findings to broader questions about the wider political system and the place in it of the representational phenomena being researched.

Very few predecessors match the study which follows in ambitiousness of aim, generality of research questions, or clarity with which important theoretical questions are addressed. The most notable exceptions are perhaps Putnam and Eulau and Prewitt.[10] Putnam examined the ideological conceptions of British and Italian MPs in order to study the nature and dynamics of social conflict and operative ideals in democratic systems. Eulau and Prewitt interviewed members of seventy-two city councils in the region around San Francisco Bay, but the theoretical interest of these researchers was not in the councilmen as individuals but in the councils as decision-making bodies and in what might be learned from them concerning the level and resolution of political conflict in representative bodies. (It is worth noting that it is not accidental that these two studies, as noted earlier, were also exceptional in their genuinely comparative research design.)

The selection of the systems to be studied and compared places the present research within the theoretical context of the politics of "developing" societies. "Political development" as such, however, is not the focus of this research. Since "developed" societies are not included among the systems studied, genuine comparative analysis of developmental problems is impossible. Nor were the questions asked of MPs, notables, or constituents designed to elicit data directly bearing on developmental processes. However, that political development is a major, if not the central, theoretical concern is apparent from the fact that the concluding chapter deals with the legislature and political development. The point to note is that the research on representatives and representation was conceived and completed with a concern for the process of political development in mind. Accepting and maintaining this theoretical orientation constitutes a significant step forward in representation research.

But theoretical problems to which the research is explicitly directed are of a different order of abstraction. These problems fall in three general categories, and their treatment, here again, represents in each case a continuation and extension of important lines of investigation begun in predecessor studies. The first category of theoretical problems, discussed in chapters 4, 5, and 6, deals with the nature, function, and dynamics of representation in political systems with elected representative bodies. Discussed under this category are legislative roles (e.g. Wahlke, Eulau, Buchanan, and Ferguson), linkages between representatives and the citizen body in general (e.g. Patterson, Hedlund, and Boynton), and the internal "legislative culture" within which representatives work (e.g. Matthews).[11]

The second theoretical focus is one which has been nominally the concern of much legislative research in the past, but which has rarely benefitted from very careful conceptualization: the policy-decision functions of representative bodies. Here the concern is not merely with the mechanics of the decision process or with explaining why certain decisions were made in certain cases (see chapter 7, e.g.). The authors also discuss how the process of making decisions and the nature of those decisions affect resource allocation for the society. Chapter 8 breaks new ground in dealing with these questions.

The third theoretical target area is one central to the important problem of political stability: public support for the legislature. Since David Easton's explication of the general concept, support for the political system has been a major object of political scientists' attention.[12] Consistent with Easton's formulation of the general concept of "the political system," however, such research has generally focused on attitudes of individuals as members of a mass public toward the system as an entity, or toward analytic components of the system as a whole (community, regime, authorities, policies). The research here, results of which are reported in part IV (chapters 9–11), builds on the important beginnings made by Patterson, Hedlund, and Boynton (1975)[13] and aims at uncovering attitudes and behaviors of the public (both as individuals and as members of various elite segments) toward specifically the representative body and the representatives themselves, ascertaining the dynamics of support for the legislature and its role in the dynamics of support for the political system as a whole.

In summary, then, this book can best be understood in light of its relationship to the generation-long series of comparative representation studies which precede it. An appreciation of the extent to which it constitutes further progress in the methodology of representation research will help the reader understand both the power and the limitations of the data on which the analysis rests, and the extent to which the knowledge it claims to add can be adjudged reliable and valid. Those additions, to repeat, relate mainly to three areas of interest, variously addressed by predecessor studies: the mechanics and dynamics of linkage between the members of the representative body and the body of the citizens they represent, the dynamics of policy determination (at least in its legislative aspects) in a key area (resource allocation), and the dynamics of support for representatives and representative bodies. All three of these topics relate directly to the central concern of the study: the nature of representation in political systems with representative bodies. Beyond these principal concerns, the study seeks to speculate and hypothesize, at least in tentative and general terms, about the implications of the findings for our understanding of still broader, more basic questions, questions having to do with political stability and political development.

Readers can judge for themselves how well the authors have succeeded in amplifying our understanding of such problems as these, as well as how much they add to our understanding of more everyday aspects of politics and government in Kenya, Korea, and Turkey. To make a significant contribution to the present stock of such knowledge is clearly a major accomplishment for any complex research project. But a further test of the success of such an intellectual venture must wait for another thirty years or so: what studies of still more basic importance, based on what still more valid and reliable kinds of data, will stand on the shoulders of this research effort? A familiar Biblical commandment is perhaps appropriate here as a wish for the results of the authors' intellectual labor: "Be ye fruitful and multiply!"

John C. Wahlke

## ACKNOWLEDGMENTS

Any large-scale research project involves a number of persons. The project on which this volume is based is a collaborative effort by a number of scholars in Kenya, Korea, Turkey, and the United States, under the auspices of the Comparative Legislative Research Center at the University of Iowa. Those of us whose names appear on the title page are indebted to a large number of persons and institutions, and it is important that we acknowledge this debt in detail. It is particularly important to note that scholars from a number of nations collaborated in the design and implementation of this study. This volume is only one product of the study, though it is intended to be the most comprehensive, comparative publication. Other monographs and articles have been published and will be published by scholars in all of the countries involved in this research.

Our principal collaborators include John J. Okumu, Director of the Eastern and Southern Africa Management Institute, Arusha, Tanzania; Seong-Tong Pai, Seoul National University; and Ahmet Yücekök, of the University of Ankara. All three of the principal collaborators participated in the design of the study at a conference held at the University of Iowa in June 1973, and all have been intimately involved in carrying out the research. John Okumu shared the responsibility for directing field work in Kenya; his knowledge and cooperation were vital to that project. Seong-Tong Pai shared responsibility for conducting the field work in Korea. Ahmet Yücekök played an essential role in the supervision of the field work and the coding and punching of data in Turkey. The size and complexity of the survey work conducted in the three countries placed a heavy burden on our major collaborators.

A number of other persons and institutions in the three countries contributed to the collection and processing of the data obtained during the course of this project. Leonard Ngugi, clerk to the Kenyan National Assembly, and

J. O. Kimoro, assistant clerk, provided advice, information, and facilities in the parliament building for our interviews. The Department of Political Science of the University of Dar es Salaam and the Institute for Development Studies of the University of Nairobi provided facilities for the directors of the Kenyan field work. The Centre d'Etudes et de Recherches Internationales of the Fondation Nationale des Sciences Politiques provided Joel Barkan with office space and computer facilities in Paris. In Korea, Young W. Kihl of Iowa State University and Byung-Kyu Woo of the Korean National Assembly assisted in directing the field work. In Turkey, Tevfik Cavdar, formerly of the State Institute of Statistics and later the State Planning Organization, helped to prepare the Turkish sample, and the Haydar Furgac Computer Center of the Faculty of Economics at the University of Istanbul provided assistance in data processing. We also wish to express our appreciation to the large number of persons in each country who served as interviewers, and to those who helped with coding and keypunching. The success of the enterprise also depended, of course, on the members of parliament, local leaders, constituents who were willing to be interviewed, and on local officials who facilitated the field work. Without their cooperation, the completion of this research effort would have been impossible.

A number of colleagues at the University of Iowa provided helpful advice in the early stages of the project and participated in the planning conference in 1973 that determined the research design: G. R. Boynton, Gerhard Loewenberg, Samuel C. Patterson, and John C. Wahlke. Several staff members and graduate students at the University of Iowa helped process the data following completion of the field work. Special mention should be made of Susan Cowart and James Gibson.

The project was supported financially by an institutional development (211d) grant awarded to the University of Iowa by the Agency for International Development, and by a grant from the Rockefeller Foundation for aspects of the field research in Kenya. The publication of this volume was also facilitated by a grant to the Consortium of Comparative Legislative Research by the Agency for International Development, and by the Consortium's director, Allan Kornberg. Neither the granting institutions nor the director of the Consortium bear responsibility for the findings and interpretations reported herein.

A special word of thanks is due to our wives, whose patience and encouragement during long periods of field research and writing went beyond the normal call of duty. The crossnational nature of this project required that they travel with us during extended periods and/or remain behind to manage our homes while we were abroad.

This volume is dedicated to Gerhard Loewenberg, director of the Comparative Legislative Research Center at the University of Iowa. As the director of the Center, Jerry Loewenberg handled the administrative chores that made this study possible, but his contribution was far greater than that. He was closely involved in developing the original grant proposal to A.I.D. and in planning the research project. It was he who urged us to undertake, and give priority to, this comparative study rather than concentrate on individual country monographs. Throughout the life of this project, he has provided— as needed—moral support, encouragement, prodding, critical advice, and friendship. Each of the persons named here played a crucial role at some stage in developing and implementing this study. Jerry Loewenberg played the crucial role in assuring that the fruits of the project would include this book.

The writing of this volume has been a collaborative enterprise, with each of us contributing factual information and interpretations to each chapter, and each of us critically reviewing each chapter. Primary responsibility for drafting each part of the book was as follows:

Part I: chapter 1, Barkan; chapter 2, Kim; chapter 3, all authors
Part II: chapters 4 and 5, Barkan; chapter 6, Kim
Part III: Turan
Part IV: Kim and Jewell
Part V: Jewell

The manuscript was read by Lloyd D. Musolf, Peter Merkl, and Richard Fenno, who generously gave their suggestions for improving this book. Mickie Wiegand, administrative secretary of the Center, Sherry Flanagan, and Dorothea Anderson helped type the several drafts of our manuscript.

# Part I

# INTRODUCTION

# Chapter 1

## LEGISLATURES, LEGISLATORS, AND
## POLITICAL DEVELOPMENT

This book seeks to determine the nature and significance of the legislative process in developing countries. As such, it is a volume devoted to the analysis of a phenomenon that is often not a factor in the political life of these societies. When the legislative process *is* a factor, the form it takes, the behavior of the actors involved, and the significance of the process are very different from those found in the industrial democracies of the West. One purpose of this volume, therefore, is to determine why, and in what ways, the legislative process in developing countries differs from that found in industrial societies; why variations exist among the patterns of legislative behavior in different types of developing societies; and why the legislative system has evolved into a component of the political systems in some of these countries, but not in others.

In seeking to determine the nature and significance of the legislative process in developing countries, this volume also attempts to bridge the distance that has emerged during the past two decades between two groups of political scientists: (1) those concerned with problems of political economy and development in Africa, Asia, and Latin America, and (2) those concerned with the function and operation of the major political institutions in the Western industrial democracies. All too often, these two groups of scholars have conducted their respective investigations in isolation from each other, and have neglected each other's work. As a result, students of political development, especially those who have devoted their efforts to the formulation of macrosystemic theories of political change, have rarely given serious consideration to the role and signficance of legislative behavior in the overall process of political development.[1] Conversely, students of legislative behavior, particularly students of legislative institutions in the Western industrial democracies, have rarely conducted their inquiries from a developmental perspective.[2]

This volume seeks to bridge the literatures of these two groups of scholars by examining the parameters of the legislative process in Kenya, Korea, and Turkey from two perspectives rather than one. The first perspective is that which regards the legislative process as a dependent variable—the phenomenon to be explained. This perspective has been the point of departure for most scholarly studies of legislative behavior, and is the point of departure for this study as well. In addition to this long-standing approach to the subject, this volume also considers the legislative process as an independent variable—the process which, at least in part, determines the shape of another phenomenon, in this instance, the systemic process of political change and development as it transpires within three developing countries. By addressing itself to the developmental consequences of the legislative process, this study pursues a line of inquiry which has largely been ignored both by students of the legislative process in the industrial democracies of the West and by students of political change in the context of Third World societies.

This volume falls within what might appropriately be termed the mainstream approach to the developmental process. The authors have largely accepted the conceptualization of political development formulated by the members of the Social Science Research Council (SSRC) Committee on Comparative Politics during the mid-1960s,[3] and later expanded upon by Samuel P. Huntington in his widely read book, *Political Order in Changing Societies*.[4] We refer to this conceptualization of political development as the mainstream approach because it has dominated the literature for almost twenty years.[5] Its basic thesis is that the process of political development consists of five closely related attributes or "subprocesses": (1) Differentiation, the process through which the political institutions of a society become more structurally complex, more specialized, and more autonomous in respect to the functions they perform. (2) Equality, the process through which political rights and obligations are extended to all members of a society over which a given political system asserts its authority, so that all may become full citizens of that system. (3) Participation, the process initiated in response to the extension of political equality, which results in a progressively larger proportion of society's members seeking to determine the content of public policy. (4) Capacity, the increasing ability of a society's political institutions to respond effectively to, "or contain the increase in participatory and distributive demands generated by the imperatives of equality," and the ability "to innovate and to manage continuous change."[6] (5) Institutionalization, the process through which the organizations and procedures for responding to and reconciling competing demands for public policy become valued by those advancing these demands, and by the public at large, to the point that they evolve into lasting mechanisms for resolving political conflict.

The mainstream conceptualization of political development focuses exclusively on those aspects of political change that transpire within the national political system. As such, it stands in sharp contrast to the neo-Marxist or "dependency" model which seeks to explain political and economic change in Third World societies in terms of the unequal economic relationships which exist between those societies and the advanced capitalist countries of the West. Despite the significance of these external relationships to the process of development and underdevelopment, we have pursued our inquiry within the framework of the mainstream approach because the legislative processes in the societies under study are fundamentally internal phenomena not directly impinged upon or determined by the factors of dependency which are the principal concern of those who employ the dependency model. Put differently, the legislative processes in the three countries examined in this study exist in the form they do for reasons other than the degree to which the political economies of these countries exist in a dependent relationship vis-à-vis the center of the international capitalist system. For our purposes, the neo-Marxist or dependency model is simply less relevant to the topic under consideration than the mainstream approach, deficient as the latter might be.[7]

Although we accept the notion that political development is a process which involves the increasing differentiation and capacity of central political institutions and the extension of political rights and obligations to all members of society, it is important to note that political development need not, and often does not, involve the growth of such institutions alone. As will be discussed at length below, political development involves not only the expansion of central political institutions to embrace those residing on the periphery of the political system, but also the reaching upward by those on the periphery and their representatives to link their local institutions with national institutions at the center. Moreover, the extent to which central political institutions become valued by members of the general public is in large part a function of the extent to which linkages are established from the periphery to the center as well as from the center to the periphery. It is in the linkage aspect of the developmental process that the roles played by legislators and the legislative process are most significant in Kenya, Korea, and Turkey.

## THE LEGISLATIVE PROCESS IN
## DEVELOPING COUNTRIES

Legislatures do not exist in roughly half of the developing countries of Africa, Asia, and Latin America, and where they are found their form and significance are quiet different from those in the West. Legislatures in both Western and non-Western countries often appear to have only an insignificant role in the making of public policy. In the industrial democracies of the West, the decline of the legislature as an institution for decisionmaking can be partly explained by the growth of the welfare state and by the prominent role these policies play in world affairs. But these explanations are not relevant in the developing countries where such conditions rarely exist. In the developed countries, legislatures have repeatedly delegated their authority to make public policy to the executive and administrative arms of government as the issues to be decided have become more numerous, pressing, and technically complex.[8] In contrast, legislatures in developing countries have either never exercised a decision-making authority, or have had that authority taken away by an executive seeking to monopolize political power.

The suppression of the legislature by the executive in many less developed countries—whether by a periodic reduction of the legislature's authority to make policy, the intimidation and/or detention of individual parliamentarians, or the suspension or abolition of the institution itself—can often, though not always, be explained in terms of the basic socioeconomic structure of these societies. With few exceptions (of which Korea is one), underdeveloped countries are extremely poor and rural in character. Most inhabitants of the countries reside in the countryside and are engaged in subsistence level farming and/or in the production of nonedible cash crops for export overseas (e.g., cotton, rubber, sisal, tea). This combination has rarely resulted in a significant measure of economic development in the rural areas of the less developed countries. Indeed, during the past decade the level of development in the rural sector in many of these countries has actually declined. In contrast, the rate of economic growth in the urban service and industrial sector in most countries has proceeded at a respectable annual average of 6 to 15 percent. From an economic standpoint, therefore, the rural areas in most developing countries are stagnant, and the disparity between the standard of living in the rural and urban sectors continues to grow.

These conditions often result in a pattern of political conflict that is characterized by intense competition between sectional, or geographical, interests. Sectional interests dominate the politics of most developing countries because the undifferentiated structure of the agrarian economies of these countries rarely gives rise to either a multiplicity of specialized interest groups or to a well-defined and articulated set of class interests. In the absence of such sources of differentiation, which are not tied to any specific locale, people tend to discriminate between one another on the basis of where they live. This is particularly true in peasant societies, where most people are rooted to a specific piece of land on which they depend for their livelihood and through which they relate to their past and obtain a large measure of their identity. Such geographical or spatial distinctions are reinforced and exacerbated when overlaid by distinctions of language, ethnicity, and/or religion. It is for this reason that geographical distinctions are a frequent source of political conflict in agrarian societies which are not divided by language, ethnicity, or religion, and within socially homogeneous areas of societies that are divided by these phenomena.

When the centrality of sectional distinctions is combined with the basic fact that most governments in developing countries have limited resources to dispense, the political process often degenerates into a volatile zero-sum game between competing regional interests none of which is willing to accept defeat. Because the capacity of the state to manage such conflict is limited, and because the state does not have the means to respond adequately to the sectional demands which are the substance of the political process, those who control the state often view political institutions which articulate the demands of regional interests as institutions which must be suppressed.

It is for these reasons that the legislature in many developing countries is so vulnerable to attack. As an institution whose members are selected to represent the residents of a series of discrete geographical units, the legislature is the political institution most likely to define political issues, and policies to resolve those issues, in sectional terms. The legislature is also perceived by executive decisionmakers as a body which lacks the expertise necessary to properly consider complex issues, and as a threat.

The extent to which the pressures of sectional conflict weigh upon the regimes of developing countries varies with the specific conditions in each. Generally speaking, these pressures will be greater where the percentage of the population living in the rural areas is higher, where the extent of land-lessness among peasants is higher, and where the per capita GNP is low. As noted above, sectional conflict is also exacerbated by ethnic and communal distinctions. This is particularly true where a large majority of the population is divided among a small number of large groups, in contrast to a situation where the population is either homogeneous (or nearly homogeneous) in its ethnic composition, or is highly fragmented into a large number of small groups of roughly equal size. Measured by these variables, sectional conflict is a more prominent feature of political life in Kenya than in Korea or Turkey. As discussed in chapter 3, Kenya's level of development is substantially lower than that of Korea or Turkey. Almost 90 percent of Kenya's population lives in the rural areas, compared to just under half of the populations of Korea and Turkey. Kenya is also highly heterogeneous in its ethnic composition, whereas Korea and Turkey are not.

Because the legislature is the institution within which sectional conflict finds its greatest expression, it is not surprising that the Kenyan National Assembly was kept on a short leash by President Jomo Kenyatta during the first fifteen years of Kenya's independence, and that it continues to have little opportunity to determine the content of public policy under Kenyatta's successor, Daniel arap Moi. In contrast, the Turkish National Assembly had a greater impact on the policymaking process prior to the military coup of

September 1980, because sectionalism was no longer the cutting edge of Turkish politics. On the other hand, the Korean National Assembly was a weak institution during the regime of President Park Chung Hee even though the Republic of Korea has not been particularly subject to sectional conflicts inside its borders. However, as discussed in chapter 3, South Korean domestic politics are greatly affected by the Communist threat from North Korea. This external pressure is a factor that overrides those conditions existing within South Korea that would otherwise contribute to the development of an independent legislative institution. As a result, the Korean National Assembly was under constant scrutiny by the government of President Park Chung Hee prior to his assassination in October 1979. Opposition parties were barely allowed to exist and the range of what was regarded as legitimate political discourse was kept purposely narrow.

## THE LINKAGE ROLE OF INDIVIDUAL LEGISLATORS

If the legislature in most developing countries is either not permitted to exist or not permitted to exercise a significant and independent role in the making of public policy, what functions does the legislature perform in these political systems? What are its prospects for survival as an institutionalized part of these political systems? And what, if any, is the significance of these powerless organizations for the developmental process?

To answer these questions, and other questions raised at the beginning of this chapter, we shall depart from what has been the usual approach to the study of legislative institutions. Instead of focusing on the process of collective decision making within the legislature, we are primarily concerned with the activities pursued by individual legislators outside the legislative chamber. We make this shift because of the relatively insignificant role the legislature plays in the policy-making process of these countries. Rather than dwell on the largely symbolic and legitimating functions which transpire within the legislature, in lieu of policy making, we think it more fruitful to concentrate our analysis on the relationship between the legislature and the general public as forged by the activities of individual legislators vis-à-vis their constituents.

In this study, the legislative process is therefore broadly defined to include not only the familiar activities of interest articulation, policy deliberation, and lawmaking, but also those activities through which legislators, by virtue of their formal status as elected members of a national government, contribute to the five principal attributes or subprocesses of political development noted in the first section of this chapter: Differentiation, the spread of political equality and participation, the growth of institutional capacity, and the process through which the organizations and procedures for resolving political conflict become valued and lasting features of the political system. Defined in this manner, the legislative process includes much more than lawmaking. Indeed, in the context of developing countries, lawmaking is an insignificant part of the legislative process.

At this point, the reader might well ask whether what we have defined as components of the legislative process in developing countries can be appropriately labeled as such, or whether many of these activities are of a nonlegislative nature, or only marginally related to the legislative process as traditionally defined. Our response is that we have included within the definition of the legislative process all activities of legislators that constitute a distinctive contribution either to the overall development of the political system or to the development of the legislature as an independent institution within the political system. Whereas the process of political development involves many actors other than legislators, and institutions other than the legislature, one of the guiding hypotheses of this study is that legislators play distinctive and sometimes unique roles in this process. To the extent that they do, it is logically impossible to exclude the activities connected with this role from what is labeled as the "legislative process" in the less developed countries.

What then, is the nature of the roles played by legislators in the subprocesses of political development? As suggested above, the contribution legislators make to the process of political development is to be found in their various activities outside the legislative chamber which affect the legislature's relationship with other central political institutions on the one hand, and with members of society on the other. From a conceptual standpoint, all such activities fall under the general rubric of linkage development—the establishment of networks for communication and the exchange of resources between the core and periphery of the political system.

Concern with the development of political linkages between the core and the periphery of the political system is a recurring theme in the literature on the politics of developing areas.[9] It draws attention to the fact that, among other things, the process of political development in the new states is a spatial phenomenon involving the extension of institutions of a national political system from one or more urban locations into rural hinterlands. Although the integration of the core with the periphery is invariably viewed as principally a "top-down" and "center-out" process, we would submit that it is also a "bottom-up" and "periphery-in" process involving the expansion of local rural political areas to the point where the boundaries between central and local institutions intersect, and those institutions become part of a single political domain.

When political development is so conceived as a dual phenomenon involving the expansion of both the center and the periphery, the importance of the efforts legislators make to create linkages between the center and the periphery becomes clear. Three types of actors contribute to the development of such linkages in new states. By far the most numerous are government civil servants whose mission is to extend the authority of the center into the periphery. The expansion of the center, and the control of the periphery by the center, is also the mission of party cadres in those few developing countries—usually those which have recently experienced wars of national liberation—where viable party organizations function. In contrast, only legislators link the locality on the periphery of the political system to the central political institutions which constitute the system's core. While civil servants and party cadres often function as "feedback" mechanisms to apprise the center of the concerns of those on the periphery, the interests of these cadres, and their source of rewards, remain those of the center. In contrast, legislators are formally charged with representing the interests of the periphery at the center. And, where the electoral process still functions, legislators are held accountable by those who reside on the periphery.

It is from this dual perspective of the process of political development and the importance we attach to the distinctive role legislators play in this process, that we begin our analysis of legislators and political development in Kenya, Korea, and Turkey. We will determine the parameters of the legislators' roles by concentrating our analysis on three basic types of linkage activities: first, those activities concerned with establishing effective representation of the periphery at the center, a condition without which neither political equality nor participation can be achieved; second, those activities which directly and indirectly influence the allocation of resources, and ability of the center to respond to demands for change by interests on the periphery; third, the activities through which legislators contribute to the support or legitimation of the legislature and other central political institutions as valued and independent bodies.

The first of these three basic types of linkage activities is discussed in chapters 4 through 6, following brief presentations of the research design employed for this study, and the historical and political contexts within which our field work was carried out in Kenya, Korea, and Turkey. Chapters 7 and 8 are devoted to an examination of legislators and resource allocation, while chapters 9 through 12 consider legislators and public support. Before proceeding with our discussion, however, let us first define representation, resource allocation, and support, so that the reader may better know the course of analysis to follow.

## THE LEGISLATOR AND POLITICAL REPRESENTATION

In considering how the representational role of the legislator contributes to the development of linkages from the periphery to the center, we focus our attention on those activities by legislators which communicate the opinions and demands of the citizens of a political system to those who have the authority to make public policy. As defined by Hanna Pitkin, representation is that relationship through which "the people of a nation are present in the actions of its government."[10] Being present in the actions of government does not, of course, mean that the people of a nation necessarily participate in such actions, but rather that they are present and that their presence is known by those who do participate. As such, representation is a process comprised of at least two, and perhaps three, distinct components or stages which exist in hierarchical relationships to one another: (1) The process of creating the linkages through which the people of a nation become present in the central institutions of the state, where the decisions which allocate the state's resources are made; (2) the process by which the people of a nation, after achieving entry into the central institutions of the state, make their presence known by articulating their demands to those with the authority and power to make allocative decisions; and (3) the process through which the people of a nation, having established and articulated their presence in central political institutions, then participate in the policy decisions these institutions make.

These three components of the process of representation are manifested in a variety of institutional settings, of which the legislature is but one. Our concern with the way in which the legislators in developing countries create and maintain linkages on behalf of those on the periphery of the political system to the center is therefore a concern with how this small group of political actors engages in the first and second stages of representational behavior. While other types of political actors engage, or claim to engage, in representational behavior, it is our contention that this form of behavior is what usually distinguishes legislators from other participants in the political process who develop linkages between the center and the periphery of these political systems.

## THE LEGISLATOR AND RESOURCE ALLOCATION

Chapters 7 and 8 consider the roles legislators play in the process of re-source allocation—the decisionmaking process which determines the content of public policy. Recognizing that the legislature in most underdeveloped countries is a weak institution that plays only a marginal part in the making of public policy, and consistent with our decision to focus on the activities of individual legislators outside the legislative chamber, instead of on the collective activities within, we shall conceive of resource allocation as a two-stage process. The first is a stage we shall call general resource allocation, the process whereby legislators, acting collectively, produce policy outputs which deal with broad issues of national concern rather than with local interests. The second stage we shall call specific resource allocation, the process whereby the decisions to allocate state resources to a given set of problems are implemented. Allocation is accomplished through bureaucratic and political action involving administrative institutions and personnel on the one hand, and lobbying by individual legislators and the representatives of special interests on the other.

In most developing countries, where sectional conflict frequently permeates the political process, where state resources are limited, and where the level of technical expertise among legislators is low, substantial discretionary authority is granted to administrative decisionmakers on the assumption that they can make specific allocations of scarce resources on both a more rational and less emotive basis than can legislators. While there is much truth to this proposition (indeed, it is one which legislators themselves often believe to be true), the net effect is to provide further impetus for a shift in activity away from the legislature.

The same factors that lead legislators to play representational roles by forging linkages from the periphery to the center, result in their playing allocative roles, which consist mainly of lobbying with civil servants on their constituents' behalf. For example, the location of a new hospital or school, the funding for which has already been provided by an executive-level decision to make expenditures in the general field of health or education, becomes grist for the legislator's mill. Denied significant participation in the process of general resource allocation, legislators turn their attention to the specific questions of how many hospitals or schools are to be built, where, and when. That such considerations of specific resource allocation become the focus of much legislative activity is indicative both of the overall structure of developing political systems, and of the great effort legislators devote to the general task of constituency service. The significance of this pattern will be discussed at length below.

## LEGISLATORS AND SUPPORT

Chapters 9, 10, and 11 consider the broader question of support for the legislature as an institution. As discussed in the first section of this chapter, a central component of political development is the process of institutional differentiation, of which the establishment of an autonomous legislature is part. For legislative institutionalization to occur, the activities of the legislature must be valued both by the legislature's own members and by those external to the organization, in this instance, members of the public, members of locally based elites, and those members of the nation's ruling elite who determine what the substance of legislative activity shall be.

Following Huntington, we therefore view the legislature in most under-developed countries as an organization that is still in the process of becoming an autonomous institution. It is an organization that requires some critical degree of external support if it is to survive and flourish, whether in its present form, or in the more conventional sense of an institution for collective decisionmaking.

The concept of political support was developed by David Easton and has been elaborated by him in a number of his writings. Easton has spoken of support for three political objects or units of analysis: (1) the political community as a whole; (2) the regime and its political institutions; and (3) the authorities, or individual actors who are members of these institutions. He has also distinguished between what he calls specific and diffuse support.[11] Specific support is a short-term phenomenon, based on the "perceived outputs and performance of the political authorities," and it is extended only to the political authorities.[12] Diffuse support is more durable in nature, and is independent of short-run outputs and performance of the political system. It is not only directed to particular political leaders and institutions, but it "is support that underlies the regime as a whole."[13]

We are primarily concerned with the level of diffuse support for the regime and its political institutions, and more specifically for the legislature. Our goal is to assess the long-term prospects for the legislative process in the political systems of the three countries in this study. We have attempted to measure the level of support among members of the public and local elites for the legislative institution, and we have also sought to determine how clearly the legislature is recognized and how accurately it is perceived by the public. We are interested in determining to what extent the level of support to the legislature is based on short-run factors, such as satisfaction with its performance or a favorable image of its members, and to what extent it is based on more enduring factors, such as a belief in the legitimacy and value of the legislative institution. We are also interested in determining how much the activities of individual MPs can contribute to a favorable impression of, and support for, the legislature. Finally, we wish to gain some insight into the relationship between support for the legislature and for the political system as a whole. Though we lack hard evidence on this question, we will speculate about the ways and extent to which support for the legislature may be transformed into support for other institutions and for the regime as a whole.

Our analysis in chapters 9 through 11 begins with an examination of public support for the legislature and proceeds through discussions of public expectations for both individual and collective performance, the extent to which the public and elite groups are aware of the legislature's activities, the levels of public satisfaction with legislative performance, and the variety of factors that affect public and elite salience, satisfaction, and support for the legislature.

## SUMMARY

The discussion which follows examines the significance of the legislative process for what we have termed the mainstream understanding of political development. Our basic hypothesis, and point of departure as we begin our analysis, is that while the legislature is a weak organization in most underdeveloped countries, the legislative process when broadly defined encompasses unique and distinctive activities which are not found elsewhere in the political systems of these countries. Chief among these are activities performed on an individual basis by legislators outside the legislative chamber. Such activities are significant because they establish linkages for communication and exchange between the periphery and center of the political system for the primary purpose of serving the interests of the periphery.

Legislators have the opportunity to play critical roles in the processes of representation, specific resource allocation, and the generation of support for the legislature as a whole. To the extent that they actually do perform these functions, MPs contribute to the development of the political system by raising the level of institutional differentiation, accelerating the spread of political equality, and enhancing the capacity of these systems to respond to the demands made by their citizens.

In the chapters to follow we shall attempt to determine the extent to which these propositions are valid, and the conditions under which they are most likely to occur. Our discussion shall be based on a series of crossnational and intranational comparisons of the relationships between legislators and their constituents in Kenya, Korea, and Turkey in 1973 and 1974. In presenting this data we shall pay particular attention to the determinants of these relationships which are the same in all three political systems. We are as much concerned with "within systems" variations that are replicated in three countries of very different character as we are concerned with "between systems" variations that result from basic differences among the three countries. We hope to present our findings in a manner that draws attention to the factors which shape the legislative process and determine its significance for political development throughout the developing world, not merely in the three countries which have served as the locations for this study.

Before presenting our analysis of the data, it is desirable for the reader to understand the research design for this study and the peculiar conditions which existed in each of the three countries at the time our field work was carried out. It is to a brief, preliminary discussion of these topics that we now turn.

# Chapter 2

## RESEARCH DESIGN AND ORGANIZATION

We seek to determine the role of legislative institutions in three developing societies in three principal activities: representation, resource allocation, and support generation. Our decision to employ a role perspective is based on our research interest in the linkages between the legislative institution and the society in which it exists. More specifically, we are interested in the nature of relationships between the legislature and the larger political system of which it is a part. A role perspective provides a useful vantage point because it forces us to examine the legislature in its interrelationships rather than in isolation.

The role perspective adopted in this study also defines our basic research strategy. It requires us to study not only what the legislature or its individual members do in pursuit of their official duties, but 'also the expectations and actions of other relevant actors involved in the legislative process. Such actors include constituents and local notables in the legislator's district, leaders of his political party, leaders of interest groups, and civil servants. Most previous studies of the legislature focused on the role of the legislature from a single perspective, that of legislators. This is clearly a limited vantage point, because it fails to account for the beliefs and acts of relevant "others" who are integral parts of the legislative process.

The basic approach of our study is a crossnational comparison. We seek to identify similarities and differences in the ways in which the three legislatures and their members perform several key functions. How do the legislatures in each country handle the problem of representation? What roles do they play in allocating scarce governmental resources? How do they contribute to generating public support for the legislative institution itself, and for other government institutions? Our ultimate theoretical objective is, on the basis of our answers to these questions, to formulate crossnationally valid generalizations regarding the role of legislatures. In the pages that follow we discuss the methodological considerations that were particularly important to us when designing this study: (1) the selection of research countries, (2) the collaboratory organization of the study, (3) the samples, (4) the field work and interviews, and (5) the analysis.

## THE SELECTION OF RESEARCH COUNTRIES

Both theoretical and practical considerations have dictated our choice of research countries. Of the theoretical considerations, our foremost concern was the number of the research sites. We needed a broad data base of cross-national sort in order to establish the kind of generalizations that we wanted. However, we could not include as many developing legislatures as might ideally be called for in a truly comparative design because of the limited financial resources and research staff at our disposal. Our methodological dilemma was how to derive crossnationally valid generalizations from the data collected in a small number of countries. As we proceeded, we became convinced that this problem could be resolved by means of a comparative design based on the differences between the countries.

"The most different systems designs," Przeworski and Teune argue, "eliminate factors differentiating social systems by formulating statements that are valid regardless of the systems within which observations are made. As long as these statements continue to be true in all systems, no reference to systemic characteristics is made." They go on to state that the most different systems design, "which seeks maximal heterogeneity in the sample of systems, is based on a belief that in spite of intersystemic differentiation, the populations will differ with regard to only a limited number of variables or relationships."[1] In our three-country comparative study we have adopted the most different systems design.

For the reasons stated above, we tried to build into our research as much country difference as possible. Our three countries—Kenya, Korea, and Turkey—are located at different corners of the developing world: one in Africa, another in East Asia, and still another in the Middle East. Not only are these three countries very different from each other in their culture and history, they also differ in the political milieux in which their legislatures functioned at the time of our field investigations in 1973 and 1974. Indeed, significant differences existed in their legislative histories, their party systems, their electoral systems, and the constitutional powers of their legislatures.

Of the three countries under study, Turkey has the longest history of a legislature in its modern form, with its origin going back to as early as 1876.

Until the Turkish National Assembly was disbanded in September, 1980, by the National Security Council, consisting of military leaders, Turkey experienced a form of parliamentary rule for seventy of the previous seventy-two years. In Korea and Kenya the establishment of a modern legislature came at a much later date. The Korean National Assembly was created in 1947 by the first popular election in the nation's history. The Assembly functioned until May 1980, when it disbanded itself in the aftermath of the assassination of President Park Chung Hee and the assumption of power by Chun Doohwan. The shortest legislative experience examined was Kenya's, where the first popularly elected legislature did not come into existence until 1960. Party systems also varied greatly among our three countries. While Kenya was typical of the weak single-party regimes found in sub-Saharan Africa, Turkey and Korea were good examples of multiparty and a modified two-party systems, respectively.

With respect to electoral systems, there was also wide variation. In Kenya, a single-member district is used, but in both Turkey and Korea, members of parliament were elected from multimember districts.

The Turkish system combined elements of proportional representation and multimember constituency. Boundaries of electoral districts coincided with those of provinces, the basic administrative unit, the appropriate number of legislative seats being allocated to each province on the basis of its population. In each province, political parties offered their lists of candidates during the election, and the number of seats won by each party was determined by the proportion of the popular votes each received.

The multimember districts in Korea were very different. Here, the boundaries of electoral districts were usually not coterminous with the boundaries of administrative units, and often cut across several such units. Two legislative members were elected from each district on the basis of plurality vote. In addition to the MPs elected directly from two-member districts, one-third of the members of the Korean National Assembly were appointed by the president with the approval of the National Conference for Unification. In designing our study we made an effort to ensure as much variation as we could by deliberately selecting countries which were different from each other in the several key political dimensions that we have discussed above.

Considerations of feasibility also influenced our choice of the three countries. From the outset, the objectives of this study required that it be a collaborative effort involving scholars from different countries. We envisioned a study involving a series of large-scale interview surveys of the kind often regarded in developing countries as politically sensitive. The collaboration and participation of local scholars was thus essential for the success of the study. These scholars bring to the project not only expert knowledge of their countries, but also experience and associations critical to carrying out surveys of the mass public and various elite groups. It is also important when conducting research overseas to establish ties with major universities or research institutes. Because the authors of this volume had previously enjoyed particularly close ties to scholars at such institutions in Kenya, Korea, and Turkey, these countries became the primary sites for our study. Following a series of consultations between those of us at Iowa and our colleagues in Kenya, Korea, and Turkey, the three countries were selected as final sites for this study, and an international research team was formed.

## ORGANIZATION AND COLLABORATION

This study was conceived and executed as a collaborative effort between American and non-American scholars. Overseas collaborators were involved at every phase of our research. The formulation of key research problems, the development of survey instruments, and the implementation of field work have all been carried out on a collaborative basis.

This collaboration began in June 1973, with an intensive three-week conference held at the Comparative Legislative Research Center at the University of Iowa. The participants in the conference included the principal collaborators from Kenya, Korea, and Turkey, and the scholars associated with the Center. We discussed the general theoretical orientations for the proposed research, considered the political context specific to each of the research countries, explored the basic concepts underlying the study design, and compiled an inventory of data to be collected. Survey instruments were also agreed upon, as were the general sampling procedures to be employed in administering the survey parts of the study. The decision to use a common set of survey instruments in the three countries raised the important question of equivalence.

Much of the field work was to be conducted in the languages of the countries under study, and involved the task of translating questionnaires that were initially drafted in English. In order to ensure a measure of equivalence and to avoid the slippages that often arise in the process of such translations, our overseas collaborators translated the instruments into their own languages before they left the planning conference, and later made arrangements to check these translations through a back-translation procedure employing others with the relevant native language competence. It was also agreed that the survey instruments developed at this meeting would be pretested in each country and that the results of such pretests would be incorporated into the final form of our survey instruments. In this manner, the basic design and fieldwork procedures of the study were worked out through close collaboration among the members of our research team.

## THE SAMPLES

Parliamentarians are only one group of important actors in the legislative system. Other important groups may include the residents of the constituencies the MPs represent, local notables who are the best informed and most politicized residents in these constituencies, and who often serve as intermediaries between the government and the general population, and higher civil servants who staff key positions in the central government bureaucracy. We chose to concentrate on MPs, local notables, and constituents in this study because they appeared to be the most significant actors shaping legislative politics in Kenya, Korea, and Turkey. We also interviewed civil servants in Korea and Turkey, and will report on the findings of that research elsewhere.[2]

### CONSTITUENCY SAMPLES

Although there were some minor variations in the sampling procedures used in the three countries, the overall strategies were uniform.[3] In each country we selected twelve to fourteen electoral districts on the basis of several important characteristics: the degree of urbanization, the level of industrialization, the degree of party competition, geographical proximity to each nation's capital, and other cultural or ethnic characteristics relevant to each country. We tried to include as many electoral districts as practicable, being mindful of the fact that the districts selected in each country should be reasonably representative of all constituencies. We then proceeded to interview between 150 and 300 adult citizens in each district. Where possible, respondents were randomly selected from the voter registration lists. This procedure produced a sufficient number of cases in each district to analyze the nature of linkages between the constituents and their MPs in matched pairs. We interviewed the following numbers of constituents: 4128 in 14 districts in Kenya, 2276 in 12 districts in Korea, and 2007 in 14 districts in Turkey.

### LOCAL NOTABLE SAMPLES

Interviews with local notables were conducted after the completion of the constituency surveys. Local notables were influential and prestigious persons in their communities. Their prominence was often derived from the formal positions they occupied or from informal status based on wealth, family connections, or age. Local notables were drawn for interview by two different methods. First, we asked the respondents in our constituency survey to nominate those individuals whom they considered to be most respected and influential in their districts. Each respondent was allowed to give up to five such names. A "reputational" method, relying on the frequency of nominations by constituents, thus served as one basis of selecting local notables.

We also identified local notables by using a "positional" method. Under this method, notables were selected primarily because of the formal positions they occupied in the local community. These included local party officials, heads of local administration, chiefs of police, school principals, religious leaders, leaders of mass media, and leaders of important social organizations such as veterans' associations, agricultural cooperatives, etc.

The "reputational" and "positional" methods together yielded some forty to fifty names in each district. We conducted a total of 453 interviews of notables in Kenya, 465 in Korea, and 285 in Turkey.

## PARLIAMENTARIAN SAMPLES

A major focus of our study is the behavior patterns of the legislators themselves, especially their interaction with constituents, local notables in their electoral districts, and senior civil servants in key government agencies. Interviews with members of the parliaments as they existed in the three countries at the time of our field investigations were thus a crucial component of our study.

The three legislatures were markedly different in size. The lower chamber of the Turkish Grand National Assembly had 450 deputies, making it the largest legislature in the three countries. The Kenyan Parliament was the smallest with 170 members, of which 158 were elected popularly and twelve appointed by the President. There were 219 members in the Korean National Assembly at the time of our fieldwork. Two-thirds were elected; the remainder were appointed by the Executive.

When selecting MPs for interview, we began by first trying to interview all the MPs who represented districts where we had conducted surveys of constituents and local notables. We supplemented this sample with additional interviews of as many other MPs as possible. The interviews with the first group of MPs were essential, because we wanted to match their attitudes and behavior with the expectations of their constituents. The MPs included in our second group, those in whose districts we did not conduct mass surveys, were chosen on the basis of several considerations: their party affiliation, the method of their recruitment (elected or appointed), their leadership position (backbencher or frontbencher), the geographic location of their district, and finally, the level of urbanization of their district. We completed a total of twenty-eight MP interviews in Kenya, 119 in Korea, and 104 in Turkey.[4] Although the total number of MP interviews varies a great deal from country to country, we were able to interview most of the MPs who represented districts where we surveyed constituents and local notables, and thus satisfied the essential requirement of our study design.

## FIELDWORK AND INTERVIEWS

Fieldwork was conducted in the three countries in 1973 and 1974.[5] It consisted of gathering three different types of data: interview data from our surveys, aggregate data, and documentary data relating to various aspects of legislative activity. The principal components of our field effort were the interview surveys, which required the most time and energy of our research teams.

### INTERVIEW PROCEDURES

Our principal overseas collaborators served as the fieldwork directors or codirectors in their respective countries. They assembled their country teams, which included other local scholars who joined the project and groups of students who served as interviewers in the field.

The student interviewers were recruited from both undergraduate and graduate departments of political science, sociology, and anthropology at local universities. These students were trained in a series of orientation sessions to be thoroughly familiar with the survey instruments as well as with their roles. In recruiting students, we gave preference to those who had some prior experience in interview surveys. Another consideration was students' familiarity with the region in which we planned to conduct the study. We therefore tried to make use of students from our sampled constituencies. All of this was designed to maximize the rate of successful interviews.

In Kenya, we had to translate our instrument into ten different languages and obtain interviewers fluent in each. Language differences in Korea were not as great, although there were significant differences in regional dialects. Employment of students who spoke the dialect of the survey areas was essential to securing reliable data in Korea. In Turkey all interviews were conducted in standard Turkish.

Once selected and trained, the survey teams were led into electoral districts by the principal field director or other collaborating scholars. All interviews conducted by student assistants were supervised by the field director or collaborating scholar. Field directors also had to explain the purpose of the survey to the community leaders or to the officials in charge of the area as well as obtain their cooperation.

Interviewing elites required a different strategy. We decided against the use of student interviewers for our surveys of MPs and civil servants for several reasons. Elites are busy people and are not likely to grant personal interviews to undergraduates. The chance of obtaining an interview, as well as the reliability of the results are enhanced when interviewer and interviewee are of equal status. When interviewed by a university professor, elites are more likely to reflect seriously about the questions posed. Their answers can be probed more deeply without offending their sense of self-importance. Student interviewers also tend to be too submissive when interviewing elites. All interviews with members of parliament and civil servants were therefore conducted by either the principal fieldwork director or his collaborating scholars.

The interview schedules or instruments used for different sample groups were essentially similar.[6] We employed many identical items in all interviews in order to generate comparable data across nations and across sample groups. It took roughly one-and-one half hours to complete each interview.

## AGGREGATE AND DOCUMENTARY DATA

We recognize the significance of the sociopolitical context in which both the legislature and its members function, and accordingly have made an effort to gather statistical data on both the social and political ecology of each constituency. We collected information on socioeconomic characteristics of electoral districts, including such factors as the degree of urbanization and industrialization, per capita income, and level of education. Also collected were data pertaining to political variables such as election turnout rates, partisan competition, and other relevant political tendencies. We tried to gather public policy data wherever possible, including per capita tax collection, per capita government expenditure, and the like. This kind of aggregate data proved extremely useful in subsequent district-by-district data analysis.

No less important than the socioeconomic characteristics of the districts are the structural characteristics of the legislature itself. We have gathered, from published documents as well as from official reports, information on procedural rules governing legislative behavior, committee organization and composition, leadership patterns, staff service and organization, the contents and origins of legislative bills, the verbatim record of debates, and biographical backgrounds of all MPs. This kind of data has helped us understand the institutional context in which MPs perform their duties.

Before creating our data files in their final form, we also crosschecked selected characteristics of our samples, especially of the constituency samples, against the aggregate data that we had collected. In the Turkish constituency data, we oversampled the urban population as a result of the different sampling procedure followed in Turkish cities. We weighted the Turkish sample to conform to the actual distribution of the population between urban and rural areas as reported in the 1970 census.

Altogether our fieldwork in the three countries yielded twelve different data files: three constituency files, three local notable files, three MP files, two higher civil servant files, and one professional staff file, the data for which were collected only in Korea. These files provide our primary source of data analysis in this study. Given the theoretical concerns of this study, the reader should also note that no attempt has been made to update the data base to account for the changes in regime that have occurred in Korea and Turkey after the surveys described above were completed. Historical events relevant to our interpretations of the survey data are, however, considered up through 1982.

*Chapter 3*

# THE NATIONAL SETTINGS

The purpose of this chapter is to provide the reader with a brief background of the political history of Kenya, Korea, and Turkey. Emphasis is on the circumstances of national independence, the geographic and socio-economic characteristics which have had a bearing on political life, the development of the political system, and the evolution and current status of the legislature in each country. The discussion which follows is but an overview of these subjects, but one which the reader who is unfamiliar with one or more of the three countries will find useful as a prelude to an examination of how each nation's legislative process works.

## KENYA

**POLITICAL SETTING**

Kenya achieved its independence from Britain in 1963 after a period of seventy years of colonial rule. The transfer of power was hastened by the Mau Mau nationalist insurgency in the early 1950s, and was accomplished through a series of elections held between 1958 and 1963, through which the numbers of Africans elected to the Legislative Council was repeatedly increased until they constituted a preponderant majority of the legislature.

This process, which Britain attempted to replicate in virtually all of her colonies during the 1950s and early 1960s, was one through which local political leaders were to be trained and gain experience in the workings and folkways of parliamentary government. What was at stake was not the mere transfer of the power to govern, but the transfer of British political institutions, which were regarded as both the cornerstones of democracy and the sine qua non of political development in those territories which had been under British rule.

Kenya was granted independence under a constitution which called for a set of institutions that closely resembled those at Westminster. These included a bicameral parliament, whose members were elected from single-member constituencies; a cabinet form of government composed of senior members of the majority party in the lower house of parliament and led by the party leader; a loyal opposition and shadow government; a politically neutral civil service which would loyally serve whatever party controlled the cabinet; and an independent judiciary. The constitution also provided for a regional or federal form of government through which power was to be shared between the national government and a series of regional entities having their own civil service and controlled by their own local assemblies. This departure from the Westminster model was written into the constitution at the insistence of the Kenya African Democratic Union, the opposition party at the time the constitution was drawn up, a party which drew most of its support from Kenya's smaller tribes on the Indian Ocean coast, in the Rift Valley, and in the far west.

As is the case elsewhere in Africa, the transfer of British political institutions to Kenya has not been complete, primarily because the structure of politics in a plural and agrarian society such as Kenya is very different from that in a highly industrialized society such as the United Kingdom. The formation of political parties in Kenya, for example, did not take place as an expression of conflicting economic interests based on occupation or class, but as an expression of conflicting sectional interests based on tribe. The ethnic basis of Kenyan parties has also been particularly pronounced because of the way the British phased electoral politics into the country during the 1950s.

Following the declaration of the Mau Mau state of emergency in 1953, the Kenyan African Union (KAU) led by Jomo Kenyatta was banned and Africans were not permitted to organize parties on a nationwide basis until 1960. Prominent African leaders with a nationwide following, such as Kenyatta, were also jailed. Thus in 1957 and 1958, when Africans were elected to the Legislative Council for the first time, parties were only permitted at the district or local level, to conform to the new legislative districts which were created for these elections. As these constituencies were coterminous with local administrative boundaries, which were in turn coterminous with ethnic boundaries, the local parties which formed were almost invariably homogeneous in the ethnicity of their members. As such, the parties were rarely organizations which espoused a particular set of governmental programs, but were, rather, ethnic political machines created to secure the election of a particular individual as representative of the ethnic group.

The result was that when nationwide party organizations were finally legalized in 1960 as a prelude to the elections for the first African-controlled parliament in 1961, the parties which formed were little more than coalitions of the local machines that had emerged in the preceding three years. One coalition, the Kenya African National Union (KANU), was primarily an alliance of the political leaders of three of Kenya's four largest tribes—the Kikuyu, the Luo, and the Kamba, which respectively accounted for approximately twenty-one, eighteen, and twelve percent of the population. The alliance also included the Embu and Meru which together comprise only six percent of the population, but whose peoples are linguistically and culturally related to the Kikuyu. KANU claimed to be the legitimate heir of KAU, and within a short time was able to draw on the political base of its predecessor.

The other coalition was the Kenya African Democratic Union (KADU), which was basically a melange of all other ethnic groups in the country. One of these, the Luhya in the west, was numerically strong but historically divided among several subgroups. Compared to KANU, KADU's support was scattered. Its leadership was inexperienced in comparison to that of KANU, which had long been involved in nationalist politics.

Ideologically, KANU and KADU were similar in that they both were nationalist organizations which demanded Kenya's independence, and both accepted the capitalist economy implanted in Kenya during the period of colonial rule. Both (especially KANU) wanted the return of European-owned land, but both were prepared to permit the continued residence in Kenya of the white settler community if they chose to stay.

Indeed, the only major difference between the two parties was that KANU insisted on Kenyatta's early release from detention while KADU did not. KANU also preferred a unitary form of government, while KADU favored a federal form designed to protect the interests of the smaller tribes. Were it not for the British, in fact, who believed that a multiparty system was essential for the successful transfer of British political institutions, and for the settlers who feared that KANU and Kenyatta would nationalize their land, KADU would never have come into existence.

Of the two coalitions, KANU was the first to organize, in May 1960. The organizational conference was attended by all of Kenya's ethnic bosses, and it was only after the leaders of smaller tribes failed to obtain positions of leadership in KANU that they formed a rival party.

Given the distinctions between the two parties, or lack of them, it is not surprising that once Kenya became independent under a KANU government, members of KADU began to desert the opposition benches in parliament for the benches of the majority party. The prime task of an MP in the new system was not to follow his party's program (for in most cases there was no program), but rather to build a personal following and obtain resources for his district. Opposition MPs were at a decided disadvantage in pursuing these goals, and one by one they were lured across the parliamentary aisle and into the KANU fold by promises of rewards such as resources and appointments to junior cabinet posts and boards of government regulatory agencies.

KADU's power in the House of Representatives was steadily eroded, as it was at the regional level where Kenyatta's government employed every method of delay at its disposal to forstall the implementation of the regional plan.

By November 1964, KANU controlled sufficient majorities in both houses of the legislature to pass several constitutional amendments which provided for the dissolution of the regional form of government and the merging of the two chambers of parliament into a unicameral body. The latter was accomplished by providing each representative and senator with a seat in the new 170-seat National Assembly. The constitution was also amended to provide for a republican form of government with a president (Kenyatta) and a vice-president, both of whom had to be elected members of the National Assembly. All of these changes went into effect on the first anniversary of Kenya's independence on 12 December 1964. Except for minor changes, the constitution has remained fundamentally the same ever since.

Accompanying the constitutional changes of 1964 was the voluntary dissolution of KADU "in the interests of national unity." In fact, the dissolution occurred because the party became an irrelevancy after a majority of KADU representatives joined the ranks of KANU. With the exception of a three-year period between 1966 and 1969, Kenya was a de facto one-party state from 1964 until 1982 when opposition parties were formally banned by law.

For the better part of Kenya's independence, therefore, Kenyan politics have been dominated by one party, KANU. It is more accurate, however, to describe Kenya in terms of its being a "no-party state," because the ruling party has remained a loose coalition of local political bosses and their personal machines, and has virtually no organization worthy of the name. Party meetings, especially at the district branch level, are rarely, if ever held. The party's finances are nil. In parliament party discipline does not exist; the main line of cleavage is between the members of the front bench and the backbenchers who frequently vote against motions brought by the leaders of their party.

As in several other African states, Kenya has regularly held parliamentary elections within a single party framework, but here again the framework is relatively loose. Whereas in Tanzania all candidates must be screened by the party's national executive and committed to the party's goals, and the number of candidates per constituency is limited to two, in Kenya there are no such constraints. Parliamentary elections, which were held in Kenya in 1969, 1974, and 1979, resemble primary elections in the southern United States, where upwards of a half dozen or more candidates contest a single seat on a strictly individual basis.

In such a system, the winners are usually those who command significant patronage and resources which they have committed to constituency service on a regular basis.[1] Thus, the main mechanism of control available to the party leader is his manipulation of the flow of patronage. Kenyatta was a master at this, and was able to construct an elaborate network of political clients through which he maintained the loyalty of subordinates at the regional, national, and grass roots levels of the political system. It is mainly for this reason that he was content to let KANU fall into disuse rather than expend his energy attempting to wield its diverse, and at times unruly, factions into a cohesive force.[2]

Given the weakness of KANU and Kenyatta's penchant for controlling the political process through clientelist means, the day-to-day governance of Kenya has largely been carried out by the civil service, especially the Provincial Administration. A creation of the British, the Provincial Administration is the main mechanism of state control and state presence in the countryside. For 90 percent of the population, it is the only government. It consists of eight provincial commissioners (PCs) and their staffs, who are the supreme state authorities in their respective regions. The role of the PCS is probably most analogous to that of the French prefect. They are assisted by a group of district commissioners (DCs) who play a similar role in each of Kenya's forty-one administrative districts. The DCs and their immediate staffs are in turn assisted by a vast network of government chiefs who are their agents at the location and sublocation levels of administration. In contrast to the PCs, DCs, and their staffs, who are now men wi⁺ college degrees and who are posted to areas outside of those in which they were raised, the chiefs are usually men with no more than secondary education and are long-term residents of the areas in which they work.

Under Kenyatta the Kenyan system thus became progressively decentralized in respect to activities which were regarded as purely political, or representational, while they became increasingly centralized in respect to activities which were viewed as administrative in nature. Because the line between these two spheres was often blurred, it was inevitable that conflicts would occur between political leaders, especially MPs, and senior members of the Provincial Administration. Since both regarded Kenyatta as "the father of the nation" and were dependent on his patronage, Kenyatta was able to resolve these conflicts, usually to the disadvantage of the MPs. As Kenya's first president, Kenyatta was able to govern Kenya in a manner which led some observers to refer to him as "the last of the colonial governors."

On 21 August 1978 Jomo Kenyatta died, and with his passing Kenya entered a new phase of its history. Kenyatta was succeeded by Kenya's Vice President Daniel arap Moi under a provision of the constitution. A non-Kikuyu, and a one-time leader of KADU, Moi had served as vice-president for twelve years. The new president attempted to rule Kenya in much the same manner as had Kenyatta, the major difference being an attempt at increasing administrative control by deemphasizing the role of the provincial commissioners and relying more on the senior administrator at the district level, the DC.

Moi has also stated that the organization of KANU needs to be revitalized. Elections for party offices were held in 1979 for the first time in almost a decade, but whether the party will become a significant factor in Kenyan politics remains to be seen.

Moi's ability to manipulate other political leaders through the control of patronage is also somewhat less than Kenyatta's. In addition to being a non-Kikuyu, the new president is not regarded with the sense of awe that was accorded his predecessor. He is also of the same generation as other leading political personalities. By necessity, his rule has been of a more collective nature than that of Kenyatta, one in which both KANU and the National Assembly play a greater role.

## GEOGRAPHY AND SOCIOECONOMIC FACTORS

Of the three countries considered in this study, Kenya is the most agrarian, and the least urbanized and economically developed. With a per capita income of $220 per year, her population is also the poorest. Kenya's land area is 219,788 square miles, about the same as that of France. In 1980, Kenya's population was 15.6 million. However, Kenya's annual rate of population growth, estimated to be between 3.9 and 4.1 percent, is the highest in the world, and poses serious problems for the years ahead. Half of the country's population is under fifteen years of age. Ninety percent reside in the countryside where they engage in small-holder agriculture, or agriculture-related activities such as petty trade.

Kenya's topography and climate do not conform to the stereotypes of tropical Africa, but rather to those of southern California and neighboring areas of the southwestern United States. Except for a strip of land roughly ten miles wide along the Indian Ocean coast, Kenya has no jungle. Most of the country is semidesert which receives less than twenty inches of rainfall per year. A plain of scrub and dry grassland stretches westward for 300 miles from the coastal strip to Nairobi where it reaches an altitude of 5,000 feet.

The area immediately west and north of Nairobi consists of highlands, some of which reach an altitude of more than 8,000 feet. This area is the home of the Kikuyu, Kenya's largest ethnic group. It runs approximately 100 miles from north to south, and is thirty miles wide. The highlands are bounded on the north by Mount Kenya and the Abaderes Mountains (which are heavily forested and which were the sanctuaries for the Land Freedom Army during the Mau Mau Emergency), and on the south by the Masai plains. On the west lies the Rift Valley, a geological fault thirty miles wide which bisects Kenya from north to south and which stretches across eastern Africa from northern Ethiopia to Zambia.

A second major highland area, and the primary site of European settlement, is located to the west of the Rift Valley. The extreme west of the country consists of well-watered lowlands around Lake Victoria and Mount Elgon to the north. This area is one of the most densely populated in the country. The northern half of Kenya, like the eastern half, is semi-desert.

Kenya's population is 90 percent rural, but occupies only about 11 percent of the country's territory. Less than 2.8 percent of the country's land is arable or well watered. Another 7 to 8 percent is classified as "good" by the Kenyan government, meaning that it receives sufficient intermittent rainfall to sustain peasant agriculture. The net result is that there is only a combined average of 0.5 hectares of arable and good land per person, an amount which is steadily declining as a result of rapid population growth. Moreover, because farmland is distributed unequally, more than a fifth of the rural households in Kenya are landless.

Despite population pressure on the land, and despite the fact that Kenya possesses no mineral wealth to finance her development, the Kenyan economy is one of the healthiest in Africa, and achieved impressive rates of growth in some of its sectors after independence until 1978. Between 1964 and 1977 Kenya's gross domestic product rose at an average annual rate of 6 percent at constant prices. As in most developing countries, the highest rates have been in the manufacturing sector where the average annual growth rate has been 9 percent.

Of greater significance, however, is the commercial agricultural sector where the rate of growth during the nineteen seventies was 5.4 percent. Kenya is the leading African producer of both coffee and tea, which rank first and third as earners of foreign exchange. Unlike most African countries, Kenya is also virtually self-sufficient in food, and in years of high rainfall is an exporter of food to neighboring countries. In years of severe drought, however, such as 1980, Kenya must import cereals to meet the needs of her people.

Only in the subsistence sector, where the average annual rate of growth between 1964 and 1976 was 3.14 percent, has Kenya's economic growth not kept pace with her increase in population. The marginal rates of growth in this sector, which are declining, are partly a function of the increasing population pressure on the land. More than a quarter of the population is still engaged in the subsistence sector, which is now the weak link in the Kenyan economy. The subsistence sector generates most of Kenya's unemployed, of whom there are 350,000 new members each year.

The future of Kenya's economy thus lies in the continued expansion of manufacturing and commercial agriculture as well as in the country's service sector with its important tourist industry. Tourism is presently Kenya's second greatest earner of foreign exchange, a situation which permitted Keyna to maintain a relatively even balance of payments until 1979 despite habitual deficits in her balance of trade. The rate of expansion in tourism, however, has declined since the late 1970s as the cost of air travel to Kenya has risen sharply, a result of the increases in world fuel prices.

Kenya's opportunities for rapidly expanding her manufacturing sector are also limited both by her small internal market and by unstable and deteriorating economic conditions in neighboring countries. Finally, the high cost of petroleum, which now accounts for 30 percent of Kenya's imports, poses serious problems for Kenyan balance of payments. The fall in the world prices of coffee and tea which commenced in 1979 and accelerated in 1980 has compounded this problem. Although generally regarded as a success compared to other African countries, Kenya's fragile economy remains vulnerable to weather and other external factors it cannot control.

## THE LEGISLATURE TODAY

The present form of the Kenyan National Assembly dates from the constitution of 1964 which merged the two houses of the legislature established before independence. The Assembly which resulted consists of 170 members, of whom 158 are elected from single-member constituencies, and twelve are nominated by the president. Of the twelve, one has always been Kenya's attorney general.

The rules and procedures of the National Assembly are virtually identical to those of the British Parliament, and are set forth in the Assembly's Standing Orders. As in Britain, the proceedings are presided over by the speaker, assisted by several parliamentary clerks (all of whom continue to wear the robes of office, though the use of wigs has largely ceased). Members of the government occupy the front bench to one side of the speaker. Because there is no opposition party, backbenchers scatter themselves throughout the remaining benches in the chamber. As in Britain, each session is officially opened by the recitation of prayers and the placement of the ceremonial mace on a bracket at the side of the table with the dispatch boxes. Until 1974 the language of debate was English, which remains Kenya's official language and continues to be used in the texts of all parliamentary bills. Between 1974 and 1978 parliamentary debates were conducted exclusively in Swahili, Kenya's national language. Debate today is in both English and Swahili, and nowhere is the mix of colonial practice and African response better symbolized than in the Assembly when cries of "Bwana Speka" fill the air.

The work of the National Assembly is almost totally controlled by the government through the vice-president who is the official leader of government business. As the leader of government business, the vice-president is also the chairman of the Sessional Committee which sets the agenda of the House. Backbenchers, however, participate vigorously in Assembly debates, and as noted in the previous section, often vote against government-sponsored bills. Backbenchers also make full use of the question period which is held once a week when the Assembly is in session, and through which they closely cross-examine government ministers and assistant ministers on the operation of their ministries.

Bills introduced to the National Assembly must pass through three readings and be signed by the president before they become law. While the president does not have the formal power to veto a bill, his failure to sign is tantamount to a veto. Because of this provision, and because the government controls the Assembly's agenda, only one private members bill passed by backbenchers has been signed into law since 1969. Several private members bills have been beaten back by the government, occasionally through a curious process of legislative cooptation whereby the government introduces a bill that is similar to a popular measure which has been previously introduced by a backbencher, and then passes the new bill instead of the original. A case in point is the Parlimentary Elections Act of 1974 which sought, among other things, to limit the possibilities of election fraud, and which had been passed by the House, but not signed by President Kenyatta.

It is not surprising that backbenchers often feel frustrated by this situation. In fact, in recent years backbenchers have periodically attempted to do an "end-run" around the Government by passing resolutions to set up independent parlimentary commissions of inquiry to probe into issues with which they have been particularly concerned. Most notable among these was the formation in 1975 of a commission to investigate the assassination of J. M. Kariuki, a popular backbencher and leading government critic. Commissions have also been set up to investigate the spread of corruption within the civil service and the explosive issue of land distribution. The usual government response to such commissions has been to attempt to frustrate the work of such groups. Several backbenchers who were particularly critical of the government and of the prime movers behind the commissions were detained, or became targets for legal harassment. However, following the ascension to power of Daniel arap Moi in 1978, the level of antagonism between backbenchers and the government declined. Calls for commissions of inquiry into governmental operations have largely ceased, and there are no longer any MPs in detention. Several former legislators, however, were detained in 1982.

The Kenyan National Assembly is normally in session for four to six months per year. As in Britain, parliamentary elections must be held every five years. The Assembly is called into session by the president, and he may dissolve it and call for new elections at any time. Because Kenya is a one-party state, elections have heretofore been held at the maximum interval of five years. In addition to the Sessional Committee mentioned above, there are six committees which deal with various aspects of parliamentary business from reviewing the annual budget of the government to running the cafeteria in the MPs' lounge. Of these, only the Budget Committee is important.

In view of the government's control of the legislative process, it is clear that the National Assembly is not an important arena for public policy, but rather, an arena for the discussion and ratification of policies made elsewhere. Under Kenyatta policymaking was largely left to individual ministers who were heavily dependent on senior civil servants in their ministries, including some expatriate advisors. The cabinet rarely met, as Kenyatta sought to orchestrate, on an individual and highly personal basis, the relationships between its members. In this context, the role of the MP increasingly became one of emphasizing constituency service in an effort to build one's local political base, and increase the value of one's support to the president at the center. Kenyatta encouraged this, and on several occasions made extensive public statements to the effect that this was what MPs should do.

In decentralizing the political process and letting the party fall into disuse, Kenyatta limited the power of the Assembly but at the same time allowed it to function as a free and well-publicized forum for debate. To date, President Moi has done the same, although the cabinet now plays a greater role as a collective decisionmaking body. The Kenyan National Assembly is thus still in the process of becoming a fully developed institution. After fifteen years it has established itself as a highly visible, and perhaps permanent, feature of Kenyan political life. But, the Assembly's ultimate role, and that of its members, have yet to be determined.

# KOREA

## POLITICAL SETTING

The unconditional surrender of Japan to the Allied powers in 1945 marked the end of her thirty-five-year-long colonial rule over Korea. Japanese colonial rule in Korea was ruthless and despotic, and provided very little opportunity for Korean participation in any significant aspect of politics. It was the harsh rule of triumphant conquerors over defeated subjects and in many respects was even harsher than the colonial rules of the Western powers in Africa and Asia.[3]

Although there were numerous resistance movements both inside and outside the country, a majority of the Korean people did not have any real opportunity to participate in politics or to acquire the experience of self-governance. By the time Korea was liberated from Japan, there existed neither a coherent leadership group emerging from the independence movement nor active citizens who could help create a democratic form of government.

Compounding this problem was the development of conflict between the two victorious Allied powers—the United States and the Soviet Union—which ultimately resulted in the division of Korea. A general election was held in 1948 in the Southern half of Korea, under the supervision of the United Nations Temporary Commission on Korea (UNTCOK) to establish the first National Assembly. The National Assembly drafted and approved the nation's constitution, and South Korea soon joined the ranks of independent states, with Syngman Rhee as her first president.

The government created under the new constitution was a republic that contained a curious mixture of both the British parliamentary system and the American presidential system.[4] The constitution's full guarantee of basic individual rights and liberties has been interpreted by many to be an explicit attempt on the part of political leaders to establish a liberal democracy.

Despite the earnest aspirations and hopes of those who helped draft the constitution, the new government quickly fell prey to Rhee's autocratic rule. Political opposition was ruthlessly suppressed, destroying any chance which might have existed for the development of a viable two-party or multiparty system. The legislature was overshadowed by the executive and became increasingly a rubber stamp organization.

The Student Uprising of 1960 brought down Rhee's regime and ushered in a new political era. The Democratic Party, an ineffective opposition force under the Rhee's autocratic rule, emerged victorious in a national election in 1960 and formed a new government. The Democratic Party's rule was riddled with factionalism and impotent, and was overthrown by a junta in June 1961.

The rule of the Democratic Party was brief, and its ineffectiveness caused social and political disorder, but it was the most liberal and democratic period in the nation's postwar history. During the Democrats' rule, the legislature was the focal point of politics, and exercised a great deal of power as the constitution prescribed. Key policies were decided in the National Assembly rather than in the executive branch.[5] For the first time in the nation's history there was a real prospect of establishing a parliamentary democracy. However, the successful military coup of 1961 put an abrupt end to this brief liberal period in Korea.

The military junta ruled Korea for two-and-one half years, after which junta leaders decided to perpetuate their control by becoming politicians themselves. Leaders of the junta discarded their military uniforms and competed in the 1963 national election as members of the newly created Democratic Republican Party (DRP). To no one's surprise, the party won a majority of the vote and formed a new government. This regime, while not directly controlled by the junta, was still a government by the soldiers in mufti. The executive gained enormous power under the Democratic Republicans, and the legislature and the judiciary were reduced to subservient roles.

The political performance of the DRP regime is difficult to assess. The regime did not make any pretension that its primary goal was to establish a western style liberal democracy. It argued that because of sociopolitical conditions peculiar to Korea, Korean democracy must necessarily take a different, non-Western form. Korean democracy, as it was articulated in the 1972 Revitalizing Reforms, was a democratic form of government adapted to the particular conditions and needs in Korea. These conditions and needs included the pressing problem of national security in the face of aggression from North Korea, rapid economic development by means of centrally directed plans, and the maintenance of political stability through consensus building under government guidance. One important characteristic of the DRP regime was its exceedingly high concentration of political power in the executive and its administrative apparatus which was justified in terms of the enormity of the problems confronting the country.

## DEMOGRAPHIC AND SOCIOECONOMIC FACTORS

Korea is a relatively small but densely populated country. In a territory no larger than that of Great Britain, Korea had an estimated population of 51 million people in 1975. Of these, roughly 35 million live in South Korea.

The Korean society has a long history, and a highly homogeneous culture. Unlike developing societies in south and southeast Asia and Africa, there are no significant cultural or ethnic cleavages in Korea. Korea has no important ethnic minorities nor are any major languages spoken other than Korean.

Koreans are a highly literate people; their current literacy rate reaches well over 90 percent. Because free primary school education has been provided in recent years, there is virtually no illiteracy among the younger generations. Further, enrollment in secondary and postsecondary schools has rapidly expanded in the last three decades as Korean society has become more affluent. College degrees are intensely sought after, because they provide the most effective avenues for social mobility. The premium value placed on college education has resulted in an intense admissions process to select universities known as the "examination hell." The demand for college education has led to a rapid increase in the number of colleges and their enrollments. In 1975 there were some 230,000 students enrolled in 116 colleges and universities in Korea.

South Korea is rapidly becoming an urban society. More than half of South Korea's population lives in urban areas. In the two decades following the end of World War II, urban growth proceeded at an explosive rate—averaging an annual increase of 5.2 percent between 1945 and 1965. This figure is considerably higher than the national population growth rate for the same period, and indicates that emigration to the cities accounted for a significant part of the increase.

One important aspect of the urban growth relates to the disparate growth rates for cities of different sizes. During the postwar period, urban growth has been concentrated in a few primary cities such as Seoul, Pusan, Taegu, and Inchon. Seoul, the capital city, has shown one of the highest growth rates. Between 1955 and 1960 Seoul grew at a rate of almost 7 percent per year. Most smaller cities have not grown so fast, and some have even lost residents through migrations to larger cities.

Expansion in communications and transportation facilities has reinforced the homogeneity of Korean culture. South Korea has a relatively compact territory. As a result of the construction of several arterial expressways during the last decade, there is no longer any journey within Korea which cannot be made in a single day.

Means of social communications have expanded rapidly. Telephones are widely used, even in many villages in the countryside. Radios are common household items everywhere. Television sets have become increasingly popular, even in remote hamlets. As recently as 1965 there was approximately 1 television set per 1,000 persons; by 1974 there were 49 sets per 1,000.

The impetus for these demographic and social changes was the impressive economic progress that occurred in Korea in the 1960s and 1970s. Until two decades ago, the Korean economy was barely recovering from the war of 1950–1953. Burdened with high defense expenditures and with a predominantly agricultural economy, the government found it difficult to achieve any substantial economic progress. The situation changed, however, in the 1960s, when the new military regime came to power. With a singleminded determination and careful management, the new government successfully implemented a series of industrialization plans which resulted in remarkable growth in the iron and steel, cement, mining, heavy machinery, shipbuilding, and electronics industries. Equally impressive were the regime's achievements in building economic infrastructure; extensive highway systems, multipurpose dams, river basin development projects, and port facilities. The success of these programs was facilitated by a diligent citizenry and a favorable international market.

Economic growth in Korea began to accelerate in the early 1960s, reached an unusually high annual rate of 17 percent in 1973, and averaged above 10 percent from 1965 through 1975. During this time, the Korean economy underwent a transformation from a predominantly agricultural economy to a more advanced industrial economy. Per capita income increased from 87 dollars in 1962 to 531 dollars in 1975, the year after the data for this study were collected. The growth rates in industrial sectors and export industries were particularly large. Total exports in 1960 amounted to 32 million dollars; in 1973 they reached a level of 3.2 billion dollars, a one hundred-fold increase over their 1960 level.

The government's role in these achievements has been crucial. It has selected strategic sectors of the economy for concentrated capital investment, employed tax and credit policies favorable to capital formation, implemented major public works to strengthen the infrastructure, and taken active part both in promoting trade and attracting foreign capital. These efforts have been and continue to be centrally managed by the Korean government through a series of comprehensive economic plans, and during the Park regime were proudly referred to as "the managed miracle."

Koreans have undoubtedly achieved a measure of economic prosperity. But a crucial question remains for the future: how equitably should the fruits of economic progress be distributed among the population?

## PARTIES, ELECTIONS, AND THE LEGISLATURE

A multiparty system has been in operation in South Korea since 1948. In the first few years following the independence a multitude of political parties, often small and poorly organized, appeared on the Korean political landscape. According to one estimate, there were 344 such organizations.[6] Gradually, these groups disappeared or were absorbed into larger and more organized political parties.

With the establishment of the Rhee regime in 1948, party politics evolved slowly into two basically cohesive groups, one in support of President Rhee's leadership, and the other opposed. This was the beginning of the loose two-party system which continues to exist in South Korea, and which encompasses independent and minor opposition in addition to the two main organizations.

In one sense the Korean party system may be characterized, to use Scalapino's term, as the one-and-one-half party system.[7] Since 1948 no opposition party has attained power through elections. Although there have been three changes in government, all have been the result of military coups. In more than a dozen elections held since 1948, the government party has not failed to gain a majority of seats in the National Assembly. The dominance of the government party and the lack of opportunity for opposition parties to capture power are the characteristics which define the one-and-one-half party system.

The party situation in the National Assembly at the time of our field study was no exception to this pattern. Members of the government parties—the Democratic Republican Party and the Society for Revitalizing Reforms (a quasi party consisting of the Assemblymen appointed by the president)—together commanded a two-thirds majority in the legislature. The New Democratic Party, the main opposition party, controlled fifty-four seats. The remaining nineteen seats were divided among a minor opposition party and independents.

The Society for the Revitalizing Reforms, one of the twin pillars of government strength, requires further comment. The party came into existence following a constitutional revision approved in a 1972 national referendum. The revised constitution, known as the *Yushin* (Revitalizing Reforms) Constitution, effected some drastic changes in the procedures for selecting members to the National Assembly. Under the revised constitution, two-thirds of the members of the legislature (146) were popularly elected from district constituencies. The remaining seventy-three members were appointed by the president, with only a nominal endorsement by the National Conference for Unification, a two thousand-member body under direct control of the president.

The seventy-three appointed members banded together as a parliamentary group, the Society for Revitalizing Reforms, and functioned for all practical purposes as an alter ego of the governing Democratic Republican Party. Thus, the government was assured a majority in the legislature because it had one-third of the Assembly seats before elections even began.

Under the *Yushin* Constitution the National Assembly became an even weaker body than it once had been. The formal powers of the legislative branch enumerated in chapter 6 of the constitution included the rights of legislation, interpellation, concurrence to the conclusion of treaties and the declaration of war, and approval of government budgets. The offices in the legislature were organized to include a speaker, two vice-speakers (one of which was given by convention to the opposition party member), and the chairmen of thirteen standing committees and special committees. The committee chairmanships have traditionally been occupied by the leading members of the government parties. The routine legislative work is performed by a relatively large staff in the secretariat.

This legislative bureaucracy was headed by the secretary-general, an office of cabinet level rank with a staff of more than 1,000 persons. At the head of this staff were the senior counsellors, numbering between 30 and 40. The senior counsellors were the core of the professional staff, each being an expert in a legislative subfield. Senior counsellors were normally assigned to the standing committees, but occasionally to the special committees as well. They helped legislators to draft bills and provided expert counsel on various legislative matters.

### LEGISLATIVE PROCESS

During the DRP regime of President Park Chung Hee, the concurrent power of the president and government bureaucracy emasculated the other two branches of Korean government, the legislature and the judiciary. Although the National Assembly was empowered in the matters of legislation, most bills originated in the executive branch, and their passage was almost always assured in advance due to the government's control of two-thirds of the legislative seats.[8] In this respect, the National Assembly could not be considered as exercising a full power in lawmaking.

Yet the National Assembly was regarded as an important representative institution by the public. The public was relatively well informed about the legislature, and accorded it a high level of support.[9] The National Assembly was considered to be established and certainly an institution worth maintaining. This is probably one of the main reasons that regimes of the past did not dissolve the legislature and why the National Assembly was reconstituted after the coup of 1980.

Individual members of the Assembly, especially those elected popularly from district constituencies, could not ignore their representative duties.

District constituents expected their assemblymen to perform tasks which ranged from securing jobs to bringing public works projects to their home districts. Those who slighted their representative duties, and thus failed to meet constituents' expectations, were not likely to be returned in the next election. The incentive for representative behavior was derived, therefore, from the public's awareness of, as well as its expectations of, the legislature. These conditions existed and persist in Korea, engendered in part by the spread of a liberal political ideology during the last three decades, and in part by the increasing levels of education.[10]

Although the National Assembly did not usually take initiatives in law-making during the regime of President Park, it did attach a seal of legitimacy to the policies enacted by the executive. Moreover, the very existence of a legislative body and periodic elections provided a sense of participation for the public. This was very significant in a political setting like South Korea's, where other channels of citizen participation were not widely available. The legitimizing function of the National Assembly was critically important to the Park regime, and is a major reason why the regime and its successor under President Dwon have tolerated the legislative body.

During the Park regime, the National Assembly also served as an important public forum. Since government exercised tight control over the news media, the legislature served as the only alternative arena for public debates on important issues of the day. To be sure, there were many constraints, both legal and de facto, on the range of issues that could legitimately be discussed in the National Assembly. The Assembly was prohibited by law, for instance, from raising any issue so fundamental that it touched on the nature of the regime itself. Insofar as the issues did not challenge the legitimacy of the governmental structure established in accordance with the Revitalizing Reforms, the National Assembly considered any issue for debate.

During the Park era there were reactions, especially by concerned intellectuals and opposition assemblymen, to the continuing decline in the fortune of the legislative body. In journalistic parlance the tendency was given the name, "Kukhoe sinychwa," meaning that the legislative branch had become a maidservant of the executive.

Although executive dominance of the National Assembly had been discussed in the past and a few proposals put forth, no concrete moves were made to reinvigorate the legislative institution.[11] Indeed, after the adoption of the 1972 *Yushin* system it became even more difficult than it had been in the past to raise such an issue. After 1972 any proposal to change the constitutional status of the legislative branch ran the risk of being perceived as a violation of the political taboo against challenging the basic structure of the *Yushin* government. Because a change in the constitutional status of the legislature was imperative to any attempt to strengthen the body, its power could not be increased as long as the *Yushin* constitution remained intact.

The *Yushin* system, based on a strong executive, was justified on two grounds. The first was national security. Having suffered through a fratricidal war from 1950 to 1953 and still fearful of North Korean aggression, the people in South Korea were acutely concerned with national security. Their sense of vulnerability was made more acute by the United States' plan to phase out American troops stationed in Korea.

The *Yushin* system was also justified by the need for rapid economic development. The Park regime sought to pull the country out of a stagnant economy by achieving rapid industrialization through centralized economic planning. Three five-year economic plans were drafted and implemented by the Democratic Republican regime, each concentrating on the growth of strategic industrial sectors. Planning and implementation of such ambitious economic plans required a strong and efficient government bureaucracy, and thereby provided another persuasive argument for a strong executive.

Now that South Korea has achieved a measure of economic prosperity, the need for rapid economic development will become an increasingly less persuasive argument for an executive-centered system. However, the security argument may continue to be an important factor in the years to come.

The collapse of the DRP regime in October 1979, following the assassination of President Park Chung Hee, brought an end to the *Yushin* system. In the months following the assassination, South Korea witnessed a brief and frantic period of political realignments, reflecting an upsurge in popular demand for a new democratic order. However, this unrest was brought to an end when military officers who had remained loyal to President Park quickly and forcefully reasserted their claim to power. A national referendum in October 1980 resulted in Korea's current constitution which specified the present governmental structure, including the National Assembly.

## TURKEY

### POLITICAL SETTING

In the hopes of regaining lost status in European politics and lost territories, the Ottoman Empire entered the First World War on the side of the Central Powers and was defeated in 1918. The Allied occupation of Turkey during the First World War, and a Greek effort to invade western Turkey, led to the development of Turkish political-military resistance organizations which were often led by nationalist officers, generally known as the Defense of Rights Associations. The associations were united in the fall of 1919 by Mustafa Kemal Atatürk. The resulting Executive Committee ruled the Turkish Independence Movement until the Grand National Assembly opened in 1920. The Sultan's government, a captive of the Allied occupation, lost its power and collapsed in 1922.

The new National Assembly included remnants of the last Ottoman Chamber of Deputies along with three new members from each province. It served as a constituent assembly and, until the Republic was established in October 1923, also as the governing body.

The politics of the country for the next 23 years was dominated by the Republican People's Party (RPP), the political successor of the Defense of Rights Associations. Two experiments with other new parties in 1924 and 1930 were quickly aborted because they became vehicles for proponents of the former regime.

The single-party period was one of extensive social reform in Turkey. At the end of RPP rule, Turkey emerged as one of the most secular countries in the world and, with the exception of Israel, the most socially and economically advanced country in the Middle East.

Turkey avoided involvement in the Second World War through an intricate system of alliances. The war, nevertheless, did affect Turkish domestic and political life. The Second World War saw full scale mobilization in Turkey, more authoritarian rule, and shortages of many industrial goods, conditions that led to dissatisfaction with the RPP. Growing conflicts with the Soviet Union led Turkey to search for closer ties with Western democracies to insure her security, and it was believed that such ties would be improved by political liberalization. Other developments, not related to the war, facilitated Turkey's transition to competitive politics. One was the death in 1938 of Atatürk, the undisputed and charismatic leader of the Republic. Another was the view held by prominent RPP leaders that the single-party period was a stage in the process of becoming a western-style democracy. The fact that the proponents of political liberalization and competition were prominent members of the RPP contributed to its success.

In the first elections contested by several parties, held in 1946, the RPP was seriously challenged by the new Democratic Party; in the 1950 elections the Democratic Party won a sweeping majority. During the next ten years, despite its electoral successes, the Democratic Party became more authoritarian, introduced deep cleavages into the society, and brought the national economy to a state of bankruptcy. Turkish lack of experience with competitive politics led to continuing tensions between the government and opposition. The Democratic Party had come to power by catering to those voters, particularly in rural areas and small towns, who were critical of the modernizing trends introduced by the RPP. As the Democratic Party sought to maintain its power, it began to violate the rules of the game and increasingly antagonized the modern elites in Turkish society. There were student demonstrations, the military was brought in to establish law and order, and in May 1960 the Democratic Party government was overthrown by a committee of military officers calling itself the National Unity Committee.[12]

A constituent assembly convened by the National Unity Committee prepared a new constitution which was adopted by the voters in the fall of 1961.

The elections that followed produced the first coalition government (led by the RPP) in Turkish history. The 1965 and 1969 elections, however, were won by the Justice Party, one of the parties set up to court the votes of the now-defunct Democratic Party.

As student radicalism became increasingly violent during the 1960s, the Justice Party governments were unable to control it. In March 1971 the Turkish chief of staff and the commanders of the armed forces issued a joint communiqué asking the prime minister to resign for having failed to bring law and order to the country. But instead of assuming direct control, the military leaders pressed for and secured the formation of civilian cabinets which were accorded reluctant votes of confidence in the National Assembly. The refusal of the Assembly to appoint the military chief of staff as president upon the expiration of the term of the former president marked the turn of the tide in favor of civilian dominance of politics. Elections, due in October 1973, were held on time.

Because no one party was able to achieve a controlling majority in the National Assembly after the 1973 and 1977 elections, the country was ruled by coalition governments during this period. The coalitions were themselves not very stable. With the exception of one coalition established by the RPP with a number of independents, parties of the radical right, one religious and one with racist tendencies, were important partners in these governments. Their influence was greater than their numbers might suggest, creating at times high levels of tension between the government and the secular-oriented, social democratic opposition of the time. Reliance on fringe parties to produce majorities created lasting instabilities in the political system. The period of coalitions, particularly after 1974, was also marked by increasing political violence of both mass and individual terroristic variety by extremist groups on both left and right.

On September 12, 1980, the National Security Council, consisting of the highest ranking officers of the Turkish armed forces, disbanded the Grand National Assembly. The military leadership promised to reinstitute competitive civilian politics, control terrorism, restore confidence in public institutions, and prepare a new constitution which would correct the inadequacies of the constitution of 1961. A new constitution was drafted with the assistance of a constituent assembly and ratified in a national referendum in the fall of 1982.

## GEOGRAPHY AND SOCIOECONOMIC FACTORS

At the time of the establishment of the Republic, Turkey was a rural society with an agricultural economy. Two trends have been visible since the beginning of the Republic, becoming stronger after the Second World War and particularly during the 1960s. First, Turkey is being urbanized at an accelerated rate. The exodus from the villages has had both urban-pull and rural-push dimensions, but in either case, urbanization has taken place at a more rapid pace than the economic development in urban areas would warrant. This has resulted in urban unemployment, growth of shanty towns around the cities, insufficient municipal services, and a host of related problems. The migrations from the countryside have also introduced neo-traditional elements into urban politics that have to be taken increasingly into account.

Second, Turkey is becoming rapidly industrialized. Turkish industry initially developed as a means of import substitution, but it is now becoming increasingly oriented toward an international market and is growing in sophistication. This has also brought new forces into politics, such as labor unions and business associations.

At the time of the founding of the Republic, 90 percent of the citizens were estimated to have been illiterate. This figure had gradually declined to about 45 percent by 1970, and is expected to decline more rapidly in the future. Literacy is highest among urban males and lowest among rural females. As the importance of nonverbal communication has increased in public life, so have the pressures to learn to read and write.

Since the Islamic-Turkish part of the Ottoman Empire comprised the territory on which the Republic was established, Turkey is a relatively homogeneous society. There are some Kurdish-speaking people in the eastern provinces and a few Arabic-speaking persons in the southern provinces. It is also in these regions that traces of an earlier tribal organization may be found and that politics may sometimes be dominated by traditional families. Nationality, as it is understood by the Republic, is political and acquired by being a Turkish citizen. Basing politics on ethnic differences is not viewed with favor by the political culture or by the law. Thus, ethnic divisions may be appropriately treated as cultural phenomena with minor political consequences.

The geographic proximity of the country to the Soviet Union has in the past caused apprehension, not only toward the Soviet Union and her allies, but also toward various types of socialist thinking. This inclination has broken down, particularly since the 1960 Revolution. While the propagation of communist ideologies and the establishment of communist parties are still illegal, organizations and publications preaching the teachings of Marx, Lenin, Mao, and others are widespread and enjoy an uneasy existence. Democratic Socialism, on the other hand, has gained wide appeal, and the RPP has itself adopted a social democratic platform.

In recent years, many Turkish workers have gone to Germany. This exportation of labor has helped reduce domestic unemployment while bolstering the hard currency reserves of the country. The social and political consequences of having workers abroad have not yet become clear, although it is thought that this might hasten modernization in the villages as workers return home.

## POLITICAL PARTIES

Although political parties existed during the later stages of the Ottoman Empire (a constitutional monarchy had evolved in 1908, following a brief two-year experiment in 1876), the parties of the Republic have not been their descendants. As was previously explained, the first political party to have been established, just before the Republic was proclaimed, was the People's Party, which later added "Republican" to its name. The RPP, with a nation-wide organization, included many of the former Ottoman officers, bureau-crats, and intellectuals, as well as some local elites who were committed to the Republic and to the values it represented. While aspiring to achieve eventual popular representation, the party initially worked to ensure the survival and development of the Republic through propagation of its values and introduction of radical changes in various areas of public life.

The Democratic Party, mentioned earlier, was born among the ranks of the RPP, and initially represented various shades of opinion. After it gained power in 1950, however, the party began to emphasize private enterprise rather than state economic activity. It encouraged foreign trade and invest-ment and catered to the preferences of the more traditional voters, with programs, for example, to fund the construction of mosques and the opening of teacher training schools. When the Democratic Party was closed follow-ing the 1960 Revolution, a number of parties emerged seeking the votes that it had previously won. The chief contenders in 1961 were the Justice Party and the New Turkey Party. The Justice Party proved to be the more success-ful, and in the 1965 elections it emerged as the victor.

Turkey is a country going through rapid social and economic change, and as a consequence its political organizations have often appeared to be tem-porary alignments of forces. While organizations bearing the same name survive, their policies and constituencies undergo change. The RPP, for example, ever since the development of multiparty politics, had sought a program that would have wider appeal to voters than its long-established policies of secularism and modernization. Prior to the 1965 elections, the RPP announced that it would pursue a "left of center" policy. As the mem-bers of the party sought to define that policy more precisely, splinter parties appeared. One of the most serious splits occurred in 1971 over the question of whether party leaders should support the effort of military leaders to form a civilian national coalition movement. Despite these divisions, the RPP in 1973 won one-third of the vote and the largest number of Assembly seats in the election.

The Justice Party also experienced rifts in its ranks. One such division forced the resignation of the Prime Minister, Mr. Demirel, in 1970; when he formed a government without the dissidents, they established a new Demo-cratic Party.

Three other parties deserve mention. The Turkish Labor Party, formed prior to the 1965 elections, was the first socialist party in the country's politics. It was ravaged by internal ideological quibbles, and then was closed by the Constitutional Court in 1971 for having preached the establishment of the domination of one social class over others. Since that time other socialist parties have been established with no visible backing.

The National Order Party, established prior to the 1969 elections, represented the religious reaction to a secular, and rapidly urbanizing and industrializing society. Although it was closed by the Constitutional Court for using religion for political purposes, it reemerged in the 1973 elections under the name of the National Salvation Party and succeeded in becoming the third largest party in the country. It has been a member of the major coalitions that have ruled the country since then.

The third party of note, the National Action Party, is a national socialist party with a tightly controlled paramilitary youth organization that has given it formidable power in street politics. It gradually, if modestly, increased in electoral support during the late 1970s, and became an essential part of coalitions led by the Justice Party.

The current state of flux in the Turkish society and economy was reflected in the lack of stability among the Turkish political parties with regard to their numbers, their constituents, and their ideologies. While the Justice Party subscribed to economic development by private enterprise, the RPP emphasized the development of a welfare state and attached more importance to public enterprises and cooperatives as ingredients in realizing its goals. The National Salvation Party (NSP) worked to further the role of religion in public life. Along with the Democratic, the Reliance, and the National Action parties, NSP was also inclined more in the direction of private enterprise.

Two effectively organized interest groups in Turkey, business and industrial labor, have in the past accorded support to the Justice and the Republican People's Parties, respectively. This support, which has never been solid, was breaking down, particularly on the part of business, prior to the assumption of political power by the military leadership in the fall of 1980.

The 1973 and 1977 elections suggest that both the RPP and the Justice Party have fared better in more economically developed and industrialized provinces, mostly in western Turkey, while the votes have been more widely dispersed in the rural and less developed regions.[13] The RPP has appealed more to industrial and urban workers, the salaried middle class, small farmers, farm workers, and intellectuals. The Justice Party has appealed to business, large farmers, and persons in professions and service sectors. The Democratic Party has received small business support. The National Salvation Party has been supported by various groups having trouble coping with social change.

The current military government abolished all existing parties. Their leadership and MPs have been banned from forming or joining newly formed political parties for specific periods. New parties for the elections that were expected to take place late in 1983 were in the process of being formed.

## THE LEGISLATURE

The first Turkish legislative body was established in 1876, and operated intermittently with little power but with some popular participation until the end of the Ottoman Empire. The National Assembly that convened in Ankara in 1920 was a constituent assembly, and subsequently played a major policy role in the government of the new Republic. The constitution of the Republic formally gave the National Assembly supreme power in the political system. It elected the president, gave a vote of confidence to the cabinet, and made laws. However, as in other parliamentary systems, the legislature came increasingly under the influence of the executive and party leadership. There was an indirect system of election of deputies, involving party slates.

Between 1923 and 1945 a number of changes made the political system more competitive: suffrage was extended to women, freedom to associate was established, and direct elections were instituted. The coming of multiparty politics did not significantly affect the domination of the parliamentary parties by party leaders or the ability of parties to discipline their deputies. Occasionally, however, revolts did break out among deputies against their parties' leaders.

The National Unity Committee closed the Assembly in 1960 and convened a new constituent assembly, which sought to create a constitutional structure that could not be so easily misused by the majority party. While multimember districts coinciding with provinces were retained, representation in each was made proportional. A Senate of the Republic was created, with members elected for staggered six-year terms. The president was chosen by the parliament for a nonrenewable seven-year term. During this period primaries were developed in the provincial party organizations to nominate deputies, a practice which weakened the control of the national parties. In order to avoid political interference, the judiciary was given control over running elections. A Constitutional Court was established with power to declare acts of parliament unconstitutional and to outlaw parties that violated the constitution or laws.

The period from 1960 to 1980 bears the marks of ambivalence as to how much faith could be placed in a legislature if its powers were not checked by other political institutions. While rhetoric placed the legislature, particularly the National Assembly, which is the lower chamber, at the apex, a system inspired by a model of checks and balances was in fact created.

Parliamentary political parties, and their leaderships in particular, were the main actors in the political life of the country. While parties and leaders have been blamed for the difficulties of the country on frequent occasions, it is important to note that the idea of a parliamentary system itself has never been seriously challenged. Even the military governments which have intervened on three occasions have promoted the idea that Turkey should be a parliamentary democracy.

The constitution of 1960 gave the legislative authority exclusively to the Grand National Assembly, stipulating that this authority could not be delegated to other branches of government. Legislation was broadly defined as the making, changing, or repealing of laws. Approving the budget, deciding to issue legal tender, finalizing death. penalties, and declaring partial or general amnesty were also specifically mentioned, as were deciding to use armed forces and approving international treaties. Laws were to be made by simple majorities of those present in both chambers, except that the budget required an absolute majority. A constitutional change required approval by two-thirds of the entire membership, and no constitutional change could be made regarding the republican form of government. Laws became operative upon being signed by the president of the Republic, who could choose to veto them, which he had done on a number of occasions. Vetoes could be overridden by simple majorities.

Laws were subject to review by the Constitutional Court, which could find them either partially or entirely unconstitutional. The Court could not initiate procedures itself, but could have cases referred to it from a number of groups specified in the constitution.

The president was legally charged with appointing a prime minister, who in turn chose a council of ministers and submitted the list for presidential approval. Technically, the cabinet took office by the affirmative action of the president, but it prepared a program and sought a vote of confidence from the lower chamber of the legislature as a matter of course. Failure to get a vote of confidence directed the president to reinitiate the process of forming a government.

A constitutional change was introduced in 1971, enabling the Council of Ministers to receive authorization from the legislature to issue decrees having the validity of laws in a given area of policy for a defined period of time. Though this change might have undermined the legal exclusiveness of the legislature as a lawmaking body, the executive tended to be the hub of lawmaking in any case. Most proposals originated in the government, and those coming from the government had a greater chance of being enacted into law. Proposals that did not have government backing, on the other hand, had little chance of getting to the floor, and when they did, were likely to be rejected. This is not to suggest, of course, that the government was insensitive to the sentiments of its parliamentary party or parties, but rather that the government was the agency that determined the priorities.

Legislative oversight of the executive was exercised by addressing questions to the ministers in oral or written form, requesting general discussion on a particular topic or area of policy, initiating parliamentary investigations of ministers, or engaging in a parliamentary review of government activities. Review procedures, which could originate only in the National Assembly, could be included in the agenda by a simple majority vote. An absolute majority was needed to depose the cabinet or one of the ministers. Parliamentary investigation of ministers, on the other hand, was conducted by a joint committee of both chambers, and decisions were reached at a joint session.

Just as the political system favored the government vis-à-vis the legislature, so parties were favored over individual legislators in the chambers. Legislators were expected to submit their own proposals to the leaders of their parliamentary caucuses for approval before presenting them to the officers of the legislature. Speakers for parties were given priority over those who wanted to speak on their own behalf, both in the by-laws and in deed. The legislator was expected to comply with all the decisions of his party with regard to how he should vote. Failure to do so resulted in disciplinary sanctions, including expulsion from the party. The constitution specifically prohibited party caucus decisions on removing the immunity of a representative or bringing ministers under parliamentary investigation, but even in this case party sentiment weighed heavily in the decision of the individual legislator.

Apart from the differences in the composition and the election methods explained earlier, some other differences between the prerogatives of the two chambers were significant. Budget proposals, unlike all other proposals, were first discussed in the Senate, then in the National Assembly. In either place, no amendments increasing public expenditure or decreasing public revenue could be introduced. In case of conflict between the two chambers, the matter went to a conference committee, but the National Assembly was given the final say on which proposal would become law. Giving a vote of confidence, as noted before, was a privilege of the lower chamber.

The Grand National Assembly convened without invitation the first day of November each year. Both chambers went in and out of session simultaneously. Vacation could not be longer than five months a year. Extraordinary sessions could be called by the president at his own initiative or upon the request of the Council of Ministers.

Elections for the National Assembly were held every four years. Elections for one-third of the Senate, on the other hand, were held every two years, at which time by-elections for the Assembly could also be conducted. Candidates of parties and the order in which they appeared on the ballot were determined by a primary in which delegates chosen from members of the parties of each subprovince participated. The national party organization could veto candidates and recommend the placement on the ballot of other candidates, not to exceed 5 percent of all the candidates advanced by a party.

Parties that had received 5 percent or more of the popular vote in the last election, and which had succeeded in electing enough representatives to form a caucus of ten representatives, were entitled to receive grants from the treasury in amounts determined by law.

The votes were tabulated according to a modified d'Hondt system of proportional representation where the vote each party had received was successively divided by $1, 2, \ldots n$, where $n$ is equal to the number of representatives to be elected from that province. The quotients for all parties were then rank ordered, starting with the highest until $n$ quotients were ranked. The number of times each party's quotients appeared in the rank ordering was the number of seats that party would get. Since places of candidates on each party's list were already ranked through a primary, it was then a matter of procedure to identify the individual winners.

## POLITICS AT THE TIME OF THE STUDY

Field work in Turkey commenced seven months after the elections in 1973. No party had gained a majority in the elections: the RPP had won 186 seats; the Justice Party, 149; the National Salvation Party, 48; the Democratic Party, 45; and others, 22. Ideological differences and personality conflicts among leaders of parties made it very difficult to form a coalition for almost two months. After lengthy negotiations, the RPP and NSP succeeded in forming a coalition headed by Bülent Ecevit of the RPP which stayed in power for nine months. It was during their rule that the Turkish armed forces intervened in Cyprus in response to a takeover by Eoka supporter Nikos Sampson. While this resulted in an upsurge in the popularity of the government, it did not overcome the major differences between the two partners. The Ecevit Government resigned in September 1974.

It took more than three months to form a new coalition headed by Süleyman Demirel of the Justice Party. This government also had many elements of instability in it. Tensions between the RPP and the coalition partners, which called themselves the "parties of the right," were high.

At the time of the study, the country faced two major problems. The first was an inflation rate of about twenty-five percent which the government was unable to control. Second was the embargo of American military assistance to Turkey which followed the Cyprus intervention.

# Part II

# LEGISLATORS AND POLITICAL REPRESENTATION

# Chapter 4

# THE MEMBERS OF THE LEGISLATURE

We begin our discussion of representation and the relationships legislators forge between their constituents and central political institutions with an analysis of the backgrounds, predispositions, and ambitions of the central actors in this process, the legislators. As noted in chapter 2, our samples of legislators from Kenya, Korea, and Turkey were not selected on a random basis, because our objective was to interview all MPs from the constituencies in which we conducted our surveys of local leaders and the general public, and because of political events in the three countries at the time of our study. While our samples of parliamentarians are highly representative of the universe of legislators in each country, we must approach our data with some caution and regard the results reported herein as tentative conclusions to be validated by further research.

## CHARACTERISTICS OF LEGISLATORS

### SOCIAL BACKGROUND

Political leaders throughout the world are invariably better educated and higher in socioeconomic status than members of the general public. The legislators from Kenya, Korea, and Turkey interviewed for this study are no exceptions. Consistent with the situation in other countries, they are also overwhelmingly male; and their median age is somewhat less than that of top government officials. Most members of our three samples are also long-term residents of the districts they were elected to represent. More than three-quarters of the legislators in each of the three countries had resided in their districts for more than a decade, while at least two-fifths had resided in their districts for more than twenty years.

Within these expected parameters, however, there are several significant variations among the legislators of the three countries, variations which appear to be closely related to the different levels of economic development each country has achieved and to the history of the legislature within each political system. Thus, in table 4.1 we find that Kenyan legislators tended to be significantly younger and less educated (as measured by the number of years spent in school) than their counterparts in Korea and Turkey, while the Korean respondents[1] were the oldest and by far the best educated. Similarly,

**TABLE 4.1.**

**Demographic and Social Background Characteristics of Legislators (percentages)**

|  | Kenya | Korea[a] | Turkey |
|---|---|---|---|
| **Sex** | | | |
| Male: | 100 | 95 | 98 |
| Female: | — | 5 | 2 |
| N = | (28) | (83) | (104) |
| **Age** | | | |
| Under 30: | — | — | — |
| 31–40: | 31 | 11 | 21 |
| 41–50: | 58 | 56 | 45 |
| 51–60: | 12 | 28 | 32 |
| Over 60: | — | 5 | 2 |
| Median age: | 45 | 48 | 47 |
| N = | (26) | (82) | (98) |
| **Education** | | | |
| Less than 9 years: | 8 | — | 15 |
| 10–12 years: | 52 | 4 | 7 |
| 13–16 years: | 36 | 48 | 78 |
| More than 16 years: | 4 | 49 | 1 |
| Median education: | 12 | 16 | 15 |
| N = | (28) | (82) | (104) |
| **Occupational rank (Hollingshead)** | | | |
| High  1 | 26 | 52 | 63 |
| 2 | 4 | 21 | 16 |
| 3 | 41 | 9 | 12 |
| 4 | 19 | — | 3 |
| 5 | — | — | 1 |
| 6 | — | — | 6 |
| 7 | 4 | — | — |
| Low  8  (unemployed) | 7 | 18 | — |
| Median rank: | 3 | 1 | 1 |
| N = | (27) | (82) | (103) |
| **Length of residence in district** | | | |
| 1–10 years | 21 | 11 | 26 |
| 11–20 years | 4 | 44 | 20 |
| 21 or more | 74 | 41 | 54 |
| N = | (23) | (80) | (96) |

a. Elected members only.

Kenyan parliamentarians were more likely to have pursued occupations of lower prestige immediately prior to their election to parliament than were Koreans or Turks. Kenyans were also more likely to have been long-term residents of their constituencies, a reflection of the fact that more than 80 percent lived in rural areas and had occupations that did not afford them a high degree of geographic mobility.

These variations suggest that recruitment into parliament is from a wider range of social strata in Kenya than in Turkey, and from a much wider range in Kenya than in Korea. This hypothesis is further supported by examining the family background of MPs and the degree of intergenerational mobility experienced by the legislators from the three countries.

As indicated by table 4.2, the fathers of Kenyan legislators were significantly less well educated than their counterparts in Korea and Turkey. While half of the Kenyans' fathers had received no formal schooling, half of the fathers of Korean and Turkish legislators had received a primary school education or more. The occupational rank of the fathers of Kenyan MPs was also much lower than the occupational ranks of the fathers of Korean and Turkish respondents. More than half, in fact, were peasants. Despite these variations, legislators in all three countries are drawn disproportionately from the middle and upper middle classes. This is true even in Kenya where, although more than half of the respondents indicated that their fathers were peasants, more than 40 percent were sons of men who had been employed in one of the three highest categories of employment.

**TABLE 4.2.**
**Socioeconomic Background of Legislators' Fathers (percentage)**

|  | Kenya | Korea | Turkey |
|---|---|---|---|
| Father's education |  |  |  |
| Less than 5 years | 64 | 52 | 33 |
| 6–9 years | 25 | 14 | 26 |
| 10–12 years | 7 | 18 | 33 |
| 13–16 years | 4 | 12 | 1 |
| More than 16 years | — | 4 | 7 |
| Median education | — | 4 | 8 |
| N = | (28) | (82) | (97) |
| Father's occupational rank |  |  |  |
| High:  1 | 12 | 14 | 7 |
| 2 | 4 | 20 | 22 |
| 3 | 27 | 40 | 28 |
| 4 | — | 1 | 10 |
| 5 | — | — | 9 |
| 6 | 4 | 17 | 23 |
| 7 (including peasants) | 54 | 9 | 1 |
| Low:  8 (unemployed) | — | — | 1 |
| Median rank: | 7 | 3 | 3 |
| N = | (28) | (81) | (102) |

It would thus appear that, while legislative recruitment remains an open process in the three countries, drawing from and supplied by all strata of society, it is also a process with an increasingly narrow and entrenched social base. As economic development proceeds and is accompanied by the almost inevitable increase of inequality, and as successive generations of parliamentarians are elected to office, legislatures in Kenya, Korea, and Turkey—as in other less developed countries—will be increasingly composed of members of the emerging socioeconomic elite. Though the legislature is an institution to which one gains entry via popular election, our data clearly suggest that legislative recruitment in these countries is not significantly different from the recruitment processes of other institutions, such as the civil service, the educational system, and large firms in the private sector. What effects these changing patterns of legislative recruitment will have on the ability of parliamentarians to forge linkages from the periphery to the center of these political systems will be discussed in chapter 5.

In the types of constituencies they were elected to represent and in their party affiliations, the legislators in our three samples were a diverse group. As indicated by table 4.3, most of the members of the three samples were elected by rural constituencies, or constituencies which were only partly urbanized at the time of our surveys. Here again, there were marked variations among the three countries. These variations reflect the different levels of economic development each country had reached, and parallel the data presented in tables 4.1 and 4.2. It is not surprising, therefore, that almost all of the Kenyan legislators represented rural constituencies, while those from Korea, and especially those from Turkey, were more evenly divided among rural, urban, and mixed areas.

Even more interesting was the tendency of different types of constituencies to elect similar individuals as representatives. A comparison of the background characteristics of legislators from rural, semiurban, and urban constituencies reveals few significant differences in the dimensions of age, education, occupational rank, and length of residence in the district. In view of the rapid rate of urbanization in the three countries, and the high mobility of urban residents, we had expected legislators from urban constituencies to be

**TABLE 4.3.**
**Type of District (Constituency) Legislator**
**Was Elected to Represent (percentages)**

|        | Kenya | Korea | Turkey |
|--------|-------|-------|--------|
| Urban  | 4     | 21    | 38     |
| Mixed  | 11    | 26    | 26     |
| Rural  | 86    | 53    | 36     |
| N =    | (28)  | (83)  | (104)  |

younger and to have resided in their districts for shorter periods than their counterparts from rural districts. Neither of these expectations was consistently confirmed by our data. MPs from urban and semi-urban areas were somewhat better educated and had pursued more prestigious occupations than MPs from rural constituencies, but the differences were limited—measuring five to ten percentage points—and could be attributed to sampling errors.

Ecological differences between constituencies might be expected to explain differences in the political and ideological orientation of MPs. Like most other African countries still under civilian rule, Kenya is a one-party state in which almost 90 percent of the population resides in the countryside. In such countries, political cleavages tend to occur along sectional and ethnic lines rather than along the lines of class. Opposition parties in these countries have disappeared from the scene partly because there have been few questions of policy on which these parties had significant differences with the party in power. Opposition MPs frequently deserted their parties when opportunities arose to join the governing party and partake of the state's resources and patronage, which the governing party controlled. As only fifteen of Kenya's 158 parliamentary constituencies are within urban areas, it is not surprising that the country is ruled by a one-party system, and that MPs from urban areas have not founded a second party to advance the special interests of the people who elected them to office.

In contrast to Kenya, Korea and Turkey are more urbanized and economically developed societies, and both are industrializing. Historically, economic development, and industrialization in particular, have accelerated the level of differentiation among the members of society and given rise to political cleavages that cut across cleavages of sectionalism and ethnicity. Ideological differences emerge under these circumstances, with the result that urban residents begin to elect representatives who hold different ideological positions and who are members of different parties from those elected by their counterparts in the countryside. This tendency is illustrated by table 4.4. It is most prominent in Turkey, where a majority of the MPs from urban areas were members of the social democratic Republican Peoples' Party, while a majority of the legislators from rural constituencies were members of the conservative Justice Party.

The classic left-right, urban-rural dichotomy, however, was not repeated in Korea. As discussed in chapter 2, socialist and radical parties on the left of the political spectrum were prohibited in Korea due to fear of communism and aggression by the communist regime in the North. Korean parties consequently operated in a truncated political spectrum ranging from the center/right to right.

The Democratic Republican Party, which was the governing party before the military takeover in 1980, and the New Democratic Party were virtually identical in terms of ideology, and addressed themselves to the same class interests. Given these conditions, it is not surprising that MPs from urban and rural areas did not overwhelmingly support one or the other of the two major parties. On the other hand, it is noteworthy that a majority of the MPs from urban constituencies were members of the opposition New Democratic Party which, though not a party of the left, was highly critical of the conservative Democratic Republican government, and drew some of its most vocal support from intellectuals and other residents of Korean cities, where dissatisfaction with the government of President Park was most pronounced. To many of these people, voting for candidates of the New Democratic Party was a means of registering protest about the existing political order rather than a way of supporting an alternative program from an opposition party.

In sum, the membership of the legislatures in Kenya, Korea, and Turkey seemed to be evolving in a manner similar to that which occurred earlier in Western Europe. As development proceeded, ideological and class distinctions superceded those of sectional interest, and the socioeconomic background of MPs became more restricted. We expect that the emergence of an upper-class oligarchy, such as Robert Michels found within the German Social Democratic Party[2] or such as emerged more recently within the parliamentary British Labour Party, will be replicated in those developing countries where the process is allowed to play itself out.

## CAREERS

Being a legislator is but one relatively short-term role in the careers of most MPs in the three samples. To understand the perspectives these people bring to their work, it is therefore useful to examine briefly the context of their lives in which these roles are played. As indicated in table 4.1, the

TABLE 4.4.
Party Affiliation of Legislators by Type of Constituency
(percentages)

|  | Urban | Semi-Urban | Rural |
|---|---|---|---|
| Korea (elected MPs) |  |  |  |
| Democratic Republican | 41 | 43 | 46 |
| New Democratic | 53 | 33 | 41 |
| Other | 6 | 24 | 14 |
| N = | (17) | (21) | (44) |
| Turkey |  |  |  |
| Justice | 21 | 48 | 60 |
| Republican People's | 69 | 33 | 24 |
| Other | 10 | 19 | 16 |
| N = | (37) | (27) | (39) |

median age for the legislators who comprised the three samples ranged from forty-five to forty-seven years. Most members of the samples assumed their positions in their late thirties or early forties, after having pursued other careers for a decade or more. We have also noted that the members of our three samples are disproportionately drawn from prestigious occupations, particularly in Korea and Turkey.

In terms of specific occupations, there are, however, several variations among the three countries, and among legislators of different political parties —the only variable which significantly affected legislative recruitment among our three samples of legislators. As is shown by table 4.5, more than half of the Kenyan respondents were civil servants or businessmen prior to entering the National Assembly.

In Korea, the civil service was also a significant source of legislators, though primarily from the right-wing Democratic Republican Party. The Democratic Republicans also drew a significant proportion of their representatives from the educational system and the military. In contrast, the most important source of opposition MPs was the party organization. Forty-two percent of the MPs of the centerist New Democratic Party were recruited after having served as full-time party workers.

Still a different situation was found in Turkey, where the largest number of MPs entered the legislature after pursuing legal careers. This was especially

TABLE 4.5.
**Occupation of MPs at the Time of Their Election to Parliament (percentages)**

|  | Kenya | Korea (elected MPs) | | Turkey | |
|---|---|---|---|---|---|
|  | KANU | New Democrats | Democratic Republicans | Republican Peoples P. | Justice Party |
| Specific categories |  |  |  |  |  |
| Civil servant | 29 | 12 | 25 | 11 | 19 |
| Teacher | 14 | 9 | 25 | 11 | 7 |
| Journalist | 4 | 12 | 3 | 4 | — |
| Lawyer | 7 | 12 | — | 41 | 29 |
| Military | — | — | 19 | — | 5 |
| Businessman | 25 | 9 | 11 | 13 | 21 |
| Leader of an interest group | 7 | — | 6 | 7 | — |
| Party employee | — | 42 | 11 | — | 5 |
| Other | 14 | 6 | — | 13 | 14 |
| General categories |  |  |  |  |  |
| Managerial | 54 | 21 | 56 | 24 | 45 |
| Professional | 25 | 32 | 28 | 57 | 36 |
| Political (Party) | — | 42 | 11 | — | 5 |
| Other | 21 | 3 | 5 | 19 | 14 |
| N = | (28) | (34) | (36) | (46) | (42) |

common among the MPs of the RPP. A high proportion of MPs of the conservative Justice Party were also lawyers, although the Justice Party recruited many of its parliamentarians from the civil service and business community as well.

This review of the data presented in table 4.5 suggests that the specific pattern of legislative recruitment in any one country was a function of conditions unique to that country, rather than a result of generic differences between that country and others. An occupation which was a major source of MPs in one country was usually a minor source in the others. If there existed a pattern of variation within each of our three samples, or between them, which can be explained in terms of the differential impact of one or more of the independent variables which is evident in all three samples, such patterns were not easily discerned.

However, upon collapsing the occupational data into a small number of analytical categories, a clearer picture emerges. In the lower part of table 4.5 we find that in all three countries about half of the parliamentarians of the right-of-center and conservative parties entered the legislature after managerial careers in the civil service, the military, or business. Conversely, parliamentarians of parties on the left were more likely to have been elected to the legislature after pursuing a career in one of the professions (teaching, law, journalism). Regardless of their party affiliation, three-fourths of the legislators in each of the three samples had held managerial positions or been professionals prior to their pursuit of a legislative career.

The data presented in these tables reveal another significant feature of the process of legislative recruitment in the three countries. With the exception of the Korean MPs from the New Democratic Party, few legislators entered parliament after pursuing careers which were explicitly political in nature, though many were officers in the political parties to which they belonged. It is especially interesting that few MPs had been leaders of interest groups, given that such groups invariably make demands for allocations of state resources and consequently are involved in the political process.

Although most legislators are men of high status, a distinction must also be made between those who are members of the national political establishment and those who are only prominent notables within their local constituencies or minor leaders of other types. With the exception of the few legislators who are ministers or junior ministers of executive departments, most MPs fall into the latter category.

Given their career backgrounds, most legislators in the three samples are thus men of status, but not usually men of power. We have already discussed why legislators are not important decision makers in these countries, nor in most other developing political systems. Perhaps as a result of this situation, and of the limited resources available for allocation by the governments of these societies, there is also an extremely high turnover in the membership of the legislature. Table 4.6 shows that two-thirds of the members surveyed in Kenya and more than half of these in Turkey were serving their first terms at the time they were interviewed.

There are a number of explanations for high turnover, and they are not equally important in each of the three countries. Some members do not seek reelection, and some are either denied renomination by their party or defeated by the voters. Some of those who do not seek reelection may be discouraged and disillusioned by the limited opportunities they have to influence policy making. Some may consider the legislature to be only an intermediate step in their careers.

In Kenya, which had the highest rate of turnover, members were elected from single-member districts where their performance was exposed to close public scrutiny. Because they had little power to make public policy, and because the government lacked the resources to provide them with the services they sought for their districts, most MPs in Kenya were unable to "deliver the goods" to their constituents. This often resulted in electoral defeat. Approximately half of the Kenyan MPs who sought reelection in 1969, 1974, and 1979 were defeated. As a result, the Kenyan legislature is composed largely of inexperienced newcomers, but is dominated by a small group of MPs who are party leaders and government ministers and who have survived the electoral process. In Kenya and other countries where this occurs, the legislature may be unable to expand its authority to make public policy, and may have difficulty in generating widespread public support.

In Turkey there were other explanations for the high turnover of legislators, in addition to what could be explained by voluntary turnover. In the large multimember districts individual MPs were under less pressure to, and had less responsibility to provide services to their constituents. They had, however, to satisfy local party organizations, and ran the risk of losing the renomination bid to delegates from local parties. During the 1970s in Turkey, new political parties emerged whose candidates were usually persons without previous experience in the legislature. The various divisions within the

**TABLE 4.6.**
**Number of Terms Elected to the Legislature**
**(percentages)**

|                    | Kenya | Korea | Turkey |
|--------------------|-------|-------|--------|
| One time           | 68    | 28    | 59     |
| Two times          | 23    | 37    | 20     |
| Three times        | 9     | 21    | 9      |
| Four or more times | —     | 14    | 14     |
| *N* =              | (22)  | (83)  | (101)  |

Republican People's Party, for example, led to the replacement of experienced legislators with new members. Thus in the elections of 1977, only two-
thirds of the members of the Turkish National Assembly sought reelection.
In the fourteen provinces which served as the research sites for our study,
only 114 of 168 incumbents sought reelection, and of those, 32 percent lost
their seats. Put differently, less than half of the outgoing MPs from these
provinces returned to the new parliament after the elections.

## IDEOLOGICAL ORIENTATIONS AND
## CONCEPTIONS OF DEVELOPMENT

Although most MPs in Kenya, Korea, and Turkey are not men of power
at the national level, their values are important insofar as they are regarded
as leaders within their local communities and spokesmen for these communities in the legislature and other central agencies of the state. Because they are
intermediaries charged with forging linkages between the mass public on the
periphery of the political system and the top decision makers who control
the institutions of the state, the beliefs of the MPs are of interest, especially
their definition of economic and political development.

Members of parliament provide an effective feedback service, without
which top decision makers cannot govern. Regardless of whether decision
makers accept the views and demands expressed by legislators, they must at
least listen to what MPs say if they are to develop strategies through which
their policies will be effectively implemented at the grass roots, and if they
are to continue to command public support. Thus, while most MPs in our
samples did not participate significantly in the decisionmaking process, they
contributed substantially to the creation of the context within which that
process occurred. Their value orientations in turn affected the manner in
which they did this, and we now turn to a review of these.

We are primarily concerned with two types of value orientation which
MPs bring to bear on their activities: (1) their basic conception of economic
development, and of how it may best be achieved; and (2) their conception of
what constitutes the ideal policy for the society and culture in which they
live.

As we noted in chapter 1, political conflict in most developing countries is
a conflict over what constitutes economic development and how development
can best be achieved. The first of these questions is macro systemic and
philosophical in scope, and involves an ideal conception of the economic
sector in the "good society." The second is practical and specific in scope and
focuses on the alternative strategies and policies a state might pursue to
achieve the conception of economic development to which it subscribes.

## CONCEPTIONS OF ECONOMIC DEVELOPMENT

By the mid-1970s the political leadership within most developing countries subscribed to one of two broad definitions of economic development. Generally they defined economic development either as the achievement of self-sustained growth of the GNP or as a combination of self-sustained economic growth and an equal distribution to all members of society of the wealth that is created. On a more global and philosophical level this has been translated into the distinction between capitalist and socialist models of development.

In operational terms, the choice that must be made by policymakers in developing countries is usually between an economy expanding at an annual rate between 5 and 10 percent, with marked inequalities in the distribution of wealth, and one expanding at only 1 to 4 percent, but with less severe inequalities of distribution. Rapid economic growth is an inherently unbalanced process. It involves three forms of inequality, which are most acute in the poorest and smallest non-Western countries.

First, rapid growth requires a concentration, in one or a very few locations, of the capital and human resources necessary for development. Economic growth is easier to achieve, and hence more rapid, in areas where some development has already occurred. Consequently, rapid growth leads to regional inequality, as nations invest their limited resources at locations where the payoffs are greatest. The net result is often a widening disparity between developed, urban areas and underdeveloped, rural areas. Given that political cleavages in these societies are usually along sectional lines, exacerbated by ethnic considerations, economic policies stressing rapid growth are likely to generate considerable opposition. New resources are limited, and competition for them becomes a zero-sum game.

The second inequality incurred by systems defining development as economic growth is the attendant rise of inequality between different strata of society, and the ultimate formation of classes that are potentially antagonistic. Class inequalities are likely to parallel regional inequalities, with urban residents being better off than rural residents. But there are also class conflicts within regions: between the commercial bourgeoisie and the proletariat in the cities, and between a trader/commerical-farmer bourgeoisie and a large peasantry in rural areas.

Third, countries defining economic development primarily as growth also require greater foreign participation in the development process than do other countries. Some writers argue that this leads to further underdevelopment of Third World countries, by increasing their dependence on major western industrial economies, and on the institutions of the international capitalist system which these economies have spawned.

Those countries that try to achieve both growth and equality face other problems, most of which result from the slower rate of economic expansion, often approaching stagnation. Thus, while many developing countries have embraced socialist modes of development, most have done so at a rhetorical rather than at an operational level. Kenya and, at times, Turkey are examples of this tendency.

Given the choices facing policymakers in developing countries, where do the MPs in our three samples stand? When asked to choose between growth and regional equality, a large majority of the MPs from all parties except the Democratic Republican in Korea opted for the latter. Sentiment for promoting regional equality, even if efforts to achieve such equality were accompanied by a slowdown in growth, was particularly strong in Kenya and among the members of center and left-of-center parties in Korea and Turkey. It is not surprising that the concern for regional equality was substantially greater among MPs who were on the left, or on what was regarded as the left of the political spectrum in their countries, than among MPs on the right or far right. A concern for regional equality, however, is basically a reflection of the fact that in most developing countries the fundamental source of political cleavage is conflict between sectional interests. Given the relative levels of development in Kenya, Korea, and Turkey, it is also not surprising that Kenyan MPs as a group, rather than by party, were the most concerned about minimizing regional disparities. As we shall see in a moment, this concern is especially interesting in light of the tolerance Kenyan MPs expressed for inequality between people of different socioeconomic strata.

Turning to the choice between economic growth and the elimination of class inequalities, social democratic MPs in Turkey and opposition MPs in Korea who were regarded as being relatively, if not substantively on the left, consistently favored equity over growth. In contrast, MPs of conservative parties, including MPs of the Kenyan African National Union, overwhelmingly favored growth over equity.

In sum, MPs who were members of parties on the left were concerned with both regional and social inequities, and believed that the elimination of these two forms of inequality should take precedence over economic growth. Conversely, MPs who were members of parties on the right were inclined to tolerate a high measure of social inequality to achieve a rapid expansion of the economy. These MPs were often unwilling, however, to accept regional disparities, particularly if they lived in a political system where the deepest political cleavages are sectional ones. MPs from right-of-center parties thus opted for what is often termed the "trickle-down" model of economic development, provided their districts participated in the process. Such a conception of economic development has been the basis of economic policy in all three of the countries included in this study as it is in most of the developing world.

This is a model that invariably gives considerable latitude to a capitalist class of entrepreneurs, while encouraging state intervention to eliminate regional disparities—particularly in the provision of social welfare services. On the other hand, MPs opting for a socialist development model choose one requiring state intervention in almost all aspects of economic life for it to become a reality. The important point, however, is that regardless of the model of development preferred, most MPs—with the notable exception of the Democratic Republicans in Korea—define economic development as a process requiring at least some state participation, particularly in lessening regional inequalities. As we shall see in chapter 5, this concern for eliminating regional inequalities is paralleled by a strong commitment by most MPs to serving their district first and the nation second. Their emphasis on constituency service reflects the fundamentally sectional nature of political conflict in developing societies.

To close our discussion of MPs' conceptions of economic development, we present a summary table showing the distribution of MPs by party on an index of capitalism versus socialism (table 4.7). The index is an additive scale consisting of MPs' responses to four statements on economic development.[3] The summary index points to the marked ideological differences between MPs of the major parties. More interesting for our consideration, however, is the relatively moderate capitalist orientation of Democratic Republican MPs in Korea, and Justice Party MPs in Turkey. This moderate, almost centerist, conception of economic development by MPs of parties on the right is partially the result of the concern shared by all MPs for minimizing regional disparities for the reasons outlined above.

It is useful to note, however, that while MPs on the left included regional balance in their conception of economic development because they are ideologically committed to the creation of an egalitarian society, MPs on the right do so primarily for tactical reasons. As indicated by table 4.4, parties on the left of the political spectrum in both Korea and Turkey draw the bulk of their support from the major urban centers with their emergent industrial working class and highly differentiated class structure. Thus, while MPs of left-of-center parties are most committed to the abstract goal of an egalitarian society, their supporters are geographically concentrated in the major metropolitan areas. Conversely, while MPs of rightist parties generally favor economic growth at the expense of equality, they must concern themselves with the spatial if not the class dimension of equal distribution, because the source of their political power is geographically dispersed.

Table 4.7 also shows the great similarity between the ideological distribution of Kenyan MPs and those of the Democratic Republican and Justice parties in Korea and in Turkey. In all three countries MPs representing rural constituencies and right-of-center parties give priority to growth over equality, while expressing concern about the geographical distribution of new economic enterprises. Conversely, in Korea and Turkey, rapid economic expansion and urban growth have produced left-of-center parties committed to a more egalitarian economic and political system. The data consistently suggest a strong relationship between MPs' conceptions of the ideal economic system and the constituencies and parties they represent.

## CONCEPTIONS OF POLITICAL DEVELOPMENT

As we have emphasized, political leaders in most developing countries are confronted by an unceasing flow of demands greater than can be met by their limited resources. These demands are particularly intense when they are sectional in nature, and they lead to pressures for distribution of resources to foster economic development that threaten governmental policies for economic growth. Political leaders frequently must choose between policies that may require a measure of coercion and authoritarian rule and ones that are direct responses to popular, particularly majoritarian, demands.

To determine how legislators in developing countries are likely to resolve this dilemma, and to learn how they think the political system ought to run, the MPs in our samples were asked to agree or disagree with three statements which measure the extent to which they favor democratic or authoritarian rule. Their responses were then added together to yield a summary score for an index of democracy vs. authoritarianism. The distribution of these scores is presented by party in table 4.7.[4]

TABLE 4.7
MPs' Conceptions of Economic and Political Development (percentages)

|  | Kenya | Korea (elected MPs) | | Turkey | |
|---|---|---|---|---|---|
|  | KANU | New Democrats | Democratic Republicans | Republican Peoples P. | Justice Party |
| Capitalism |  |  |  |  |  |
| 1 | 13 | 3 | 8 | — | — |
| 2 | 38 | 11 | 58 | 9 | 34 |
| 3 | 42 | 46 | 31 | 65 | 63 |
| 4 | 8 | 40 | 3 | 26 | 3 |
| Socialism |  |  |  |  |  |
| Authoritarianism |  |  |  |  |  |
| 1 | — | 3 | 8 | — | — |
| 2 | 13 | 3 | 11 | — | 13 |
| 3 | 29 | 17 | 61 | — | 16 |
| 1 | 58 | 77 | 19 | 100 | 71 |
| Democracy |  |  |  |  |  |
| N = | (24) | (35) | (36) | (46) | (38) |

A quick review of the data indicates that most MPs lean toward a democratic conception of the most desirable type of political system. As in industrial societies, members of left-of-center political parties are especially fervent in their democratic orientations insofar as these orientations involve a fundamental belief in the appropriateness of majoritarian rule, coupled with belief in the right of the individual to express dissent. The strong democratic orientations expressed by MPs of all parties, however, suggest two interesting conclusions about the way legislators perceive the political process.

First, it would appear that MPs in developing countries subscribe to the view frequently expressed by parliamentarians in industrial societies that legislators and the legislature constitute a bulwark against the authoritarian tendencies of executive power. By rejecting the view that society is better ruled by a "few enlightened leaders than by the will of the masses," the members in our three samples seem also to be saying that their role as parliamentarians is an inherently democratic one. As directly elected representatives of the citizens in their home areas, MPs do not accept the view that the executive, with its great resources of administrative and technical expertise, should make public policy entirely on its own.

A second interesting feature of MPs' opinions about how the political system ought to function is that legislators of opposing political parties diverge much less in their beliefs about the political rules of the game than they do in their values about economic relationships. Because MPs' attitudes about the economic system are in large part a function of the types of constituency they represent, we may expect MPs from different constituencies to diverge much less in their conceptions about the political system than in those about economic development. Put differently, legislators in developing countries appear to be more likely to arrive at a consensus about what constitutes the political dimension of development than about what constitutes the economic dimension.

# Chapter 5

# LEGISLATORS AND REPRESENTATION

In chapter 1 we argued that legislators in developing countries perform a distinctive and necessary function when they establish linkages from the periphery to the center of the political system. The establishment of these networks for communication and the exchange of resources is a necessary first step in the representational process. If we are to determine the extent to which legislators in Kenya, Korea, and Turkey contribute to the representational process, we must identify whether and in what manner these legislators seek to create the linkages of which the representational process is composed.

To make this determination, we shall focus on the activities of individual legislators as they carry out their respective conceptions of what constitutes, and what should constitute, the legislative role. Put simply, we shall attempt to answer the questions of whether and how legislators in developing countries contribute to the representational process by first determining what these legislators do and why. We shall describe the legislators' conceptions of their roles and try to determine to what extent their behavior fulfills these role expectations.

In chapter 6 we will compare these findings with the role expectations held by constituents.

## LEGISLATORS' DEFINITIONS OF PURPOSIVE ROLES

In all countries where the legislative process is a significant component of political life there exist at least five distinct sets of expectations of what the role of legislators should be: (1) the formal role as specified by the country's constitution and/or by the rules of procedure which regulate the legislative process; (2) the self-definition of the legislative role which each individual legislator articulates for himself or herself; (3) peer expectations of the legislative role; (4) the legislative role as defined for each legislator by his or her constituents; and (5) the legislative role as defined by referents outside the legislature and outside the districts each individual legislator represents. These include the expectations of the executive, the civil service, major interest groups, and the public at large.

In this study we are principally concerned with the second and fourth sets of role expectations, because of our interest in the linkages legislators establish from the periphery to the center of the political system. The establishment and perpetuation of these linkages is largely a function of the relationships between legislators and their constituents, and so the ways in which each of these groups views the role of the legislator constitute our main concern. The reader should, therefore, remember that our discussion of legislative role expectations is a selective and partial one. It is not, nor does it pretend to be, a comprehensive study.

To determine how the legislators interviewed for this study conceived of their roles, we commenced our interviews in all three countries with an open-ended question: "How would you describe the job of being a legislator—what are the most important things you do?" The responses, which are presented in table 5.1 by the political parties to which the respondents belong, indicate that legislators usually defined their roles in terms of two functions—lawmaking and representation.

The data also suggest that legislators conceive of their roles as being quite different from those of members of the executive on the one hand and of the civil service on the other. None of our respondents, for example, thought that it was his or her duty to shape public opinion, an important component of political leadership in new states, and one normally assumed by the head

TABLE 5.1.
MPs' Descriptions of Their Purposive Roles (percentages)

|  | Kenya | Korea | Turkey |
|---|---|---|---|
| Lawmaking, legislating | 48 | 42 | 49 |
| Performing "constitutional" and legally defined duties | 8 | 5 | 9 |
| Policymaking, participating in key government decisions | 12 | 16 | 7 |
| Representing the voters, and/or various interest groups | 60 | 41 | 22 |
| Helping to shape and guide public opinion | — | — | — |
| Assisting in the implementation of government policy through close cooperation with the executive | 8 | — | 5 |
| Checking and balancing the power of the executive branch | 4 | 27 | 5 |
| Initiating plans for economic and social development | 20 | 1 | 6 |
| Helping to achieve overriding national objectives (i.e., unity, national identity) | — | 10 | 18 |
| *N* = | (25) | (83) | (102) |

*Note:* Percentages often total to more than 100 because some respondents gave multiple answers to this open-ended question.

of state and/or by cadres of the ruling political party, where such exist. While some respondents expressed a desire to participate in making of key government decisions, the principal function of the executive, it was not a major concern. Nor did more than a handful of our respondents feel that they should play a significant role in the implementation and administration of policy, the main reponsibility of civil servants.

Upon considering the two activities cited most often by our respondents, it seems somewhat strange and formalistic that they placed so much emphasis on lawmaking, given the relative weakness of the legislatures in the three countries. A closer examination of table 5.1, however, suggests why our respondents replied to our query in the manner they did.

First, legislators in Kenya, Korea, and Turkey did not appear to equate lawmaking with policymaking. While almost half of the MPs in each country defined their roles in terms of lawmaking, no more than a sixth (and usually much less) defined their roles in terms of policymaking. It would thus seem that lawmaking is perceived by the legislators as the process through which policies made by others are ratified and legitimized via translation into law.

The most significant differences among MPs from the three countries lay in the importance attached to representing the voter, ranging from 60 percent in Kenya, to 41 percent in Korea and only 22 percent in Turkey. These differences can perhaps be explained by differences in the electoral systems and by alternative methods of linkage available to constituents. Single-member district systems (Kenya) and to a lesser extent two-member districts (Korea) provide more direct contacts between voters and their representatives than is likely to occur in large multimember districts (Turkey).

It is important to recognize that the legislator is only one of a number of channels available to voters who seek to gain benefits or to influence decisions of the government. Voters may also work through local party organizations, voluntary organizations in the community, local leaders of various kinds, or even local agents in the bureaucracy. Moreover, it is possible that some citizens will go through intermediaries, such as local leaders or local party organizations, in order to contact their legislators, rendering an MP's representation of constituents quite indirect.

Local party organizations played an important linkage role in both Korea (especially for the governing party) and Turkey. Constituents in these countries often contacted local party officials instead of MPs or (especially in Turkey) as a way of getting their message to MPs. The importance of the party organization in both Korea and Turkey helps to explain why legislators in those countries were less conscious of a representative role.

Upon examining the data further to determine whether MPs of different backgrounds and affiliations defined the role of the legislator differently, we found few variations in the patterns of response that were replicated in all three countries. The only variable to give rise to significant variations in the ways members of the three countries defined their roles was that of party affiliation, but these variations were largely due to conditions specific to one of the three political systems considered in this study. For example, the ideological position of an MP's party had little effect on the way they conceived of their roles. Although in all three countries MPs from parties on the left and right of the political spectrum held very different conceptions of what constitutes the good society, their conceptions of the role of the legislator were roughly the same.

On the other hand, MPs who were members of the governing party in their country at the time of our survey tended to place greater emphasis on lawmaking than did members of the opposition. Such an orientation is what one would expect, given that these MPs had the votes in the legislature to enact legislation and were in part elected to translate their party's policies into law.

Conversely, MPs belonging to the opposition expressed the reverse position. In Korea, more than half of the members of the opposition New Democratic Party defined the role of the legislator as providing a check and balance to executive power. This finding is hardly surprising given the extent and methods by which the government of President Park dominated the Korean political system. But it was not a view expressed by backbenchers (the functional equivalent of an opposition) in Kenya. The fact that the Turkish system is basically a parliamentary one helps to explain why MPs in that country were not concerned about checking executive power.

Variations in the social backgrounds of MPs—their occupations, education, or age—resulted in no consistent or significant differences in the ways they conceived of their roles, nor did variations in the types of constituencies MPs were elected to represent. Representatives of urban and rural districts conceived of the legislator's role in similar terms, though MPs who were members of parties that drew a disproportionate amount of their support from rural areas were somewhat more likely to define their roles in representational terms than were members of parties supported by the residents of rural areas.

## ROLE BEHAVIOR OF LEGISLATORS

After questioning our respondents about their purposive roles, we asked them a series of questions about the activities to which they devoted the bulk of their time. The purpose of these questions was to obtain both a detailed description of what our respondents did and a measure of the extent to which this behavior was consistent with their roles as they initially defined them.

To determine the activities on which MPs spent most of their time, the members in the three samples were first asked to rank six activities frequently cited as important components of a legislator's role in Kenya, Korea, and Turkey. The results of the survey are given in table 5.2.

A review of the table suggests that none of the six activities dominated the attention of the respondents in all three countries, though two—obtaining resources for one's district and interceding with civil servants on behalf of one's constituents—occupied the time of 43 to 60 percent of the Kenyan and Korean MPs. Conversely, only one activity, helping to resolve local conflicts, was consistently ignored.

As was the pattern with the respondents' descriptions of purposive roles, MPs of different social backgrounds and affiliations and representing different types of districts did not differ significantly or consistently in respect to the role behavior they reported. Further examination of the data, however, indicates that in choosing to concentrate their efforts on different activities, the members of the three samples tended to cluster themselves by selecting activities that were similar in type. The inclination of MPs to cluster themselves on the basis of the activities to which they devoted most of their time is revealed by crosstabulating the respondents' first and second choices of these activities. Upon so manipulating the data, one finds that the respondents tend to cluster themselves within two broad groups which we shall henceforth refer to as the "internals" and the "externals." As can be seen from a review of table 5.3, the great majority of the respondents who said explaining government policy was their most important activity also indicated that debating and amending bills was the second most important activity on their agendas. Conversely, a majority of those who said that legislation was their most important activity indicated that explaining government policy was their second most important duty.

By contrast, a majority of those who devoted their principal efforts to obtaining resources for their districts said that their second most important activity was contacting civil servants on their constituents' behalf. And the great majority of those whose principal activity was contacting civil servants said their next most important effort was obtaining resources for their districts. Given these clusters, we shall label the first group of respondents (those who confine the bulk of their activities to discussing government policy and legislating) as "internals," and the second (those who obtain resources and intercede with civil servants) as "externals."

In reviewing the distribution of the data in table 5.3, the reader will note that respondents who indicated that their most important activity was expressing the views of their districts do not fit neatly into either of the aforementioned clusters. However, because of the low $N$ of our country samples, we have decided to apportion these respondents to the internal and external clusters on the basis of the activity they regard as the second most important. It is then possible to present a typology of legislators' behavioral roles and a distribution of the three country samples across this typology (see table 5.4).

## TABLE 5.2.
### Activities to which Legislators Devote Most of Their Time (percentages)

| | Kenya | | | Korea | | | Turkey | | |
|---|---|---|---|---|---|---|---|---|---|
| | First choice | Second choice | Total | First choice | Second choice | Total | First choice | Second choice | Total |
| Explaining policies to voters | 15 | 11 | 26 | 15 | 10 | 25 | 39 | 11 | 50 |
| Proposing, debating, and amending bills | 19 | 15 | 34 | 23 | 15 | 38 | 30 | 13 | 43 |
| Expressing the views of the people in my district | 15 | 19 | 24 | 14 | 20 | 34 | 3 | 35 | 38 |
| Obtaining government resources for my district | 44 | 15 | 59 | 15 | 28 | 43 | 7 | 33 | 40 |
| Interceding with civil servants on constituents' behalf | 7 | 37 | 44 | 33 | 27 | 60 | 22 | 6 | 28 |
| Resolving local conflicts | — | — | — | 1 | — | 1 | — | 3 | 3 |
| N = | (27) | (27) | (27) | (80) | (80) | (80) | (101) | (101) | (101) |

TABLE 5.3.

**Most Important Activities: First Choice by Second Choice (percentages)**

| Second choice | First choice | | | | | |
|---|---|---|---|---|---|---|
| | Explaining policy | Debating bills | Expressing views of district | Obtaining resources | Contacting civil servants | Resolving conflicts |
| Explaining policy | — | 38 | 10 | 10 | 4 | — |
| Debating bills | 25 | — | 43 | 20 | 6 | — |
| Expressing views of district | 40 | 38 | — | 17 | 16 | 100 |
| Obtaining resources | 26 | 6 | 19 | — | 74 | — |
| Contacting civil servants | 9 | 14 | 29 | 53 | — | — |
| Resolving conflicts | — | 5 | — | — | — | — |
| $N =$ | (65) | (66) | (21) | (30) | (49) | (1) |

We believe that the categories of internal and external legislators are valuable in analyzing representation for several reasons. In order to understand representation we need to know what legislators actually do, and our question about how they spend their time (though imperfect) is our best measure of their activity. We have found (table 5.2) that in fact some members tend to concentrate their time on activities within the legislature, while others concentrate on activities outside the legislature. We recognize of course that some members (perhaps many of those who are unclassified) devote much time to both. We believe, nevertheless, that this distinction between internal and external priorities in MPs' activities is the most useful analytical technique, given our data. No other distinction between the kinds of roles legislators play was apparent in all three countries. Consequently, we will devote considerable attention in the rest of this chapter to determining which characteristics are useful in distinguishing between these two types and how they differ in actions and beliefs.

## COUNTRY VARIATIONS BY ROLE BEHAVIOR

As shown in table 5.4, the typology embraces between 69 and 84 percent of the MPs surveyed in each of the three countries, proportions that support the use of this dichotomy as an appropriate scheme for distinguishing among the behavioral roles of most legislators. Most interesting are the differences among the countries: the much larger proportion of externals in Kenya, the larger proportion of externals in Korea, and the larger proportion of internals in Turkey. In trying to explain these differences, we might compare electoral structures, party systems, legislative-executive relations, or basic socioeconomic differences among the three countries. In choosing which roles to emphasize, individual members may be guided by their own preferences; the demands made on them by colleagues, other political actors, and constituents; and the realistic possibilities for effective activity within or outside the legislature. Because our typology is a relative ranking, it is affected by variables that encourage or deter internal activities, as well as by those that have an impact on external activities.

Earlier in this chapter, in our analysis of purposive roles, we noted several factors that help to determine how many members emphasize representing voters. These same factors should help to determine how much time members devote to external activities. Consequently, the higher proportion of "externals" in Kenya may result partly from the use of single-member districts and the absence of such linkage vehicles as strong local parties. The multimember districts and strong local parties in Turkey may discourage Turkish MPs from devoting as much time to external activities. The priority attached to internal activities, on the other hand, is certainly affected by the opportunities available to members to participate in debates, offer amend-

ments, and have some impact on the policymaking process. These opportunities were greater in Turkey than in Kenya and Korea, where policymaking is dominated by the executive.

The level of economic development in the three countries would also
appear to have some effect on the priorities that legislators assign to internal
and external matters. Due to factors discussed in chapter 1, we would expect
that the more urbanized and industrialized the country, the more likely the
legislators are to devote time to internal matters.

As noted in chapter 1, political conflict in agrarian societies usually occurs
between competing sectional interests, geographically defined, rather than
between competing economic interests, functionally defined. As a result,
legislators in agrarian societies are most likely to define the constituencies
they represent in geographical or sectional terms, while those in industrial
societies define their constituents in terms of the different economic interests
located in their districts, interests which usually exist in other districts as
well.

Where legislators perceive the interests of their constituents in geographic
terms, as in Kenya, the main task of the legislator, if he is responsive to
constituent demands, is that of obtaining resources for his district and helping
individual constituents with their problems. This role does not require devotion to the task of policymaking, but rather to the specific distribution of
resources already allocated by the policymaking process to his district. Most
of these activities occur outside the legislature, and thus can be described as
external.

Where legislators define the needs of their constituents in terms of the
demands made by the leading economic interests in their districts, as they do
in Turkey, their main task is to shape the outcomes of the policymaking
process so that the resources allocated by that process are directed to interests
of the kind located in their districts. This means that the legislator must be
concerned with the making of public policy as it occurs in the legislature (if
indeed it does) and within other institutions at the center of the political
system, such as the executive branch.

**TABLE 5.4.**
**A Typology of Legislators' Behavioral Roles by**
**Country (percentages)**

|                | Kenya | Korea | Turkey |
|----------------|-------|-------|--------|
| Internals      | 28    | 28    | 46     |
| Externals      | 54    | 42    | 23     |
| Not classified | 18    | 30    | 31     |
| N =            | (28)  | (83)  | (104)  |

If external and internal priorities of legislators were based entirely on the level of development, Korean MPs should be approximately as internally oriented as those in Turkey. We have already suggested, however, that other factors (such as executive domination of policymaking and the structure of the electoral system) may reduce the internal orientation of Korean legislators.

The relationship between the level of development and behavioral roles that we have found at the national level appears to be replicated at the district level. Legislators from rural districts tend to be externals, while those from more urban and more economically developed areas tend to be internals. We were unable, however, to determine whether the behavior of the members in our three samples was primarily a function of the overall level of development in their respective countries or of the level of development in the districts they represent. Upon controlling for the effects of both variables, we found that the impact of each appeared to be roughly the same.

## PERSONAL BACKGROUND VARIABLES

Among the personal background variables that might be expected to affect behavioral roles, we found that social status and ideology (see chapter 4) had no effect. We did find, however, that older respondents were more likely to be internals than externals. A major reason for the positive relationship between the age of MPs and their propensity to be internals is the correlation between age and political experience.

Older MPs have been elected to office many more times than younger legislators,[1] and are therefore more likely to occupy leadership positions in their parties and in the government, should their party be in power. As such they are more likely to be concerned with questions of basic policy than are younger MPs, questions which require them to concentrate their efforts on activities which transpire within the legislature and at the center of the political system. The data suggest a strong and clear relationship between being a party leader and being an internal. The MPs who have held party office at the national level, or who have been officers of their parliamentary party, are more likely to be internals than are legislators who have merely held staff positions or positions within local party organizations.

## RELATIONSHIP BETWEEN MPS' PURPOSIVE AND BEHAVIORAL ROLES

There ought to be a positive relationship between the purposive and behavioral roles of legislators, that is between what they think are the most important parts of their job and what they say they devote most time to. Table 5.5 shows this to be the case. The internals are more likely to rank as important those parts of the job that would appear to arise within the legislature: lawmaking, legal duties, and implementing government policy. Policymaking, however, was mentioned more often by externals. Those classified as externals were also more likely to mention representing voters, checking the executive branch, and initiating plans for economic and social development, plans that would presumably be focused on the district. The fact that externals gave more attention to checking the executive branch is interesting, for it is a function that while not strictly internal, is more national than local in its focus.

When legislators were asked which activities they would like to spend more or less time on, there was a slight tendency for internals to prefer internal activities and for externals to mention external activities. It is clear, however, that some members would like to spend more time on types of activities substantially different from those that now take up their time. One reason for this is that in countries with the most externals—Kenya and Korea—many legislators wanted to play a more active role in policymaking through debate and amendment of bills; in Turkey, where there were more internals, many MPs said that they should spend more time getting government resources for the district.

There was, as we would expect, a much closer correlation between the internal-external dichotomy and the MPs' responses to a question about whether national or district problems occupied most of their time. Almost 78 percent of the externals said they concentrated on district problems, and 56 percent of the internals said they concentrated on national problems. The different types of issues which occupied internals and externals further suggests

TABLE 5.5.
MPs' Descriptions of the Role of the Legislator by the
Roles Legislators Actually Play (percentages)

|  | Internals | Externals |
| --- | --- | --- |
| Activities pursued by internals |  |  |
| Lawmaking, legislating | 61 | 29 |
| Performing "constitutional" and legally defined duties | 9 | 4 |
| Policymaking, participating in key government decisions | 8 | 15 |
| Assisting in the implementation of government policy |  |  |
| through close cooperation with the executive | 6 | 3 |
| Total | 84 | 51 |
| Activities pursued by externals |  |  |
| Representing the voters and/or various interest groups | 30 | 44 |
| Checking and balancing the power of the executive branch | 8 | 18 |
| Initiating plans for economic and social development | 1 | 8 |
| Total | 39 | 70 |
| Other activities | 12 | 12 |
| N = | (77) | (73) |

Note: Percentages total to more than 100 because of multiple responses.

that internals are basically oriented towards the center of the political system, while externals face the periphery. This distinction will be explored further below.

## THE LEGISLATOR IN THE DISTRICT

In order to understand more specifically how legislators represent their constituents and what variations occur in representation, we will present data on the legislators' descriptions of what they do in their districts: how often they visit, to whom they talk, what topics are discussed. We will make comparisons among countries, and also look for differences reported by internals and externals. Subsequently, in chapter 6, we will explore constituent views of the MPs' visits to their districts.

Let us begin by examining how frequently legislators visit their districts. Not all legislators can make frequent visits. First, there is the problem of distance. Some electoral districts are far from the capital. Transportation systems, like distance, may either facilitate or impede travel to a legislator's constituency. Second, the amount of time each deputy may devote to visiting his constituency varies. Those in leadership positions, for example, may have less time for visits than do backbenchers. It may also be argued that legislators whose seats are insecure may be more motivated to visit their districts than those who experience fewer difficulties in getting reelected.

Our data show that most legislators visit their districts one or more times each month. Although all Kenyan districts are located within a day's travel of the capital, it is still remarkable that 96 percent of the Kenyan deputies visited their districts three times or more a month, indicating the importance they accorded to being available to their constituents. It is also somewhat surprising to discover that almost half of the elected Korean deputies did not feel the need to visit their districts, despite the fact that most Korean districts are easily accessible. Seventy-six percent of the Turkish legislators visited their districts once or twice a month. Those paying more frequent visits were from provinces which are either near the capital or easily reached by rapid transport systems.

Contrary to what might be expected, we do not find that externals visit their districts more often than internals do. Neither do we find evidence from our Kenyan and Korean data to support our expectation that backbenchers would visit their districts more because they had more time available. While we might also expect that the frequency of visits by a legislator to his district might be determined by his expectations about the prospects for reelection, this line of reasoning is not borne out by the data. Those Turkish and Korean deputies who anticipated opposition to their renomination (the question was not asked in Kenya) did not appear to visit their districts any more frequently than those who expected no such opposition. Thus, easy access to transportation determines frequency of visits by deputies to their districts in Turkey, but not in Korea, where strong personal electoral machines eliminate the need for frequent visits to the constituency.

What do legislators do when they visit their districts? Whom do they see or who tries to see them? The answers to these questions will help us identify the linkage patterns between the legislators and the constituents. We asked legislators in Kenya, Korea, and Turkey whether they saw most of their constituents individually or in groups when they visited their districts. Kenyan deputies most often saw their constituents both individually and in groups, Korean deputies individually, and Turkish deputies in groups.

Table 5.6 shows that Kenyan and Korean legislators demonstrated remarkably similar activity patterns when they visit their districts. They asked constituents about their problems and in some cases informed them about new laws. By contrast, Turkish legislators most frequently mentioned informing citizens about new laws, and also often said that they asked them their opinions about legislation.

We also see a difference in emphasis in constituent visits between internals and externals. Internals were most likely to inform constituents about new laws and policies; two-thirds of them either informed constituents about laws or sought their opinions. By contrast, two-thirds of the externals said that their most important activity was to find out about constituent problems, and only 4 percent of them gave top priority to discerning views on legislation. In other words, internals used their district visits to facilitate and support their legislative activities within the central institutions of the political system, while externals used the visits to become better informed about the needs and demands of their districts.

The differences in the mode of legislators' interaction and the type of activities they conducted when visiting their districts suggested that systemic

TABLE 5.6.
Legislators' Most Important Activity when Visiting District (percentages)

| Activity | Kenya | Korea | Turkey | All countries | |
|---|---|---|---|---|---|
| | | | | Internals | Externals |
| Asking constituents' opinions about legislation | 4 | 2 | 22 | 22 | 4 |
| Asking constituents what problems are troubling them | 72 | 75 | 16 | 31 | 66 |
| Informing constituents about new laws and policies | 16 | 15 | 54 | 44 | 16 |
| Others | 8 | 8 | 8 | 3 | 14 |
| N = | (25) | (83) | (102) | (77) | (73) |

characteristics may affect the behavior of legislators. Kenya, as noted earlier, has the least structured and formalized political party. The Kenyan deputy does not have intermediary institutions between himself and his constituents. He meets them both in groups and as individuals, consults them about their problems, and then tries to assist them. The Korean MP, on the other hand, belongs to a well-organized and disciplined party at the parliamentary level that has no counterpart at the local level. Instead there is often a personal political machine, the members of which the Korean MP consults for information on district problems.

The Turkish deputy not only belongs to an organized and disciplined parliamentary party, but also to a national party organization that is well organized on the local level. The fact that several deputies represent the same province (for example, forty-three deputies represented Istanbul in 1977) means that a single deputy does not have a clearly defined constituency, at least not in geographic terms. When a Turkish deputy visits his district, he will typically go to the headquarters of the local party organization, talk to the party activists, and bring them news from Ankara, often explaining how new legislation and government decisions may be exploited for local ends. Personal problems are sometimes brought to the member, but local party leaders tend to most of these.

The analysis we have presented above is given added support by an examination of whom the MP tries to see or who tries to see him most often when he is visiting his district, and of what the topics of conversation are.

As indicated in table 5.7, Korean and Turkish MPs saw party officials (members of their political machines in Korea, and local party leaders and activists in Turkey) when they visited their districts. Kenyan MPs saw party officials and local leaders of various kinds, many of whom constituted the local personal machine of the MP in the district. Korean MPs also mentioned seeing village heads and other traditional leaders, suggesting their importance as a source of support.

Kenyan MPs often mentioned contacts with local civil servants, such as district or subdistrict commissioners, for two reasons. First, these public officials have an important role to play in the planning and execution of development projects, and it is therefore important for the MP to maintain close relations with them. Second, MPs act as transmitters of constituency problems and desires, interceding with them on behalf of constituents. The Korean deputy, though to a lesser extent, also devoted some time to visiting with civil servants. Turkish deputies, however, did not report such contacts, since this was ordinarily done by local party leadership. It is also true that in Turkey, provincial and subprovincial governors, for example, perceive themselves as nonpartisan employees of the state, and shy away from close relations with deputies who are political figures.

If we divide the MPs from all countries into internals and externals, it is clear that the former make a concerted effort to contact party officials, while the latter seek out other local notables, such as leading businessmen, leaders of interest groups and social organizations, and village headsmen and chiefs. Sixty-two percent of the externals in our study contacted party officials first when visiting their home districts, while only 38 percent of the internals did so. This may be because the party leaders, though functioning at the local level and often parochial in their roles and interests, are often part of a national organization which is directed at the center; the other local leaders are not only located on the periphery, they are actually much more interested in the purely local problems that are of particular concern to externals.

The topics deputies discussed when visiting their districts also confirmed the influence of systemic constraints on modes of interaction with constituents (see table 5.8). Kenyan deputies most often discussed district matters, whereas Koreans discussed partisan matters, consulting with members of their personal political machines.

Turkish legislators, on the other hand, talked most about national political matters. We suspect, however, that the concern with national matters was somewhat exaggerated, while district problems were somewhat deemphasized, as a consequence of the Turkish intervention on Cyprus. Yet the basic pattern was probably unchanged, since more than 60 percent of the interviews were, in fact, completed a month before the military action.

Internals and externals also differed in the subjects they discussed with the people they made a special effort to see. The distinctions here were somewhat blurred, because the subjects discussed also varied with the type of persons MPs saw, but when talking to local leaders other than party officials, externals were more likely to discuss local issues and personal matters than were

TABLE 5.7.
Who Legislator Sees when Visiting District (percentages)

|  | Kenya | Korea | Turkey |
|---|---|---|---|
| Village head, traditional leader | 0 (0) | 13 (19) | 4 (6) |
| Local social leaders | 14 (23) | 5 (6) | 15 (15) |
| Business notables | 4 (0) | 5 (21) | 1 (2) |
| Party officials | 21 (8) | 61 (16) | 50 (41) |
| Civil servants | 36 (38) | 6 (23) | 0 (2) |
| Others | 4 (4) | 6 (9) | 31 (32) |
| None in particular | 14 (15) | 0 (0) | 0 (0) |
| N = | (28) | (83) | (95) |

Note: Percentages do not add to 100 because categories of minor importance in all countries have been eliminated. Figures in parenthesis indicate second ranked activity.

internals, and less likely to discuss issues of national concern. When talking to party officials, however, there was little difference between the two types of legislators, as both were particularly interested in discussing partisan matters. These findings suggest again that internals tend to be oriented towards the center of the political system, while externals look to the periphery.

## FOCUS OF REPRESENTATION

Students of American legislatures, and a few studying other countries, have sought to determine how legislators make choices among various groups that they represent or have responsibilities toward.[2] Particular attention has been paid to the distinction between trustees, who follow their own convictions, and delegates, who take instructions from a particular constituency. These distinctions are particularly meaningful in those legislative bodies (such as the United States Congress and state legislatures) in which members play an important decison-making role and have some freedom to choose among various groups that make demands on them. The greater the range of answers to such questions in a legislature, the greater the variety and complexity of roles there are; where there is consensus on representational focus, or on other types of roles, we can conclude that legislative norms are strong enough to prevent much diversity.

A comparison of representational roles in several legislative bodies should be useful because it would demonstrate how much consensus there is in each body and provide some basis for estimating the importance of various factors in the decision-making process. In other words, it is one important clue to understanding how legislators represent and whom they represent.

There are some limitations, however, in the utility of such role analysis—

**TABLE 5.8.**
**Topics of Discussion when Visiting District (percentages)**

|  | Kenya | Korea | Turkey |
|---|---|---|---|
| National political matters | 0 (0) | 3 (6) | 49 (44) |
| District matters | 71 (75) | 22 (53) | 24 (27) |
| Campaign matters | 7 (8) | 7 (1) | 0 (0) |
| Partisan matters | 7 (0) | 47 (9) | 14 (14) |
| General matters | 0 (17) | 8 (7) | 4 (1) |
| Personal matters | 0 (0) | 11 (21) | 1 (6) |
| Other | 14 (0) | 1 (1) | 8 (9) |
| *N* = | (14) | (74) | (79) |

*Note*: Figures in parentheses indicate second ranked activity. Figures may not add to 100 due to errors in rounding.

particularly on a crossnational basis. The choices that a legislator makes in choosing among competing foci of representation may be more complicated than can be captured in a few brief questions. Legislators may give the answers that they think are expected of them, rather than completely frank responses. Legislators in different political cultures may interpret questions differently. While these problems are inherent in all crossnational studies based on questionnaires, they seem particularly applicable to the study of representative roles.

We must also recognize that the average member of the legislature in each of the three countries we are studying played a modest role in the decision-making process. The strength of executive authority in Kenya and Korea, and the strength of party in Korea and Turkey, limited the choices that MPs could make on legislative matters. Undoubtedly, many legislators paid less attention to legislative business then they did to constituency service.

Keeping these limitations in mind, we shall now examine the responses of MPs to a series of questions on representation. The MPs were asked, "If you had to make a choice between the views of the following groups, which one would you choose?" These five groups were on the list: "my constituents," "leaders of my party," "my personal conviction," "my party faction," and "a major interest group." The results are summarized in table 5.9, which shows the results of the forced choices among the three most salient groups—party leaders, constituents, and the MPs personal convictions. The bottom half of the table shows what proportion of MPs ranked each group high, using an additive index (one point for each time the item was chosen). It should be noted that members in Kenya were less willing to make such choices than were those in the other two countries. This is largely because the political party and party leaders are less important in that legislature, and consequently choices involving the party were not meaningful to many Kenyan legislators.

A close examination of the data shows some interesting differences among the countries. Interest groups commanded little attention in any of the countries, and, except in Korea, party factions were relatively unimportant. In Korea a strong party orientation was evident in the responses of MPs; this appears to reflect the political realities of the Korean legislature. The Korean MPs also gave higher priority to their own beliefs than they did to the views of their constituents.

The strong constituency orientations of Kenyan legislators, which we have noted throughout this chapter, were evident in the analysis of representative focus. When asked to choose between their constituents and other groups, Kenyan MPs always chose their constituents. Kenya was the only country where a majority of those responding professed to prefer the views of constituents to their own. In reality, many Kenyan legislators believe that they must remain sensitive to the general wishes of their constituency, but that, being better educated and informed, they are responsible for guiding and articulating constituency wishes. It would be incorrect to assume from this analysis that Kenyan MPs regularly vote against the party leadership, but the data do suggest that they maintain a strong constituency orientation and that they use whatever opportunities they have in the capital to advance constituency interests.

In Turkey, where MPs are elected on party slates in multimember districts, it is not surprising to find that constituency ranks relatively low. What is surprising is that, despite the strength of the party system, members ranked party leaders even lower than constituents. By far the strongest focus of representation for Turkish MPs, according to them, were their own convictions. The label of trustee would appear to fit the Turkish MPs better than it would MPs in other countries. The relatively high level of education and legislative experience among Turkish legislators probably contributes to their trustee orientation (though it is not higher than the levels found in Korea). The constitutional declaration that MPs should represent the whole nation rather than any district, together with Turkey's strong national party organization, contributes to the norm that makes a purely constituency delegate role seem too parochial. The independence that Turkish MPs expressed

TABLE 5.9.
Legislators' Focus of Representation

|  | Kenya | Korea | Turkey |
|---|---|---|---|
| Percentage of members making choice |  |  |  |
| Party leaders v. | 14 | 53 | 30 |
| my constituents | 36 | 39 | 32 |
| Personal convictions v. | 14 | 66 | 52 |
| my constituents | 25 | 29 | 15 |
| Party leaders v. | 14 | 58 | 22 |
| personal convictions | 21 | 36 | 44 |
| Percentage of members scoring high for each item on index |  |  |  |
| My constituents | 25 | 36 | 31 |
| Leaders of my party | 14 | 57 | 26 |
| My personal convictions | 18 | 53 | 63 |
| My party faction | 7 | 17 | 7 |
| Major interest group | 4 | 0 | 0 |
| *N* = | (28) | (83) | (104) |

*Note*: Legislators who were unwilling or unable to make these choices are not listed, and consequently percentages in the top part of the table do not add up to 100. The index in the bottom half of the table was constructed by counting one point for each time an item was chosen in forced choices with another item, resulting in scores ranging from 0 to 4 for each index. Those MPs with a score of 3 or 4 on an item are classified as scoring high.

with regard to party leaders may reflect some wishful thinking, though it is not an uncommon occurrence for legislators to resign from their parties over an issue and become independents or eventually join another party.

We compared the answers given by our two major categories of MPs—internals and externals—to the questions on focus of representation, but found no significant differences. In other words, those who devoted their time primarily to legislative business were not more responsive to party leaders as we might have expected. Neither were those who spent more time on district affairs necessarily more responsive to their constituents when making decisions. We will return to the topic of representative focus in chapter 6, where we will compare the choices of MPs with the preferences of their constituents.

# CONSTITUENTS AND REPRESENTATION

Representation is shaped by the interplay between representatives and constituents. In the preceding chapter, we concentrated on the problem of representation as seen from the standpoint of legislators. Now we turn to the other actors in representative linkages, the constituents. How do constituents regard the legislative institution? What kind of roles do they attribute to their MPs? How do they evaluate the performance of their representatives? What positions do they take on key policy issues, and to what extent are their preferences represented by their MPs? And what are the consequences of representative linkages in broader political terms?

Two different but interrelated topics are explored in this chapter. The first is the political subculture of representation at the constituency level. The second is the nature of linkages between the MP and his district. Let us elaborate the first topic by formulating a precise definition of legislative culture and by specifying its analytic components.

## THE CONCEPT OF LEGISLATIVE
## CULTURE

The term *legislative culture* refers to the patterns of popular recognition, role expectation, and evaluation of the legislature and its individual members. In this sense it is part of the general political culture in a society, a part specific to the representative institution. It consists of the public's belief about and attitudes towards the function and performance of the representative body. Several aspects of the concept require further explication.

The legislative culture is, first, a political subculture because it is comprised of beliefs and attitudes concerning a single political institution. In an effort to make our concept consistent with the more general Almond-Verba formulation, we too will regard the legislative culture as based on three dimensions: cognitive, affective, and evaluative.[1] Thus, the legislative culture may be described in terms of the patterns of cognition, affection, and evaluation regarding a representative body.

Second, the legislative culture focuses upon beliefs and attitudes rooted in the masses. Our attention is directed principally to the constituent attitudes and their patterns of distribution across the population, not to the system of beliefs and norms governing the behavior of legislators within a representative body. While legislative culture could be taken to mean the subculture within the legislative body itself, we wish to make it clear that in our study it refers only to the constitutents' attitudes and beliefs.

Third, the legislative culture may be described at different levels of society. One can speak of the legislative culture in a nation as a whole. In this instance, one is concerned with a general characterization of the patterns of popular beliefs and attitudes relevant to the representative institution. One may also speak of the legislative culture in a district. The district legislative culture consists of the patterns of attitudes shared by those who reside in a geographically defined area.

Just as one can describe the system of beliefs and attitudes as it exists in a district, so can one apply the same concept to a group of elites such as local notables.[2] Given the political activism and influence of local elites, the legislative culture embedded in an elite stratum may prove to be much more important than the general culture of a district in shaping representative linkages. In a crossnational comparison, the national legislative culture may be an appropriate focus, while both the district and the elite legislative cultures may be of particular utility for comparisons within nations.[3]

Fourth, the legislative culture as we define it constitutes an important part of the political milieu in which the legislature and its individual members function. Not only is the MP elected by a geographically defined constituency, i.e., an electoral district, but he also must serve his district in some way between elections. The legislative culture intervenes in the election process by playing a role in voters' decisions. It may also influence the ways in which MPs behave between elections. Obviously, MPs who operate in a legislative culture which places little emphasis on personal records are less likely to perform certain acts designed to impress the voters. The legislative culture may also influence the daily activities of MPs, the frequency and mode of their interactions with constituents.

The components of legislative culture include the public's cognition of the legislature (knowledge about the legislature and about the activities of individual MPs) and its actions, the roles that the public attributes to MPs, and the public's evaluation of the institution and its members. We shall report data on such knowledge and its distribution pattern at the constituency level.

In investigating role expectations, one cannot assume that every adult citizen has a clear conception of what MPs should do. In fact, it is more realistic to assume that citizens lack such clear role expectations. We begin, therefore, by seeking information about the extent to which citizens hold well-defined role expectations concerning MPs. We also examine the contents of their role expectations. Whom do constituents think the MPs should represent? (This is often referred to as a representational focus.) How should the MPs discharge their duties?[4] (This is usually called representational style, and refers to the MP's choice of following his own convictions or those of others.) Another aspect of role expectations is the personal qualities that constituents believe MPs should possess.

A final component of the legislative culture is the constituents' evaluation of the legislature and of its members' performance. Do constituents believe that legislators have the personal qualities that they consider important? Their judgment on this may affect their evaluation of the legislature and their support for it. Evaluative attitudes also entail the public's judgment of the performance of MPs in particular and the legislature in general.

## THE CONCEPT OF LINKAGES

Our understanding of representation is enhanced when we can determine the precise nature of linkages connecting an MP and his constituency. In the final analysis, representation refers to the manner in which the representative and the constituent are connected. The core of representation studies should therefore focus on linkages of this kind.

Linkages may be examined from three different vantage points. First, we may examine the patterns of interaction between the MP and his constituents. A description of these linkages involves an analysis of a complex interactive process and is an insuperably difficult task. It requires matching an MP with his specific home district, which in turn necessitates the transformation of the individual-level data to group-level data, the level of the constituency as a whole. Where a single member represents a district, the task of matching the data is a relatively simple matter, but it becomes a treacherous operation in multimember districts such as exist in both Korea and Turkey. Therefore, we shall pursue the subject only insofar as we can make some intuitive sense.[5]

Linkages may also be examined in terms of policy concurrences between an MP and his constituents.[6] To what extent is there agreement over key policy issues? Do MPs and constituents agree that the benefits of economic growth should be equally distributed? Do they agree that political democracy should be a principal developmental objective? Do they agree that rapid social modernization is necessary, even at the expense of valued traditions?

The last but not the least important context in which linkages may be viewed is that of role congruence or the extent to which an MP and his constituents hold a concurrent perception of the legislator's role. Since we have already made an analytic distinction between representational foci and styles, role congruence will be investigated in terms of these two analytic dimensions.

## PATTERNS OF LEGISLATIVE CULTURE

Because the legislative culture refers to the patterns of beliefs and attitudes that constituents hold toward the parliament and its members, it provides a convenient descriptive vehicle to characterize the basic public attitudes and expectations in a nation.

### COGNITIONS

How much does the public in each country know about the legislature? Is the legislature more salient to some citizens than others? To measure the public awareness of the institution, we put to our respondents three questions: how familiar were they with the history of the nation's legislature; did they know the size of the legislature; and could they distinguish the legislature from other government agencies? The relevant data from the survey are summarized in table 6.1.

TABLE 6.1.
Level of Knowledge about the Legislative Institution (percentage)

| | Kenya | | Korea | | Turkey | |
|---|---|---|---|---|---|---|
| Salience items | Local notables | Constit- uents | Local notables | Constit- uents | Local notables | Constit- uents |
| Knew the history of the legislature | 74.8 | 46.6 | 80.3 | 40.2 | 83.3 | 53.4 |
| Knew the correct size of legislative membership[a] | 56.5 | 21.6 | 62.4 | 19.2 | 83.2 | 39.3 |
| Could distinguish the legislature from other government agencies[b] | 49.9 | 21.6 | 66.5 | 2.6 | 88.9 | 56.2 |
| N = | (453) | (4,128) | (468) | (2,274) | (287) | (2,007) |

a. An answer was considered "correct" if the number indicated by a respondent came within a range of ± 10 of the real size.

b. Respondents were asked to indicate the differences in functions between the legislature and other parts of government. Those who mentioned one or more such differences were taken as being able to make such distinction.

Of the three nations the Turkish public appeared to be the best informed about their legislature. More than half of the Turkish constituents (53.4 percent) had a good knowledge of the history of their legislature; nearly 40 percent were capable of accurately indicating the size of the legislature, and 56 percent knew that the legislature is charged with distinctive functions and therefore is different from other government agencies. In Korea and Kenya the legislative institution was considerably less salient to the public.

These differences may be due to two unique features of Turkish history and politics. Of the three countries studied, Turkey's legislative history dating back to the turn of the century is the longest. During this long period the Turkish Grand National Assembly has become firmly institutionalized in the minds of the general population and is therefore now regarded as one of the key political institutions.

The second feature relates to the visibility of the Grand National Assembly. Because the cabinet system headed by a prime minister requires the support of a majority of the legislature, the executive power is constrained in a significant way by what transpires in the representative body. Hence, the Turkish National Assembly serves as a central political arena, and enjoys high public visibility. By comparison, the legislatures of Kenya and Korea are overshadowed by a dominant executive and relegated to a relatively minor role.

Among those who act as the leaders of their local communities, the legislature is a highly salient institution in all three countries. The level of knowledge of this group concerning the history, the size of membership, and the specific functions of the legislature is consistently higher than that of ordinary citizens. Further, it was the Turkish local elites who were the best informed in this regard among the elites of the three countries.

How much detailed information do constituents have about individual members of the legislature: What proportion know the name of their own MP? How specific is their knowledge of the MP's activities? We distinguish the salience of an institution from that of its individual members, because they are two different cognitive elements.

The salience of individual MPs may derive in part from what Almond and Verba have called "the subject culture."[7] This type of culture is distinguished from others by its overwhelming emphasis on the output of the political process. In a subject culture the citizen's attention is directed disproportionately to those aspects of leadership behavior that involve the delivery of political goods and services, while the input aspects of politics receive little or no public attention. Insofar as citizens perceive an opportunity to extract goods and services, they might be expected to develop an extensive body of political knowledge and become actively involved in the political process. In the specific context of representation, this would mean that constituents tend to have a good deal of knowledge about their individual members, especially when the latter act as a principal provider of goods and services. On the other hand, they would know very little about the legislative institution to which their MPs belong, a body too abstract and too remote in their cognitive maps to be of any immediate relevance.

Kenyan constituents were the best informed about their individual MPs. Nearly every adult citizen knew the name of his or her representative, while in other countries scarcely more than one-half of the citizenry could perform this task. Also, a majority of Kenyans had a definite opinion concerning the honesty and level of education of their MPs. In Korea and Turkey those able to indicate the personal qualities of their MPs were less numerous (see table 6.2).

As we shall show later, Kenyans regarded service as the single most important role of their MPs, to a considerably greater extent than did the electorates in other countries. Moreover, Kenya uses a single-member district, whereas a multimember district is used in Korea and Turkey. The differences in these characteristics may account for the higher salience of individual MPs in Kenya. It is also important to note that both Kenyan constituents and local notables were less capable of distinguishing the MPs from the officials of other government agencies than were their counterparts in other countries. Only 18 percent of the constituents and 42 percent of the notables in Kenya could differentiate MPs from other government officials. In other countries these figures were substantially higher.

**TABLE 6.2.**
**Level of Knowledge about Individual MPs (percentages)**

| Salience items | Kenya | | Korea | | Turkey | |
|---|---|---|---|---|---|---|
| | Local notables | Constit- uents | Local notables | Constit- uents | Local notables | Constit- uents |
| Knew MP's name[a] | 97.1 | 83.5 | 96.7 | 69.1 | 95.1 | 52.9 |
| Knew MP's distinctive functions[b] | 42.2 | 18.0 | 82.1 | 41.6 | 95.7 | 68.9 |
| Had a view on whether MPs are honest[c] | 90.7 | 87.7 | 30.7 | 82.3 | 85.0 | 74.8 |
| Had a view on whether MPs are well educated[c] | 91.7 | 87.5 | 57.0 | 87.5 | 91.4 | 79.2 |
| N = | (453) | (4,128) | (468) | (2,274) | (287) | (2,007) |

a. Because of the multimember system used in Korea and Turkey, the respondents were allowed to name several MPs. Anyone naming one or more of his or her MPs was included in the computations.

b. The question was designed to indicate whether the respondent could differentiate the legislators from other civil servants. Those who could clearly mention one or more differences were included in the computations. In Kenya 37 percent of the constituents and 35 percent of the local notables said that there were no differences in functions between their MPs and government officials.

c. Honesty and good education were the two personal qualities of an MP regarded as most important by the public. The MPs were, it is assumed, more salient to those who could express a view, positive or negative, on their MP's honesty (and education) than to those who could not.

The evidence suggests that Kenyans know a great deal about what the individual members of their legislature do, but very little about what the legislative institution itself does. This cognitive discrepancy appears to be due to Kenyans' preoccupation with the extraction of scarce government resources, a tendency characteristic of a subject culture, and their view of MPs as the principal agents of resource allocation.

Local notables were significantly better informed about individual MPs and their activities than were ordinary citizens. These differences were pronounced and consistent across all three countries. As leaders of their communities, opinion makers, and intermediaries between the center and their respective communities, local notables naturally keep in close touch with what MPs do.

One interesting aspect of local notable data came from Korea where the local notables showed relatively low percentages (as compared to Kenya and Turkey) on two items. Quite contrary to our expectations, less than 31 percent indicated a definite opinion concerning the honesty of their MPs, and only 57 percent expressed familiarity with MPs' educational qualifications. These figures compare very poorly with those of the general public. It is difficult to believe that the Korean notables were less well informed of their MPs' honesty and educational qualifications than was the public at large. Instead, what seems to be reflected here is notables' reluctance to reveal their true feelings about their MPs' qualities. The political sensitivity of the questions, combined with deeply ingrained cultural attitudes that discourage any criticism of a specific leader, may have caused many Korean notables to avoid the questions rather than give negative replies.

To summarize, the data on cognition revealed a distinctively different pattern in each country. In Turkey, both the legislature and its individual members were highly salient objects. In Kenya, MPs were highly salient but the institution in which they serve was not. In Korea, neither the legislature nor its members were highly salient to the public.

## ROLE EXPECTATIONS

Role expectations are an important constituent element of the legislative culture. What do constituents expect of the legislature and its members? We begin first by looking at the personal qualities expected of the MPs in the three countries. Table 6.3 lists eight such qualities rated for importance by respondents. These qualities include: a good education, personal honesty, being a community leader, a lengthy residence in the district, being a successful person in his occupation, an ability to understand the common man, an ability to work hard, and being a member of a particular ethnic or clan group.

The quality most often mentioned by constituents and local notables in all three countries was personal honesty. The second most frequently mentioned quality was the ability to work hard, followed by the ability to understand the common man and a good education. The pattern was consistent across nations and across different groups, suggesting that personal honesty, an understanding of common man, and a good education are the qualities desired everywhere, not only in MPs, but in all leaders.

What kinds of activities do constituents expect from their MPs? This question relates to one important aspect of legislative roles, generally known in the literature as the purposive role.[8] In table 6.4 the role perceptions of MPs, local notables, and constituents are compared. The activities considered most important by constituents include those matters which directly affect them. In each country, constituents listed expressing the views of the district as the most important role of the MP. They also stressed the role of MPs in bringing government projects to the district and in assisting constituents who have problems with government agencies. In all three countries the public regarded these constituency service aspects of the MP's role as the most important. On the other hand, only a minority of the constituents attributed great importance to MPs' role in lawmaking or explaining government policies. These findings are in complete accord with recent studies of the legislature in developing societies.

TABLE 6.3.
**Important Personal Qualities that Local Notables and
Constituents Expected of Their MPs (percentages)**

| Personal qualities | Kenya | | Korea | | Turkey | |
|---|---|---|---|---|---|---|
| | Local notables | Constit-uents | Local notables | Constit-uents | Local notables | Constit-uents |
| Honest | 77.7 | 84.0 | 96.2 | 91.0 | 86.8 | 77.5 |
| Hardworking | 72.8 | 71.8 | 95.9 | 92.4 | 78.7 | 64.8 |
| Able to understand common men | 79.7 | 68.9 | 91.2 | 89.9 | 83.3 | 62.3 |
| Good education | 62.5 | 67.3 | 75.4 | 73.6 | 53.7 | 61.0 |
| Community leader | 52.1 | 54.8 | 46.8 | 47.3 | 42.9 | 31.2 |
| Successful in an occupation | 40.8 | 50.4 | 45.1 | 41.4 | 44.3 | 30.6 |
| Long-term resident of district | 58.7 | 53.8 | 30.6 | 38.6 | 32.8 | 22.3 |
| Member of a right ethnic or clan group | 24.3 | 29.2 | 8.3 | 22.7 | Not asked | Not asked |
| N = | (453) | (4,128) | (468) | (2,274) | (287) | (2,007) |

*Note:* The respondents were asked to rate each quality as "very important," "important," "not important," or "don't know" in Kenya and Turkey. In Korea the data were coded without making a distinction between "very important" and "important." Only the case of "very important" was included in computations for Kenya and Turkey, while the only case for "important" entered the computations for Korea.

## TABLE 6.4.
### Role Expectations: Aspects of Legislative Activities Regarded as Important by MPs, Local Notables, and Constituents (percentages)

| Activities | Kenya | | | Korea | | | Turkey | | |
|---|---|---|---|---|---|---|---|---|---|
| | MPs | Local notables | Constituents | MPs | Local notables | Constituents | MPs | Local notables | Constituents |
| Explaining policies to voters | 10.7[a] | 74.8[b] | 68.3[b] | 30.0 | 47.0 | 34.9 | 69.4 | 39.4 | 18.2 |
| Proposing, debating, and amending bills | 32.1 | 79.5 | 65.6 | 75.0 | 67.1 | 44.2 | 41.7 | 33.4 | 18.6 |
| Expressing the views of the people in district | 28.6 | 88.7 | 84.1 | 55.0 | 63.0 | 52.1 | 51.4 | 66.9 | 45.7 |
| Obtaining government projects for district | 71.4 | 88.5 | 79.0 | 40.0 | 32.5 | 41.2 | 59.7 | 62.7 | 46.1 |
| Interceding with civil servants for district voters | 28.6 | 67.8 | 67.6 | 35.0 | 44.9 | 40.1 | 30.6 | 21.3 | 20.6 |
| Resolving local conflict | 7.1 | 56.7 | 54.6 | 0.0 | 37.8 | 25.4 | 16.7 | 25.1 | 21.2 |
| Visiting district | not asked | 77.9 | 68.8 | not asked | 30.6 | 35.8 | not asked | 46.0 | 28.1 |
| N = | (28)[c] | (453) | (4,128) | (20)[c] | (468) | (2,274) | (72)[c] | (287) | (2,007) |

a. The MPs were asked if they felt they should spend more time, about the same time, or less time on each activity listed. The percentages include those who said they should spend more time on these activities.

b. Both the local notables and the constituents were asked to rate the importance of each activity. The percentages include those indicating each activity as "very important."

c. We have examined only those MPs in whose districts we conducted the mass survey. Consequently, the size of Ns for the MPs are smaller than the totals whom we interviewed in each legislature.

The local notables had more sophisticated conceptions of the legislative role than did the constituents, and placed a higher value on MPs' role in the areas of lawmaking and explaining government policies. Nevertheless, it was still the constituency service roles of MPs that notables considered most important.

MPs defined their own roles differently than did constituents, and to a lesser degree local notables. With the exception of the Kenyan legislators, most MPs emphasized their own roles of lawmaking and explaining government policies equally, if not more than, their service roles. For instance, nearly 70 percent of the Turkish legislators regarded their role of explaining policy as very important, a striking contrast to 39.4 percent of the notables and 18 percent of the constituents. In regard to the lawmaking role, the same is true: while 42 percent of the MPs stressed this role, the comparable figures for the notables and the constituents were 33.4 percent and 18.6 percent, respectively.

In Korea, the lawmaking role was rated very highly in importance by all three groups. Among the MPs, three-fourths stressed it, making it by far their most valued role. Both notables and the constituents concurred with their MPs (67 percent and 44 percent, respectively). The importance attributed to MPs' lawmaking role in Korea should not, however, be construed to mean that the Korean legislature is an effective lawmaking body. On the contrary, its lawmaking power is in fact quite overshadowed by that of the executive. Why then did Koreans rate the lawmaking role so highly?

One possible reason is that many Koreans are profoundly disillusioned with their impotent National Assembly. They know that a strong and active legislature is the prerequisite of a liberal democracy, a form of government promoted in school textbooks in the last three decades. But Koreans also know that their legislature is nothing more than a mere rubber-stamp organization. Koreans' aspiration for a strong representative body may account for their emphasis on the lawmaking role. This response, then, might be interpreted to indicate that Koreans believe their legislature should be stronger than it really is.

Kenyan MPs provide a unique case. More than two-thirds (71.4 percent) stressed their constituency service role, especially their activities aimed at obtaining government resources and delivering tangible benefits to their districts. This role also received the highest rating from both Kenyan notables and constituents. In contrast to their Turkish and Korean counterparts, Kenyan MPs regarded other activities as much less important. Also, there was a widespread consensus on this role among the general population as well as among the legislators themselves. This aspect of representation clearly distinguishes Kenya from other countries that we have studied.

MPs represent different groups in their actions. Some MPs endeavor to represent the interests of their constituencies, while others act as agents of their political parties or other interest groups. Still others may pursue their duties on the basis of their own personal political convictions. The subject here pertains to the classical question of representational foci; whom should the MPs strive to represent in their action? In our survey we asked the respondents to indicate whether or not they felt it important for the MP to represent the interests of his district, his political party, the executive branch of government, interest groups, his advisors, or to act according to his own personal beliefs. As shown in table 6.5, different patterns of representational foci emerged in each country.

In Kenya the district was considered the single most important representational focus; almost 86 percent of the notables and 78 percent of the constituents mentioned the district. Over 73 percent of the notables considered the political party, the KANU in this case, to be nearly as important as the district. For the constituents, however, the party was not as important. In Korea also, the greatest importance was attributed to the district focus, followed next by political parties. However, the Turkish pattern was different. Political parties in Turkey were considered more important foci than were the electoral districts. This may be due to the central political role of the Turkish parties and to the multimember systems used in that country.

Of special interest is a strong emphasis placed on personal convictions in Korea. More than half of the Korean notables (56.2 percent) felt that MPs should act according to their personal convictions. Almost as many constituents (43 percent) held similar views. These figures are quite high compared to those in other countries, and suggest that many Koreans subscribe to a trustee role of representation.

**TABLE 6.5.**

**Role Expectations: Representational Focus Considered Very Important by Local Notables and Constituents (percentages)**

| Representational foci | Kenya | | Korea | | Turkey | |
|---|---|---|---|---|---|---|
| | Local notables | Constit- uents | Local notables | Constit- uents | Local notables | Constit- uents |
| Electoral district | 85.4 | 77.7 | 62.4 | 59.1 | 18.5 | 15.3 |
| Political party | 73.3 | 48.0 | 41.2 | 23.4 | 39.0 | 16.2 |
| Executive branch of government | 43.0 | 38.7 | 25.6 | 22.6 | 14.6 | 12.2 |
| Interest group | 41.7 | 41.2 | 15.2 | 12.1 | 18.8 | 9.3 |
| MP's personal advisers | 25.6 | 26.3 | 7.5 | 8.5 | 10.1 | 8.1 |
| MP's own convictions | 32.2 | 27.8 | 56.2 | 42.8 | 29.6 | 17.8 |
| $N =$ | (453) | (4,128) | (468) | (2,278) | (287) | (2,007) |

*Note:* The comparable data for the MPs were already reported in table 5.9 in chapter 5. Respondents were asked to rate the importance of each representational focus listed above. The percentages are based on those who rated any focus as "very important."

It has been suggested that such trustee orientations are particularly compatible with the prevailing norms and expectations of the leadership role in Korea.[9] Confucian ethics, still dominant in the Korean culture, extol the virtue of *chijo*, being a man of principle. Leaders are expected to stand firmly by their personal convictions, and actions leading to compromise or conciliation are regarded as egregious violations of the *chijo* code. The cultural norms of *chijo* encourage trustee orientations, making them politically appropriate and desirable behaviors.

Another aspect of role expectation is the style with which an MP performs his representative duties. Two different styles of representation have been suggested: the delegate and trustee roles.[10] These roles represent the two polar types of orientations, the delegate indicating a closer tie with the views of constituency while the trustee an inclination to act independently of the constituents' views. The orientations of those who could not be classified by either of the two role types were grouped into the 'mixed' category.[11]

The data on representational style show a different pattern in each country (see table 6.6). In Kenya a majority of the people expected their MPs to act as delegates. And, Kenyan MPs also perceived their jobs primarily in terms of the delegate role.

The delegate role was deemphasized in both Korea and Turkey. In these countries, both the public and MPs themselves considered the trustee role as most appropriate. Nearly 60 percent of both Korean and Turkish MPs defined their jobs in terms of the trustee role. Local notables of the two countries also regarded the trustee role as most appropriate, although to a slightly lesser degree than did the MPs themselves (60 percent vs. 53 percent in Korea and 61 percent vs. 51 percent in Turkey). Constituents' role expectations deviated very little from those held by their local leaders. They expected the trustee role orientations from their MPs just as frequently: 41.9 percent in Korea and 47.3 percent in Turkey, respectively.

In all three countries there was a relatively high congruence on the representational roles. Kenyan MPs, local notables, and constituents regarded the delegate role as most appropriate. In Korea and Turkey, all three groups indicated their preference for the trustee role. While different role styles were stressed in different countries, there exists nonetheless an impressive amount of agreement between the MPs and their constituents in each country regarding what constitutes an appropriate role for the MPs.

The question of role behavior is quite distinct from that of role expectations. And, so, the next question put to MPs was how they actually behave in their roles? The same question was put to constituents: On what activities should their MPs spend most of their time? Based on responses to the second question we classified the general public into two groups: one that stressed the external orientations of their MPs and the other the internal orientations.

## TABLE 6.6.
### Role Expectations: Representational Styles (percentages)

| Role styles | Kenya | | | Korea | | | Turkey | | |
|---|---|---|---|---|---|---|---|---|---|
| | MPs | Local notables | Constituents | MPs | Local notables | Constituents | MPs | Local notables | Constituents |
| Delegate | 64.3 | 52.9 | 55.8 | 20.0 | 23.1 | 30.3 | 30.5 | 17.0 | 20.8 |
| Mixed | 17.9 | 32.2 | 26.1 | 20.0 | 23.7 | 27.8 | 8.3 | 31.6 | 31.0 |
| Trustee | 17.8 | 14.9 | 18.1 | 60.0 | 53.2 | 41.9 | 61.2 | 51.4 | 47.3 |
| N = | (28) | (429) | (4,018) | (20) | (459) | (2,083) | (72) | (282) | (1,902) |

Note: The Ns for the notables and constituents in each country are smaller because the cases of no response were eliminated in the tabulations.

There was a marked discordance between what the MPs actually did and what their constituents expected them to do. In all three countries the MPs spent less time on external activities than their constituents expected them to. In Kenya, over 90 percent of both the notables and constituents stressed the external aspects of an MP's role. Yet, among the MPs themselves no more than 53.5 percent showed behavioral tendencies that could be classified as external. Although the overall emphasis placed on the external aspects of the legislative role in Korea and Turkey was quite low, more than two-thirds of the constituents in the two countries stressed the external orientation of their MPs. Only 35 percent of the Korean MPs and 21 percent of the Turkish MPs acted as externals.

### EVALUATION

Another aspect of the legislative culture is the constituent evaluation of the legislature and its members. Does the public feel that their MPs possess the kind of personal qualifications they ought to? How well do they feel the MPs are performing their job? How strongly do they support the legislature as a valid and legitimate institution? To explore the public evaluation of MPs' personal qualities, we asked them about the qualities they thought MPs should have and the qualities they thought their MPs actually did have. If the constituents said their MPs did not possess the qualities they should have, we considered this a negative evaluation.[12]

TABLE 6.7.
Shortcomings in the Personal Qualities of MPs as Perceived by
Local Notables and Constituents[a] (percentages)

| Lacking in qualities | Kenya | | Korea | | Turkey | |
|---|---|---|---|---|---|---|
| | Local notables | Constit-uents | Local notables | Constit-uents | Local notables | Constit-uents |
| Honesty | 62.7 | 64.3 | —[b] | 44.1 | 48.4 | 44.5 |
| Able to understand common people | 67.5 | 55.8 | — | 41.8 | 59.9 | 46.8 |
| Hardworking | 58.1 | 52.8 | — | 36.5 | 60.3 | 44.7 |
| Good education | 47.0 | 39.4 | — | 20.8 | 30.7 | 32.0 |
| Community leader | 33.6 | 38.9 | — | 17.7 | 26.5 | 23.7 |
| Successful in an occupation | 28.5 | 29.6 | — | 12.7 | 32.4 | 23.5 |
| Long-term resident of district | 30.0 | 33.7 | — | 11.1 | 24.7 | 20.9 |
| N = | (453) | (4,128) | — | (2,274) | (287) | (2,007) |

a. The percentages in this table indicate the proportion of respondents who thought a given personal quality very important but felt that most MPs lacked it.
b. The Korean local notable data were coded differently. Thus, comparable figures could not be presented.

Strikingly similar qualities were mentioned by all constituents in the three countries (table 6.7). Most frequently mentioned was the quality of personal honesty of the MP, but it was also one quality that was considered most lacking among legislators. Nearly one-half of the constituents in Korea (44.1 percent) and Turkey (44.5 percent) mentioned a lack of honesty among their politicians. In Kenya, almost two-thirds (64.3 percent) considered their MPs to be less than honest.

Other shortcomings mentioned included MPs' inability to understand the common people and their failure to work hard. More than one-half of the Kenyan constituents, and nearly a half in the other two countries, thought that their MPs lacked the ability to understand the common people. A large number of constituents in all three countries also felt that their MPs did not work as hard as they should. The Kenyan citizens were most critical in this regard, with nearly 53 percent showing a negative evaluation. In Korea and Turkey, too, the negative feeling was quite widespread (36.5 percent and 44.7 percent, respectively).

During our fieldwork, as well as in our personal interviews with the MPs, we were impressed time and again by the workload each legislator carried. Virtually all MPs complained about a short supply of time and staff that made it difficult to attend to all the matters they felt they should. We were left with the impression that all MPs, leaders and backbenchers, worked very hard at their jobs. Still, their constituents thought otherwise.

Local notables concurred with constituents in their perceptions of MPs' basic shortcomings. For each personal quality examined the local notables' evaluation followed very closely the pattern revealed in the constituent data. Notables also felt that the personal qualities MPs lacked most were honesty, an ability to understand the common people, and an ability to work hard. They were even more critical in some respects: the proportion of notables in Kenya and Turkey who negatively evaluated their MPs' ability to work hard and to understand the problems of the common people exceeded the proportion of constituents with similar complaints in those two countries.

The data on constituents' evaluation of MPs' job performance are displayed in table 6.8. Constituents were asked to rate the performance of their MPs on seven specific activities which we thought comprised the most salient aspects of legislators' jobs. These activities included explaining government policies to citizens, actively participating in deliberation and debate on bills, telling the government what constituents want, bringing more government projects to the district, interceding with government agencies on behalf of constituents, helping to solve community problems, and frequently visiting the district. Kenyans gave the most positive overall ratings of their MPs' performance, the Koreans the least positive.

Of the seven activities listed, constituents in all three countries regarded certain activities as more important than others, suggesting a uniform pattern of role expectations across nations. They all stressed MPs' responsibility to explain policies, make laws, represent district interests, and help district voters who have problems with government agencies. These were also the activities for which MPs received the most positive ratings.

A closer scrutiny of the data reveals that constituents tended to give MPs positive ratings for those activities about which they knew and cared relatively little. Conversely, constituents gave less favorable ratings to those activities which they regarded as the most important aspects of their MPs' jobs. For example, they gave very favorable ratings to their MPs' performance in explaining policies and making laws, processes about which they knew relatively little. Yet, they gave a much lower rating to their MPs' job performance in obtaining government projects and assisting those who had problems with government agencies, areas in which constituents had considerable personal knowledge.

Local notables, in comparison to constituents, showed markedly more favorable ratings of their MPs' performance. The difference was remarkably consistent across nations, as well as across different activity items. Why were local notables more satisfied with their MPs' performance? In part, because they were better informed about politics in general, and about the activities of their MPs in particular. Moreover, because of their status in their communities they were more likely to be in close contact with MPs than were constituents. Through this contact notables benefitted more from the services provided by their MPs, and therefore, were more satisfied.

**TABLE 6.8**
**How Well Does the Public Think the MPs Are Doing Their Jobs (percentages)**

| | Kenya | | Korea | | Turkey | |
|---|---|---|---|---|---|---|
| Types of Activity | Local notables | Constit-uents | Local notables | Constit-uents | Local notables | Constit-uents |
| Explaining policies to voters | 69.1 | 55.0 | 54.3 | 30.7 | 48.4 | 45.7 |
| Proposing, debating, and amending bills | 77.3 | 57.0 | 56.8 | 31.9 | 50.6 | 43.4 |
| Expressing the views of people in district | 69.5 | 52.4 | 50.0 | 26.2 | 52.0 | 42.5 |
| Obtaining government projects for district | 65.1 | 50.8 | 35.2 | 22.0 | 38.0 | 35.8 |
| Interceding with civil servants for district voters | 62.7 | 46.7 | 44.9 | 24.2 | 64.8 | 43.6 |
| Resolving local conflict | 56.9 | 43.7 | 46.8 | 24.1 | 39.4 | 36.1 |
| Visiting district | 63.2 | 46.2 | 39.4 | 19.0 | 43.6 | 36.9 |
| N = | (453) | (4,128) | (468) | (2,274) | (287) | (2,007) |

Note: The percentages indicate the proportions of the respondents who said their MPs were doing a "good" or "very good" job for each activity listed.

## PATTERNS OF REPRESENTATIVE
## LINKAGES

Representative linkages consist of the connection between an MP and his district constituency. Linkage patterns are the specific ways in which their interactions are organized. We will concentrate on two aspects of linkages: the degree of concurrence between an MP and his district voters in terms of their attitudes toward key developmental policies and the degree of congruence between an MP's own role perception and his constituents' role expectations.

This part of our analysis requires a district-by-district scrutiny and involves data aggregation from the individual level to the constituency level. We draw upon three different sets of data: the MP file, the local notable file, and the constituency file. And, these disparate data need to be matched by each constituency. There are some obvious difficulties in interpreting the results of such an analysis because of the difference in the electoral systems of the three countries. In Kenya, where a single-member district is used, matching a legislative member with his constituency poses little problem. In such a system it makes sense to make a direct comparison between an MP and his constituents on a range of attitudes and actions. However, where a multi-member district is used, such as in Turkey and, to a limited extent, in Korea, it becomes difficult to make a meaningful comparison of the data. Consider the problem of concurrence in policy attitudes, for an example. We can measure the attitudes of each legislator on a policy. To aggregate this information to the constituency level we have to take an average of the attitude scores for all legislative members representing a district. Some members may hold attitudes very much similar to the constituency attitudes, but others may hold opposite views. Matching the average attitude scores of MPs with constituency attitude scores poses a serious problem for interpretation. Its meaning is not as intuitively clear as it is in the context of a single-member district. Nonetheless, because of our theoretical concern for representative linkages existing in each electoral district, we will pursue the analysis of the aggregated data, mindful of the difficulties mentioned above.

### CONCURRENCE ON KEY DEVELOPMENTAL POLICIES

In chapter 4 we identified several key policy issues relevant to development: distributive policy, political democracy, and social change. Attitudes on each of these policy issues were measured from an identical set of survey items included in all of our surveys, which made it possible to develop an exact parallel measure across different population groups and across nations.[13] The resulting data indicated important variations by country and by groups within countries.

Among the MPs, the Turkish deputies supported an equitable distributive policy more strongly than did anyone else. Almost 81 percent favored such a policy in Turkey compared to only 43 percent in Kenya and 55 percent in Korea. Furthermore, in Turkey deputies favored a proequality policy more strongly than did constituents (53.8 percent) or local notables (55.6 percent). In Korea and Kenya there were no noticeable group variations in this regard; MPs, local notables, and constituents showed similar levels of commitment to an equitable distributive policy.

With regard to other policy issues, two general conclusions could be drawn from the data. One is a uniformly consistent tendency for MPs to advocate democratic values more strongly than do citizens. The other is that MPs in all three countries were more strongly change-oriented in their attitudes than were the populations they represented. Thus, MPs tended to favor the developmental policies of social modernization and democratization a good deal more than the people they led, and to favor an equitable distribution of wealth as much as, if not any more than, the general public.

The policy concurrence data are reported in table 6.9. In each district we examined three types of concurrence: between the MP (or MPs) and constituents, between the MP and local notables, and between local notables and constituents. The highest concurrence was obtained between local notables and constituents in all three countries. One could have easily predicted this result, for notables are themselves an integral part of their local communities and so are likely to share the attitudes and beliefs that prevail in these communities.

Little concurrence occurred between MPs and constituents in their policy preferences. The lack of policy agreements was consistent across countries and in some instances we even noticed strong policy disagreement. For example, in Korea, the more strongly an MP endorsed modernization policies, the greater was the level of anti-modernism among his constituents ($r = -.56$). Several similar negative correlations occurred in Turkey and Kenya.

Policy concurrence between MPs and local notables was also negligible. Although the data show a slightly greater concurrence here than between MPs and constituents, it is still true that local notables were closer in their policy preferences to constituents than to MPs. Policy concurrence does not, therefore, constitute an important basis upon which representative linkages are forged in the three countries.

## ROLE CONGRUENCE

The degree to which MPs and their constituents agree on the legislative role is an important aspect of representative linkages. In their discussion of the legislative role system, Wahlke and his associates suggest two different kinds of role consensus: interposition and intraposition.[14] They argue that "without some minimum of consensus the legislature would cease to be

## TABLE 6.9.
### Concurrence on Key Developmental Policies (Pearson *r*)

| Policy areas | Kenya | | | Korea | | | Turkey | | |
|---|---|---|---|---|---|---|---|---|---|
| | MP v. constituents | MP v. notables | Notables v. constituents | MP v. constituents | MP v. notables | Notables v. constituents | MP v. constituents | MP v. notables | Notables v. constituents |
| Distributive policy | -0.05 | -0.06 | -0.47[a] | 0.11 | -0.42 | 0.68[a] | -0.23 | 0.01 | -0.15 |
| Democratization | 0.15 | 0.37 | 0.54[a] | -0.05 | -0.01 | 0.79[a] | -0.07 | 0.37 | 0.50[a] |
| Social modernization | -0.11 | 0.13 | 0.32 | -0.56[a] | 0.01 | 0.03 | 0.07 | -0.16 | 0.32 |

a. Significant at the level of 0.05.

an institutionalized group.[15] Consequently, role congruence may serve as a measure of the level of institutionalization of a legislature.[16] The sort of role consensus that we will analyze in this section is the interposition consensus, involving the degree of agreement between MPs and their constituents about the appropriate behaviors of a legislator.

We will focus upon two "classical" aspects of the representative role. First, we will analyze the service aspect of the legislative role: how much agreement is there between an MP and his constituents concerning the importance of service functions? Next, we will examine the centrality of election district in the conceptions of both MPs and their constituents: to what extent do they agree that the district should serve as a main focus for representative actions?

Questions included in the MP survey asked whether legislators felt they should spend more or less time on a variety of legislative activities. An identical set of questions were put to constituents and local notables. Whenever a respondent indicated a service activity such as obtaining resources for district or assisting voters who had problems with government agencies a score of 1 was assigned. These scores were summed to form a 4-point index, with a high score indicating a greater emphasis placed on the service role. Finally, these scores were aggregated to the constituency level in order to compare the relative emphasis that each group placed on the service role.

A similar procedure was followed to create an index of centrality of the district. However, it should be noted that the specific items used for the index were different. The index for MPs was based on a set of forced-choice questions ("If you had to make a choice between the views of the following groups, which one would you choose?"). This was followed with a list of choices: leaders of my party vs. my district constituents, my own party faction vs. my constituents; my personal convictions v. my constituents, and so forth. The index scores were derived from the frequency with which MPs chose constituents over other groups.[17]

For obvious reasons we could not repeat the same questions in the mass survey. Because constituents do not confront the same situations as do MPs, the same set of questions would be of little relevance to most of them. Consequently, we formulated a somewhat different set of questions for constituents. Specifically, we asked them: Should MPs do what the people want regardless of MPs' own opinions? Should MPs follow their personal judgments in their actions, as they know what is best for their own districts? Should MPs act according to their own beliefs even though people in the district often disagree?[18] Although different from the items used in the MP survey, the three questions cited above were nevertheless designed to measure the same role attitude, the extent to which the general public regarded the district as a central element in representation.[19]

We report our role congruence data in table 6.10. As expected, the greatest congruence occurred between the local notables and constituents. The

**TABLE 6.10.**
Role Congruence (Pearson *r*)

| Roles | Kenya (*N* = 14) | | | Korea (*N* = 12) | | | Turkey (*N* = 14) | | |
|---|---|---|---|---|---|---|---|---|---|
| | MP v. constituents | MP v. notables | Notables v. constituents | MP v. constituents | MP v. notables | Notables v. constituents | MP v. constituents | MP v. notables | Notables v. constituents |
| Service role | -0.38 | -0.52[a] | 0.61[a] | 0.22 | 0.29 | 0.73[a] | -0.15 | 0.51[a] | 0.14 |
| District role focus | -0.29 | -0.42 | 0.62[a] | 0.07 | -0.21 | 0.27 | 0.25 | 0.39 | -0.55[a] |

a. Significant at the level of 0.05.

Turkish case, however, presents an exception to this general rule, for here local elites agreed very little with constituents ($r = 0.14$) and disagreed rather dramatically over the centrality of the district ($r = -0.55$). In Kenya there was a strong role consensus between local leaders and constituents. Correlation between the two groups was 0.61 on the service role and 0.62 on the centrality of district issue. Thus, the Kenyan notables stood very close to the members of their community in terms of their role expectations. A similar pattern was obtained in Korea but with a slight variation. While constituents and notables tended to agree on the service role ($r = 0.73$), they showed little agreement on the centrality of district issue ($r = 0.27$). Although the data do not provide unequivocal evidence, one can nevertheless draw a tentative conclusion that local elites and constitutents tend to have congruent role expectations.

Role consensus between MPs and local notables was generally low, with the exception of Turkey. In Turkey, a substantial consensus occurred between the two groups. The level of their consensus reached an impressive correlation of 0.51 for the service role, while the consensus on the centrality of the district issue attained a modest correlation of 0.39.

No such consensus was seen in Kenya or Korea. On the contrary, the data indicate strong negative correlations between the two groups in Kenya and to a lesser extent, in Korea.

The most important aspect of role congruence for our purposes is that which occurs between MPs and their constituents. In none of the three countries did we observe any significant consensus between these two groups. Evidently, MPs and their constituents did not see the legislative role in the same way.

When an MP stressed his service role, his constituents chose to ignore it. Conversely, when an MP sought to concentrate his efforts on activities other than service functions, his constituents called for a more active service role. This was particularly so in Kenya, as indicated by the negative correlations ($r = -0.38$ and $-0.29$), and to a lesser extent in Korea and Turkey.

The analysis of role congruence in each district failed to disclose strong linkages based on consensual role perspectives.[20] MPs' own perceptions did not match closely those held by the local notables and constituents. Because role congruence was conspicuously absent in all three countries as well as in all electoral constituencies that we studied, it clearly cannot form an important part of representative linkages.

## LINKAGE FORMS IN ELECTORAL DISTRICTS

Different forms of linkage may evolve in different constituencies. To properly understand linkage, we need to trace the patterns of interaction among all principal actors participating in representative relationships. Few studies have treated the subject of representation as an intergroup relationship, although virtually all have defined the term as some form of relationship. Loewenberg and Kim observed in their recent study that, "an individualistic interpretation of representation has guided a good deal of research on this subject over the past two decades, while very little work has been done on representation as an inter-group relationship."[21] Furthermore, much research has approached the subject from the perspective of legislators, thus neglecting the equally important perspective of constituents. There are only a handful of studies in which all the relevant partners of the representative relationship have been analyzed simultaneously.[22]

In thinking about the nature of representative linkages that evolve in each constituency, we begin by identifying the key participants. We consider three groups to be the most relevant to linkage formation: representatives, their district voters, and local notables. Local notables are included because they play an especially important role in developing societies as the intermediaries between the political center and the periphery. In all three countries we discovered that local notables held political beliefs and attitudes most consonant with those of their community members. Both groups agreed closely with each other on several basic values including their expectations of the legislative role.

Each of these groups acts out its unique role, exchanges support and benefits, and forges a common sense of solidarity. The ways in which the three groups interact with each other define the form of representative linkages. On the basis of the data collected from forty constituencies, we have identified four basic forms of linkages; these are shown in figure 6.1.[23]

*Multiple linkages.* Extensive contact and communication among the MP, local notables, and constituents characterize this form of representative linkage. The MP maintains a broad and frequent contact with his constituents, while he simultaneously seeks to remain in close touch with local notables. Constituents in such a district have access to two main channels through which they can take their personal or community problems to the MP: they can approach the MP directly with their requests, or they can ask their local notables to mediate such requests on their behalf. A legislator who is elected from a district with multiple linkages is likely to spend a great deal of his time in his home district providing a variety of services to constituents and local notables.

*Direct linkages.* This form is quite similar to the multiple linkage discussed above except for the lack of extensive contact between the MP and local notables. In direct linkages, local notables must compete for attention and influence with the emergent groups of professionals, party officials, and economic interest groups. In this case notables do not hold a monopoly over the role of intermediary for they must share it with new groups.

The most important causes for the decline in notables' community standing are modernization and its accompanying social effects. As the traditional authority structure has broken down, so has the stature and influence of local notables. Direct linkages are most likely to occur in industrialized and urbanized constituencies where modern forms of political organization grow rapidly, replacing the traditional roles that local notables used to perform.

Because modernization leads to an increased level of political consciousness, constituents in an industrialized district develop a higher sense of political competence than do those in socially backward districts. Residents of industrialized constituencies exhibit definite ideas about what their legislature should do and are familiar with the roles that legislatures of other advanced

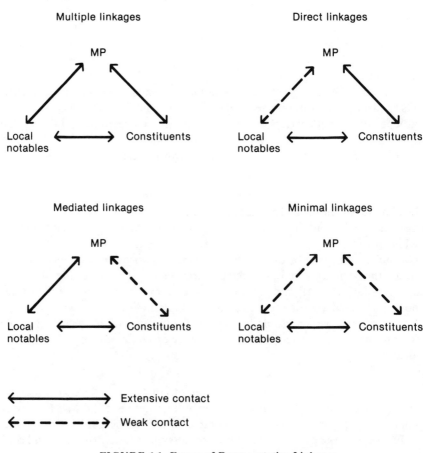

FIGURE 6.1. Forms of Representative Linkages

countries play. They also have clearer notions about what their own MPs should do and about whether the MPs deliver what they promise. When they have problems, they seek direct contact with the MPs or mediation by modern groups such as labor unions or party branches, rather than mediation by local notables who have by now lost much of their past stature and power. We expect to find more of the direct representative linkages in modernized societies and in relatively more developed regions of a country.

*Mediated linkages.* Local notables play the pivotal role in this form of linkage. Almost exclusively they fill the intermediary role within their communities. Without mediation of notables, political leaders at the center cannot reach the grassroots. The behavior of an MP serving such a district is easily anticipated. He will strive to cultivate good will among influential local notables by returning to his district as frequently as possible and by spending a great deal of his time there talking to a few select community leaders.

The MP will also strive to provide an active constituency service, mostly in response to requests coming from or mediated by local notables. He is unlikely to seek direct and personal contacts with his constituents. In districts like this, local notables are in effect neighborhood captains in what students of political development call a "patron-client system."

Representation consists of, in this context, a two-step flow of communication and contact: first, from the members of a community to their local notables, and second, from the notables to the MP. Such mediated linkages are likely to evolve in less modern and more traditional constituencies. Also, such linkages are likely to be formed by people still retaining strong emotional attachments to parochialism or tribalism.

*Minimal linkages.* The absence of significant contacts between an MP and his constituents, and between the MP and local notables, constitute minimal linkages. Between elections, the MP seldom visits his home district. Instead, his main arena of action is the nation's capital. He regards constituency service as onerous and largely irrelevant to his primary duties. Consequently, he provides only a minimal amount of constituent service. Minimal linkages are likely to evolve in places where the legislature and its members perform only a nominal constitutional role, and in areas which remain poorly integrated into the mainstream of the political life of a nation. In such areas constituents have not yet established strong psychological ties with the government at the center, and are still content in their private world of parochialism or tribal culture. They see little relevance in all that goes on outside their immediate environment, including the actions of the MPs. In fact, the people of these subcultures are excluded from effective representation for the reasons of their own making. Minimal linkages may also evolve in places where the people are disenchanted with the performance of the legislature.

**TABLE 6.11.**

**Forms of Representative Linkages Forged in Each Constituency**

| Linkages | Kenya (N = 14) | | Korea (N = 12) | | Turkey (N = 14) | |
|---|---|---|---|---|---|---|
| Multiple linkages | Kajiado-North | | Pyongtaek, Imsil, Chungju, Kongju, Kwangju | | Ankara, Canakkale, Denizli, Diyarbakir, Konya | |
| | | 7% (1) | | 42% (5) | | 36% (5) |
| Mediated linkages | Kilifi-South, Starehe, Embu-South, Mbooni, Githunguri, Kericho, Busia-East | | Kangnung | | Gaziantep, Istanbul, Samsun | |
| | | 50% (7) | | 8% (1) | | 21% (3) |
| Direct linkages | Nyakach | | Pusanjin | | Kars, Mus, Yozgat | |
| | | 7% (1) | | 8% (1) | | 21% (3) |
| Minimal linkages | Kirinyaga-West, Laikipia-West, Ikolomani, Mbita, Kitutu-East | | Seoul, Andong, Dalsong, Mokpo, Chinju | | Adana, Izmir, Rize | |
| | | 36% (5) | | 42% (5) | | 21% (3) |
| (N) = | | 100% (14) | | 100% (12) | | 99% (14) |

Note: This table lists percentages, frequencies (in parentheses), and the names of electoral districts where we conducted the mass survey.

In Table 6.11 the results of our classification efforts are displayed. After examining the interaction data, we were able to determine the specific form of representative linkages functioning in each constituency.[24] By and large, the results confirmed our initial expectations. In each of two comparably modernized societies, Korea and Turkey, we identified five electoral districts where multiple representative linkages operated. This number accounts for more than one-third of all constituencies in which we conducted research. In Kenya, the least modernized of the three countries, we could identify only one district with multiple linkages.

Of the fourteen constituencies that we studied in Kenya, we could place seven in the mediated linkages category. This suggests that the intermediary role of local notables in these Kenyan districts is crucial to representation. In other countries we found fewer cases of the mediated linkages: only one in Korea and three in Turkey. Mediated linkages were a dominant form of constituency representation in Kenya, which comes to us as no surprise; the salience of the patron-client system in Kenyan politics has been well documented by scholars, and our own data collected at the local level have corroborated the same point.[25]

We did not expect to find multiple or direct linkages in Kenya, given the importance of the intermediary role of local notables in that country. However, in one district, Nyakach, we did identify direct representative linkages. Upon closer examination it became clear that the MP representing that district was quite unique in his approach to his constituency. He held, in addition to his legislative seat, the important position of secretary general of the Center Organization of Trade Unions and deviated from the general norm by seeking direct contacts with voters. Moreover, he rejected the tradition of the patron-client network, and in so doing, angered many of his local notables. He evidently believed that he could afford to bypass the influential local notables because of his national visibility.

In Korea, two dominant forms of constituency representation were observed. One was the category of multiple linkages. This particular form of representation was identified in five districts: Pyŏngtaek, Imsil, Ch'ungju, Kongju, and Kwangju. The other dominant form was the category of minimal linkages which were identified in another five districts, including Seoul, the capital; and a southern district called Mok'po which produced a former presidential candidate, Kim Dae-jung, who had almost unseated President Park. Subsequently, Kim was charged with treason, supposedly for political reasons, and sentenced to a prison term, losing his seat in the Assembly. Because of this and other events, Mok'po constituents had reason to be disenchanted. There were also reasons for the voters in Seoul to be disenchanted. Seoulites are the best educated group in Korea, and have a relatively high political awareness. Moreover, they obtain much of their political information about politics and government from national media located in the capital which are always critical, and at times, even cynical in their political coverages. Their proximity to the centers of government, and especially to the National Assembly, tends to magnify their perception of the seamy sides of politics. This high political awareness leads them to expect high government performance. These are the principal sources of their political disaffection, manifest in their records of "protest voting" for opposition parties. Disillusioned with politics and, in particular, with the ineffectiveness of the legislature, they do not look upon its members as influential political actors, and consequently, do not try to establish close contacts with them.

We found no single dominant form of representative linkages in Turkey, other than the multiple linkages that we mentioned previously. We identified such linkage forms in five districts: Ankara, Canakkale, Konya, Denizli, and Diyarbakir. Other constituencies showed quite divergent forms of linkages. This diversity may, in fact, reflect the complex nature of representative politics in Turkey. The extremely complicated electoral system, the unique constitutional clause formally barring deputies from representing district interests, and important variations in subculture and socioeconomic condition by region are all contributing factors.

The types of representative linkages an MP forges with his constituency may have direct effect on his reelection. When the constituents and local notables are closely linked to their representative, and are satisfied with his service activities, they are likely to return him to the legislature. In Kenya, where we followed the political fortunes of individual MPs in the election of 1974, we discovered a striking pattern. Constituencies where we identified mediated linkages returned all but one of their MPs, an 86 percent reelection rate. By comparison, only one of the five MPs representing the minimal linkage districts was reelected. It seems clear that in Kenya the establishment of mediated linkages in home districts is a key factor for MPs' reelection success. Although we do not have comparable data for Korean and Turkish MPs, our evidence from Kenya is suggestive of the similar effects in these countries.

Having determined the specific forms of representative linkage characteristic of each constituency, we must now confront an important question: Why do representative linkages vary from district to district? The variables that we expect to be important in shaping representative linkages are summarized in figure 6.2.

The first group of variables includes personal characteristics of an MP such as his personal background, political experience, and basic political attitudes. The second group is comprised of the characteristics of the district: its homogeneity, modernity, partisan alignment, and cultural orientations. Equal in importance to these two groups of variables is legislative culture of a district. This group consists of ecological characteristics as well as the district's relationship to the nation as a whole. The fourth group of relevant variables consists of systemic attributes such as a nation's constitutional structure, its party system, political culture, and so forth. Loewenberg and Kim have suggested, on the basis of research in six countries, that these systemic variables are most useful in explaining variations in parliamentary representation.[26]

Unfortunately, we do not have the necessary data for a full investigation of the sources of representative linkages. We have, however, examined a few constituency-level variables and have failed to find any variables that, alone or in combination, account for a significant amount of the variation in representative linkages.[27] Our limited analysis of the sources of linkages suggests that representative linkages are the product of a complex set of interacting variables. A systematic search for the sources of linkage variation by district is beyond the scope of our study, but it is one that requires the collection of detailed personal data about the MP and in-depth observation in each district, of a kind much more detailed and intensive than we were able to collect through our structured survey.

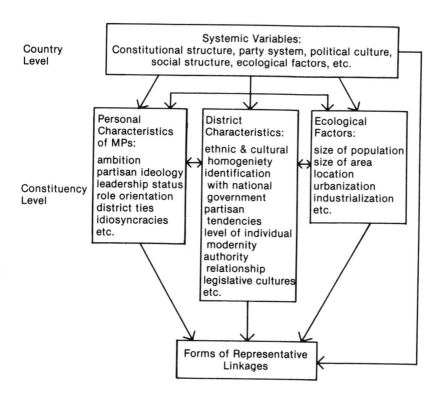

FIGURE 6.2. Variables Influencing Representative Linkages

# Part III

# RESOURCE ALLOCATION

# Chapter 7

# GENERAL RESOURCE ALLOCATION: THE ROLE OF THE LEGISLATURE AND LEGISLATORS

The legislature is one of many governmental institutions involved in resource allocation. Other actors in the resource allocation process include the executive, the bureaucracy, local governments, political parties, and independent or autonomous government agencies. The rules and patterns of interaction among actors are important factors in determining who gets what in a political system. Equally important is the internal structure of organizations competing for resources.

For our purposes, it will be useful to make a distinction between general and specific resource allocation. General resource allocation is the process by which the legislature produces outputs as a collectivity, while specific allocation refers to the implementation of policies that are determined by the bureaucracy, with some possible influence by legislators. As an example, the legislature may make a general budgetary allocation to a rural electrification program. But, the decision about which villages in which provinces will be electrified is a specific allocation; if a legislator wants villages in his district to benefit from the program he must intervene in the administrative process.

## THE LEGISLATURE AND GENERAL
## RESOURCE ALLOCATION

In order to identify the role of legislatures and legislators in the process of resource allocation in Kenya, Korea, and Turkey, we shall first examine their location in their respective political systems and the constraints which operate on their resource allocation activities. We shall then examine the perceptions of the MPs about how their legislatures make general allocative decisions and how they as individuals participate in that process. In the next chapter we will examine the role of legislators in the specific allocation of resources, that is, the efforts they make to gain benefits for their districts.

## THE LEGISLATURE AND THE EXECUTIVE

The legislature is said to make laws. Such a statement is correct in the sense that laws are not enacted without being accepted by a majority of the members of the legislature, but it often does not reflect where bills originate, who shapes them, whether and how much the legislature determines their content.

In all three countries in our study, the executive has historically played an important role in lawmaking. Executive dominance has been a conspicuous feature in Korean politics in the last three decades. Under the *Yushin* system, executive power expanded even more, giving the president the power to do virtually anything he wanted. Constitutionally, both individual MPs and the executive were empowered to submit legislative bills. In practice, however, bills submitted by individual MPs were not only few in number but also had a significantly poorer rate of passage on the floor than government bills.[1] Moreover, the National Assembly seldom amended the government bills in any significant fashion. The dominant role of the executive in lawmaking was almost complete and was built upon three factors: a constitution that favored executive power, the president's control of major parties in the Assembly, and the personal stature of the president himself.

In Kenya virtually all bills originate in government ministries. They are normally drafted by the attorney general's office, and are scrutinized by the president and his inner circle of advisors before being introduced in the National Assembly as government bills. Only rarely do individual legislators present bills on their own; only one such bill has been passed into law since 1969.

Occasionally, however, a bill is introduced by a backbencher that has widespread support in the National Assembly. Such bills, which usually challenge the government on a given issue, are vigorously opposed by the front bench. When such bills are passed, however, or when it is evident that a majority support the measure, the government often introduces a substitute bill of identical content, which it then insists be passed into law.[2]

Since bills passed by the Kenyan National Assembly do not become law until they are signed by the president, an executive refusal to sign bills that have been introduced and passed by backbenchers, coupled with the introduction of a substitute measure, effectively means that no private member bills become law regardless of whether they are passed by the legislature. On the other hand, such bills are occasionally an effective means through which the legislature, as a collective body, can influence government policy.

In Turkey, most bills originated in the ministries, were discussed in the cabinet, and were presented to the legislature as government proposals. The substance of government-backed legislation was seldom changed. Individual legislators, to be sure, were able to present their own bills, but such bills were not given priority in consideration. The traditions of parliamentary parties required legislators to clear their bills with the leadership of the parliamentary party before they submit them. The leadership of the majority party (or parties, if the government was a coalition), worked closely with the government and often acts as the government spokesman to the legislature.

In all three countries, then, the executive was the major source of legislative proposals, and the legislature was viewed as an institution which generates support for governmental action.

### DISCIPLINE IN THE PARLIAMENTARY PARTIES

The organizational structure of political parties, the nature of the relationship between the party organization and the parliamentary party, and the internal organization of the parliamentary party itself are among the factors that will promote or restrict the influence of the legislature in resource allocation.

The parliamentary parties in Turkey voted in compliance with the decisions of the party leadership. The bylaws of the Grand National Assembly treated the "party group" rather than the individual deputy as the main actor in parliamentary activity. Official spokesmen of parties, for example, were favored over individual deputies in floor debates. In the case of budgetary debates, to cite an instance, only three deputies were permitted to speak, for periods not to exceed ten minutes each, on the budget of a ministry or other government agency. Committee assignments were made by the party leadership.

Violations of Turkish party discipline were rare, given the powers of the leadership of the parliamentary party, which increased when the party was in power. The failure of an individual or group of deputies to comply with party discipline was usually a prelude to a break from the party.

Such rigid party discipline did not mean that backbenchers of the parliamentary party lacked channels through which they related their preferences to their leaders. First, individual discussions with deputy leaders of the parliamentary group of a party were always possible. Second, and more important, party leaders called meetings of the parliamentary group for discussion and consensus building. Once a decision was reached, however, the deputies were expected to obey.

In Korea, party discipline was strong, especially in the two government-controlled parties. At the time of our research, the leadership of the Democratic Republican Party (DRP) exercised tight control over its members. It was very rare that a DRP member spoke or voted against his party position.

Similarly, the members of the Society for Revitalizing Reforms (SRR), who were appointed by the president to the legislature, acted in a concerted manner, always in complete agreement with the DRP legislators. Violations of party discipline were dealt with severely, through expulsion and other sanctions. While the leadership of the two government parties were in complete control of their individual members, they did not exercise power independently. The leaders of both the DRP and the SRR were personally linked to the president, and they were in effect nothing more than the floor managers for the executive.

In the case of the main opposition party, the situation was somewhat different. The opposition New Democratic Party (NDP) insisted on strong discipline, but internal factional strife frequently impaired this discipline. The NDP was really a confederation of several factions organized around individual leaders. In the face of dominance by government parties, these factions formed an opposition coalition and acted as a cohesive unit. But on occasions when the factions disagreed, they failed to act as a disciplined group.

As described in chapter 3, Kenya is technically a one-party state but because of the organizational weakness of the ruling KANU party, it is usually more accurate to describe Kenya as a no-party state. Although there is a KANU parliamentary party composed of all members of the Kenyan National Assembly and presided over by the president, the parliamentary party rarely meets except when the president wishes to address the MPs or conduct parliamentary business in private. Under these conditions, the ruling party as an organization has little impact on the course of legislative business. Although government bills are often introduced by ministers who are also senior party officials, it would be a misinterpretation of the situation to suggest that the parliamentary party therefore influences the legislative process. Such bills are government bills, not party bills, a distinction often underscored by the fact that backbenchers occasionally vote against measures introduced by their own "party" leaders.

## PARTY ORGANIZATION OUTSIDE THE PARLIAMENT

Parliamentary parties may be extensions of a national political organization or they may constitute the essence of a political party. The existence of a national party organization may affect the role of the legislature and the legislators in the process of resource allocation in several ways. First, the party organization may bring pressures on legislators to observe party discipline. Second, local party organizations may serve as channels through which district needs are communicated to the legislators. Third, local organizations may serve as support bases for deputies mobilizing local funds for development projects, or organizing meetings or rallies when they visit the district. Fourth, party organizations may help constituents to resolve their problems with the national bureaucracy or local government. Such assistance may facilitate the work of a deputy in that many constituent problems may be handled without reaching him, thus easing his constituency service burden. Such assistance may also undermine his direct linkages with the voters, rendering him more reliant on local party bosses at his next election.

Turkish political parties had formal and permanent organizations down to the subprovincial level, with informal extensions into lower levels of administrative organization. Local party leaders often intervened on behalf of constituents to help settle their problems with officials of the national government, and guide them to the deputies representing them in the capital for additional help. They were instrumental in organizing local lobbying delegations to Ankara.

Local party organizations in Turkey were important because they determined the electoral chances of deputies. Party tickets in each province were chosen in intraparty primaries where delegates, acting as representatives of the provincial party membership, voted on candidates. The local party leadership was the single most influential group in the naming of delegates, and so exercised significant power over deputies.

Leaders of subprovincial party organizations often engaged in bargaining with each other to win province-wide support for the candidates they sponsored. Leaders of provincial and subprovincial party organizations were generally able to deny renomination to incumbent legislators who proved to be mavericks or incompetents. On the other hand, an incumbent or any other candidate who campaigned hard often won votes from delegates in the primary without the support of provincial or local party leaders.

The role of the national party organization in the nominating process tended to be defensive. It had the authority to veto candidates before a primary, and it could effectively prevent primaries in provinces where the party organization was either very weak or splintered into factions. The central party organization could also place a limited number (5 percent) of candidates on the party ticket. Such spots were ordinarily filled by prominent incumbents, incumbents who formerly belonged to other parties, or other individuals the party wanted nominated. In provinces where primaries were not held, the party would select the nominees, but this tactic was limited to provinces where the party was weak. From the viewpoint of an incumbent MP, the prospects for renomination and a position on the party list high enough to make reelection likely, depended heavily on maintaining good relations with provincial and local party leaders and activists.

Korean political parties at the time of our study were essentially parliamentary parties in character. With the exception of the governing DRP, they lacked a well-organized mass base. The Society for Revitalizing Reforms consisted of appointed members without specific district constituencies and without a need for support at the grassroots level. The New Democratic Party was poorly organized at the mass level, because it was no more than a loosely organized collection of factions. What organizations did exist at the grassroots level were often electoral machines fostered by individual politicians. These organizations are known as the *jiban* in the Korean language, and their purpose is explicitly to provide reelection support to politicians. Such organizations were not regarded as integral parts of the party organization. The governing DRP probably had the best party organization in Korea, penetrating deeply and effectively down to the villages. With professional staff at every level, the DRP was very successful in reaching voters in rural areas.

The organization of Kenya's ruling KANU party has withered. Party branch organizations at the district level, which once constituted the backbone of KANU, have—except in a few unusual cases—ceased to exist. These district-wide party organizations have frequently been displaced by the personal political machines of individual MPs. These machines in turn, are usually confined to single parliamentary constituencies, and are therefore smaller than district-wide party organizations. Where they do exist, the machines serve as feedback and support mechanisms for individual legislators.

## ORGANIZATION OF ELECTORAL DISTRICTS

Electoral districts may be organized as single or multimember districts, and the pattern is different in each of the three countries of our study. Kenya has single-member districts, and Korea elected two members in each district. Turkish electoral districts elected from three to thirty-four members each, depending on the size of the population in the district. Turkish deputies were chosen on a proportional representation system using party lists.

The size of electoral district affects the resource allocation activities of legislators in many ways. The representative from a single-member district may be more visible to his constituents, better known by them, and also the single target of constituency demands. In multi-member districts, individual legislators are less visible and consequently more reliant on the local party organization, both for electoral support and for advice on the services expected from them. A division of labor may emerge in such districts with some deputies becoming more oriented toward constituency service and others toward legislative activity.

Also important may be the competitiveness of elections in an electoral district. Where the marginal value of votes is high, we may expect the deputies to be more attentive to constituency service.

## ORGANIZATION OF THE LEGISLATURE

In accounting for the domination of the executive over the legislative branch, it is often argued that the latter does not possess the same expertise and access to information as the former. Legislative committees and staff are cited as two means which may serve to remedy the weakness of the legislature vis-à-vis the government and thus help it to acquire a greater role in the process of resource allocation.

The Turkish Grand National Assembly had twelve standing committees and several ad hoc committees. The ad hoc committees were generally established to conduct parliamentary investigations. The standing committees were viewed as procedural organizations and did not ordinarily modify the substance of legislative proposals. It is interesting to note that two of the most sought after committees were the Foreign Affairs Committee and the Committee on State Economic Enterprises. The first gave its members a chance to get into the diplomatic circles in Ankara, the second an opportunity to meet managers of enterprises who might be able to find jobs for constituents. Partly because the rate of turnover of deputies was high in recent elections and partly because committee members changed frequently, committees were unstable groupings which did not wield influence of substantial consequence.

There was one legislative committee, however, which granted its members an opportunity to affect legislation in a way which is reminiscent of the pork barreling practices in the United States: the Joint Committee on Budget and Planning. The preparation of the national budget went through several elaborate stages in the bureaucracy and was debated in this committee. Committee members introduced resolutions for changes in the proposed budget to restore funds which had been targeted for cuts in the budgets of ministries and other government agencies.

The Joint Committee on Budget and Planning included thirty-five deputies from the lower chamber and fifteen members from the Senate; the government was guaranteed thirty of these seats. The members of the committee certainly had a greater opportunity than did most legislators to influence budgetary policy in ways that would benefit the interests and constituents they represent, but the magnitude of this opportunity should not be exaggerated. Committee members who belonged to the majority party, particularly those who had seniority or held leadership positions, had an advantage over other members.

In order to limit the possibilities for log-rolling and major changes in the budget, proposed amendments were submitted first to a subcommittee, which reviewed them carefully in consultation with budgetary officials; subcommittee recommendations were generally accepted by the full committee. A further restriction on the prospects for amendment was the reluctance of the committee to recommend amendments to the investment budget.

Members who served on this committee were seldom able to have any dramatic effect on budgetary policy, but there may have been some disguised advantages. Members of the committee on Budget and Planning had opportunities to meet and work with the highest ranking civil servants of the capital officialdom. Such relationships were obviously advantageous to members who did business with members of the bureaucracy on behalf of constituents.

In summary, it may be said that while the committee system in the Turkish legislature did not constitute an instrument through which the legislature or legislators affected general resource allocation in any significant way, it did provide opportunities for legislators to affect specific allocations for their constituents.

The chief officers in the Korean National Assembly were the speaker and two vice-speakers. The speaker was elected at the beginning of each session; the post usually went to the leader of the governing party. One of the two vice-speakers was always the leader of the opposition party, as a matter of courtesy by convention.

Other main offices include the chairmanships of the standing and special committees. The standing committees were organized to parallel ministries in the central government such as the Committee on Foreign Affairs, the Committee on Home Affairs, the Committee on Education, and so forth. The committee chairmanships were always filled by influential leaders of government parties. Although every legislative member received an assignment to at least one standing committee by law, the key committee posts were controlled by government parties.

The committees were important sites in the legislative process because all legislative bills were sent to them for deliberation. On many occasions in the past the opposition party confronted the government in these committees. Even though the committees were more or less controlled by government parties, the opposition members could still frustrate government programs by obstructing committee processes.

The Kenyan National Assembly is presided over by a speaker, and has seven standing committees to facilitate its operation. Of the seven standing committees, the Sessional Committee is the only one directly concerned with the flow of legislative business in the House. Two committees, Public Accounts and Estimates, exist for the purpose of legislative oversight, while the remaining four deal with the internal management of the National Assembly and its physical plant and are of no consequence so far as policymaking is concerned.

Only two of the committees dealing with legislation and oversight meet on a regular basis. The Sessional Committee determines the agenda of the National Assembly, and meets weekly when parliament is in session. It is chaired by the vice-president acting in his capacity as the leader of government business. It is composed of twenty to thirty members, and is completely under the control of the government.

In contrast, the Public Accounts Committee is usually chaired by a backbencher. It consists of twenty-five to forty members, and meets regularly during the course of an annual session. The annual session usually begins its work between May and July and lasts from four to five months during which time the Public Accounts Committee reviews the work of each government ministry. The committee tenders an annual report on its findings, but the impact of this report on government policy is difficult to assess.

In addition to the standing committees, select committees are created from time to time to deal with specific issues. Select committees are appointed by a resolution of the house, and in recent years have been the focus of much controversy. They have invariably been controlled by backbenchers and have been a thorn in the side of the government. Select committees are the only significant mechanism backbenchers have for pressing their case against the government on specific issues. In recent years select committees have been created to investigate a number of extremely sensitive problems, a development which has often led to government intimidation and occasional detention of the MPs involved.[3]

## THE BUREAUCRACY

The bureaucracy, being the chief implementor of policy, is the major source of specific resource allocations. It is with the bureaucracy that the legislators intervene to perform constituency services. The specific resource allocation activities of the legislators are affected by the bureaucracy; its size; the scope of services it provides; the efficiency of its administration; its level of autonomy (with respect to the cabinet and political parties); and its degree of professionalism. When the bureaucracy is capable of performing the services expected of it there is less need for legislators to perform certain constituency services such as finding hospital beds for ailing constituents or getting an agricultural bank to extend seasonal credits to a small farmer. Generally, the more professional a bureaucracy, the more resistance it will exhibit toward partisan use of public funds.

As discussed at length in chapter 3, Kenya is basically an administrative or no-party state in which the state bureaucracy governs the country in a manner similar to that which characterized the colonial period. A single national civil service carries out governmental policy across the country through a hierarchy of eight provincial commissioners and forty-two district commissioners assisted by a vast network of government-appointed chiefs at the local levels.

The provincial administration above the level of the chiefs consists mainly of young administrators who have received university training within the last fifteen years. Top officers at the provincial level, however, are often older men recruited by the British during the twilight of the colonial period in the 1950s. The president presides over the entire system and works closely with the provincial commissioners, a practice not unlike that followed by the colonial governors who ruled Kenya in the past.

Some writers have suggested that the provincial administration constitutes the "steel frame" of the Kenyan state, but, as suggested in chapter 1, the network of officials is basically an instrument of the center to penetrate the periphery, not an agent to represent the periphery at the center.[4] Kenyan MPs, and to an increasing extent, members of the provincial administration, have become aware of this distinction—as did President Kenyatta and his sucessor, Daniel arap Moi.

The result of this awareness is that since 1969 the provincial administration, initially at Kenyatta's urging, has encouraged MPs to become more actively involved in community development. Such involvement has been largely limited to MPs' constituencies, but many MPs have taken advantage of this opportunity to build a local political following. As noted above, MPs concentrate their efforts in the area of constituency service because it is the one arena in which they are given a relatively free hand to operate. Provincial administrators need MPs to play such roles if they are to succeed in administering government policies at the local level, especially policies designed to stimulate grassroots development.

In Korea the bureaucracy has traditionally exercised a paramount influence in the political process, resulting in the executive dominance that we have referred to previously. Under the Park regime the bureaucracy became even more powerful than before, for the regime chose to use it as its main instrument of social change, charging it with primary responsibility for development and implementation of ambitious economic plans. This led to an unprecedented growth in bureaucratic functions and power.

Korean bureaucrats, especially those occupying key positions in central government agencies, view themselves as more than administrators who implement policies formulated elsewhere; many define their roles in terms of active policymaking and planning. Among the 225 higher civil servants inter-, viewed in Korea, 56 percent defined their roles primarily in terms of policymaking rather than in terms of policy implementing. Of the 225 Turkish higher civil servants interviewed, 42 percent emphasized their policy making roles.[5] In both countries the ranking bureaucrats appear to go beyond the classical conception of an administrator in defining their own roles. In Korea the bureaucracy is both powerful and exercises a broad control over scarce resources. Without working closely with the government officials MPs cannot hope to induce a fair share of such resources to their districts.

Unlike Kenya and Korea, modern Turkey is the successor to a bureaucratic empire. Although the Ottoman Empire lost more than half of its territories during the First World War, 93 percent of the government officials of the Empire chose to remain in Turkey and serve as civil servants after the war's conclusion. The Republic's attempts to consolidate the new regime and introduce radical changes to modernize the country resulted in the expansion of the national bureaucracy.

The distinction between government officials and the cadres of the Republican People's Party was somewhat blurred during the single-party era, since both perceived their mission to be converting Turkey into a modern society as defined by Kemal Atatürk.

The introduction of competitive politics in 1946 and the attendant ascension to political power of the Democratic Party resulted in strained relations between the government and the bureaucracy which experienced a decline in influence. The 1960 Military Revolution has been attributed in part to bureaucratic reactions to a government which was willing to compromise values such as secularism in order to gain electoral support. Although the bureaucracy, its higher civil servants in particular, has tended to reflect the political divisions within Turkish society in recent years, a majority seems to hold views closer to those of the Republican People's Party.

The existence of a competitive political system in Turkey for almost thirty years had made the bureaucracy more responsive to citizen demands. The rising expectations of the citizenry and the desires of the governments themselves to achieve a social welfare state have served in recent years to increase political pressures on civil servants. Because the resources of government are not sufficient at any given time to meet a sizable proportion of citizen demands, both deputies and local party leaders intervene with administrators on behalf of their own supporters.

While partisan pressures on Turkish bureaucrats have been increasing, many bureaucrats have clung to their tradition of professionalism and resisted the pressures to become partisan agents. A majority of Turkish citizens can distinguish the job of the civil servants from that of the deputies, and their interaction with what is essentially a well-developed, penetrating bureaucracy is more extensive than are their contacts with their legislators.

THE NATURE OF POLITICAL ISSUES

The legislature deals with issues of broader interest than the particular concerns of districts and constituents. This is not to deny that certain issues may be more relevant for some constituencies than for others, but legislatures tend to address themselves to issues of a larger scope than single district or individual constituent concerns.

The nature of the issues before a legislature is one of the determinants of the role it will play in decision making. Broad or redistributive issues leave little room for the individual legislator to be influential and may help the government lead the legislative process. Sectorally fragmented issues, on the other hand, may broaden the scope of action for legislators to influence legislative outputs. It may also be suggested that the greater the need for rapid legislative action, the more likely it is that the government will lead the activities of the legislature. Urgency calls for expediency at the expense of legislative power.

Predominance of national security issues also tends to reduce the role of the legislature in decision making. Traditionally, political systems have been averse to the display of differing domestic opinions on issues involving external threats. The emphasis on internal unity vis-à-vis the external world promotes a concentration of power in the executive branch whose decisions the legislature is asked to support. A similar emphasis is called for by unstable regimes that feel threatened domestically. The absence of conflicting viewpoints in the legislature and the support this accords national political leaders are perceived by the latter to be a vindication of their policies.

## DEFINING LEGISLATIVE ROLES

The legislative institution and its members may play an important role in managing tensions and making innovations. The discussion and debate that occur in a legislature may in itself help reduce tensions in three ways. First, the ideas and interests represented by different factions and parties may lead to outputs pertinent to the needs and demands of different groups. Second, the behavior and actions of the executive and the bureaucracy may be prompted, modified, or restrained in response to views and sentiments expressed in the legislature. Third, the simple fact that different interests and views get hearings in the legislature may provide symbolic gratification for those who fail to influence legislative outputs, or even more generally, the outputs of the political systems.

In terms of innovation, new ideas and solutions may originate in the legislature, or the legislature may be one of the first arenas where innovative ideas are expressed or adopted. The role of legislators in resource allocation is closely linked to the development of a capacity to deal with tensions and to innovate, and to manage change.

## THE LEGISLATORS AND GENERAL
## RESOURCE ALLOCATION

At the beginning of this chapter, we drew a distinction between general and specific resource allocation. By general resource allocation, we refer to the process whereby the legislature produces outputs as a collectivity. These outputs may be allocations for services which a government provides or carries out on a regular basis or they may be intended to solve societal problems which are new or which have not been dealt with before. Except in rare instances, such outputs do not address themselves to specific individuals, small groups, and geographical locations, but rather to national concerns.

The rest of this chapter deals with the roles of legislators and legislative institutions in general resource allocation. We begin with the survey data from constituents, notables, and legislators concerning the major sources of conflict in the legislature. Next we describe the perceptions of legislators about how the legislative process works: the most difficult job of the legislature, the crucial problems it faces, and the ways in which these problems are handled. Then we turn to the MPs' own participation in the process: the types of activities in which they engage and their satisfaction with the outcomes.

## PERCEPTIONS OF SOURCES OF CONFLICT IN THE LEGISLATURE

Perceived sources of conflict play a role in the resource allocation because such perceptions of MPs, local notables, and constituents influence their beliefs and attitudes about who should get what and how much. Significant variations in such perceptions are expected by country and by population groups such as constituents, local notables, and legislators.

Table 7.1 shows that the sources of conflict in a legislature were perceived differently in Kenya, Korea, and Turkey, but similarly among the different strata of the populations. Both in Kenya and Turkey, a high percentage of citizens have vague notions concerning the causes of conflict in the legislature.

**TABLE 7.1.**
**Sources of Conflict within Legislature (percentages)**

| Sources | Kenya | Korea | Turkey |
|---|---|---|---|
| Constituents | | | |
|   Human nature | 3.9 | 2.4 | 32.2 |
|   Nature of job | 27.6 | 3.4 | 6.0 |
|   Party system | 0.7 | 19.3 | 18.6 |
|   Ideology | 0.2 | 2.6 | 19.4 |
|   Social conflict | 14.9 | 0.6 | 0.7 |
|   No answer | 37.2 | 63.1 | 9.7 |
|   Don't know | 11.4 | 8.4 | 11.3 |
| Local notables | | | |
|   Human nature | 2.2 | 0.2 | 20.2 |
|   Nature of job | 43.9 | 0.6 | 13.2 |
|   Party system | 3.3 | 50.6 | 31.0 |
|   Ideology | — | 0.2 | 30.7 |
|   Social conflict | 27.1 | — | 0.7 |
|   No answer | 18.8 | 47.2 | 2.8 |
| Legislators | | | |
|   Human nature | 14.4 | 8.4 | 12.5 |
|   Nature of job | | 4.2 | 1.9 |
|   Party system | 24.9 | 77.3 | 34.6 |
|   Ideology | | — | — |
|   Social conflict | 32.1 | — | — |
|   Legislative organization | 7.1 | — | — |
|   No answer | 10.7 | — | — |
|   Other | 7.1 | 4.2 | 37.5 |

*Note:* Percentages do not add up to 100 because responses containing less than 5% of answers in all three countries have been eliminated.

Korea and Turkey have well-organized political parties represented in their national legislatures, so conflict was frequently attributed to them. In fact, party is the only source of conflict mentioned by more than a few notables and constituents in Korea. The Kenyan political party is more a label than an effective political organization in the eyes of citizens and the legislators. Intensity of political competition in Turkey, based on increasingly more divisive ideological issues, is reflected in citizen perceptions of sources of conflict in the legislature. Kenyan references to social conflict, on the other hand, can be understood in terms of ethnic and tribal differences which are absent in Turkey and Korea.

The distribution pattern of the sources of legislative conflict does not differ among strata within each country. There was, however, a tendency to cite more frequently the organizational bases of conflict as one moves up the political strata from constituents to notables to legislators. Among both constituents and notables in Turkey, and among notables in Kenya, those from urban areas are more likely to stress ideology while those from rural areas more often mention human nature or the nature of the job as sources of conflict. It should also be noted that the "no response" category among the Kenyan and Korean constituents and notables was rather high, probably reflecting the reluctance of citizens in authoritarian political environments to offer opinions about conflict.

## MEMBERS' PERCEPTIONS OF THE LEGISLATIVE PROCESS

What kind of problems do legislatures deal with in Kenya, Korea, and Turkey? In an effort to probe the question, we asked the legislators in these three countries what they thought was the hardest job for the parliament as a

TABLE 7.2

**Legislators' Perceptions of the Hardest Job for Parliament (percentages)**

| Job | Kenya | Korea | Turkey |
|---|---|---|---|
| Getting membership to agree on sound policies | 7.1 (39.3) | 16.8 (36.1) | 34.6 (17.3) |
| Preventing adoption of government policies that would hurt people | Not asked | 52.1 (18.5) | 25.0 (23.1) |
| Preventing selfish interests from blocking policies | 50.0 (10.7) | 5.0 (8.4) | 25.0 (7.7) |
| Getting constituents to accept policies essential for economic development | 10.7 (17.9) | 22.7 (22.7) | 2.9 (38.5) |
| Don't know, no answer | 32.2 (32.2) | 3.1 (14.2) | 12.5 (13.5) |
| $N$ = | (28) | (119) | (104) |

Note: Percentages of first and second choices are given. The numbers in parentheses indicate the second choices.

whole. Respondents were asked to rank the choices listed in table 7.2. Their responses provide an insight into the nature of the three political systems under study and the role of their legislatures in resource allocation.

A majority of Korean legislators saw their job as protecting citizens from governmental excesses in an executive-dominated authoritarian system of government. The Korean government became increasingly authoritarian during the nineteen seventies, despite the people's desire for greater political freedom. The Korean legislature also attempted to act as a mediator between the government and citizens. This conclusion is given support by the fact that the job which was second most frequently cited by legislators was getting constituents to accept policies essential for economic development.

In Kenya the lack of a strong political party, coupled with the ability of legislators to influence government decisions through close personal ties to the president or higher ranking civil servants, resulted in a desire among many legislators "to prevent selfish interests from blocking policies."

Turkish legislators, operating in a competitive environment, most frequently cited "getting membership to agree on sound policies" as their hardest job. During most of the nineteen seventies Turkey was ruled by coalitions. Frequent difficulties, even among members of the same coalition, in finding common ground for initiating policies may explain the emphasis on reaching a consensus on policies.

It is useful to compare answers given by members of the government and opposition parties in Korea and Turkey. In Korea nearly 90 percent of the members of the opposition party were concerned with blocking government initiatives that they believed would hurt people. Korean government parties were more concerned with getting the membership to accept sound policies, and (particularly appointed members of the *Yujonghoe*) with propagating and legitimizing the decisions of the government by getting constituents to accept economic development policies.

In Turkey government parties emphasized "preventing selfish interests from locking policies," a priority that probably reflects the frustation of government parties with the tactics of the opposition parties. The opposition, on the other hand, was more likely to mention the difficulty of getting the membership to agree on sound policies, probably because it has not been able to get the government to accept its policies. When we examine the differences between the RPP (the major government party) and the Justice Party (the largest opposition party), we find marked differences, probably because these parties both have strong ideological orientations.

## MAJOR PROBLEMS FACING THE LEGISLATURE

To identify the role of the legislature in the process of general resource allocation, we asked legislators what they thought were some of the major problems their legislatures were dealing with during the term in which the survey was conducted, who had been instrumental in bringing these problems to the legislature and where in the legislative system crucial decisions concerning these problems were made. An examination of table 7.3 shows that although the important problems legislators had to deal with at any given time varied, certain types of problems were predominant. Korean and Turkish legislators paid particular attention to problems concerning executive-legislative relationships. As previously mentioned, the main difficulty of the Korean legislature in the past was influencing the behavior of the executive, whereas in Turkey it was one of producing a viable coalition able to get a vote of confidence in the Grand National Assembly.

Kenyan legislators cited most frequently their constituency services and representational problems. Apart from the problems concerning executive-legislative relationships, Turkish legislators alluded to a number of problems, without particular emphasis on any one of them. In Korea, internal legislative questions, constitutional-legal disputes, and foreign policy issues received frequent mention. These three sets of problems are, in one way or another, tied to the uneasy relationship between government and opposition. The first two are concerned more directly with the rights of the opposition and the nature of the relationship between a government and its opposition. Foreign policy issues also constituted a major point of contention between political parties in Korea. The issues that the legislatures of Kenya, Korea, and Turkey had to deal with were issues of general concern, not specific to particular districts.

TABLE 7.3.
**What Problems Legislature Had to Deal with (First Mentioned by MPs)**
**(percentages)**

|  | Kenya | Korea | Turkey |
|---|---|---|---|
| Problems internal to the legislature | 10.7 | 16.8 | — |
| Problems concerning executive-legislative relationships | 14.3 | 37.8 | 38.5 |
| Party organization and partisan issues | 3.6 | — | 3.8 |
| Problems of interest groups | — | 0.8 | 4.8 |
| Constituency service and representative problems | 32.1 | 8.8 | 5.8 |
| Foreign policy issues | — | 17.6 | 1.0 |
| Problems of public opinion and mass media | — | 2.5 | — |
| Constitutional, legal disputes, electoral system | — | 15.1 | 2.9 |
| Other problems | 21.4 | 2.5 | 21.2 |
| No important problems for legislature | 7.1 | 5.0 | — |
| No answer, don't know | 10.7 | 0.8 | 22.1 |
| N = | (28) | (119) | (104) |

INITIATION OF ISSUES

Table 7.4 shows who was instrumental in bringing problems to the attention of the legislature. Not surprisingly, none of the legislators in our survey, except one Korean deputy, claimed responsibility for bringing an issue up. Neither were rank and file legislators often credited for having done so. In fact, again with the exception of Korean opposition parties, intraparliamentary sources were not even identified as a major source of issues taken up by the legislature. The percentage of legislators who failed to identify a specific source for the issues that were brought up before the legislature is high, further confirming that legislatures do not often define the issues they deal with, but rather respond to issues which are put before them by other organs of government such as the president, cabinet members, bureaucracy, and the media. It should be added that legislative leaders of the ruling party who often appear to be intraparliamentary sources of issues brought before the legislature, may in fact act merely as spokesmen for the president or the cabinet.

The Korean exception, where legislative leaders of opposition parties were most frequently cited as those defining issues before the parliament, requires an explanation. A semiauthoritarian political system with competing parties may find itself on the defensive, responding to challenges from opposition leaders who may be the only group in a position to make them. The government, then, may be forced to meet these challenges in order to insure its dominance.

TABLE 7.4.
**Who Brought Problem to Legislature (First Mentioned by MPs)**
**(percentages)**

|  | Kenya | Korea | Turkey |
|---|---|---|---|
| Legislative leaders of government party | 7.1 | 5.0 | 9.6 |
| Legislative leaders of opposition party | — | 36.1 | 6.7 |
| Executive branch | 35.7 | 21.0 | 10.6 |
| Party politicians outside of the legislature | 3.6 | 0.8 | 1.0 |
| Committee chairman | — | — | — |
| Rank and file legislators | 7.1 | 5.9 | — |
| Professional staffs | — | — | — |
| Public interest groups, mass media, voters | — | — | 15.4 |
| Others | — | 10.9 | 12.5 |
| No one | 7.1 | — | 8.7 |
| I did | — | 0.8 | — |
| No answer, don't know | 39.4 | 19.3 | 35.6 |
| *N* = | (28) | (119) | (104) |

Members of all parties in Korea cited legislative leaders of opposition parties more frequently than they mentioned legislative leaders of government parties, although opposition members mentioned opposition leaders as initiators more often than the others did. There were no other major partisan differences concerning who brought problems to the legislature.

In Turkey members of the governing RPP party often mentioned the executive branch or their own legislative leaders; members of the opposition Justice party more often mentioned their own leaders. It is also interesting that the RPP members mentioned interest groups more often than did other members, reflecting the RPP's closer ties with such groups.

## LOCUS OF DECISION MAKING

Turning to the locus of decision on issues, we find that decisions were most frequently made not in the legislature or by legislators but by the government or the party leadership. In all three countries, key decisions were mostly made in the cabinet or government, or by party leaders. Legislative committees were not centers of decision making, and floor debates often concerned decisions already made elsewhere.

Some Kenyan legislators identified, however, the floor of the legislature as the center of decision making. Lack of a strong party organization in Kenya, coupled with the relative independence of its parliamentary members from government control, has encouraged competition between frontbenchers and backbenchers for public resources, and has made the floor a more salient arena of decision making in Kenya than it is in Korea or Turkey.

In all three countries a large number of legislators failed to identify a single and preeminent center of decision making, which suggests that the process of key policy decisions involves a multitude of actors located in a variety of government agencies and that it is difficult to cite any one arena as more important than the others. The evidence also suggests that the legislature was not an important arena of decision making.

## ACTIVITIES OF LEGISTATORS IN GENERAL RESOURCE ALLOCATION

We have thus far examined legislators' perceptions about the legislature covering a number of topics pertinent to general resource allocation. We are also interested in the activities in which legislators engage and in their personal satisfaction with the accomplishments of the legislature. We would expect these to vary by leadership position and by party. Party leaders should be more active than rank and file members. Those of the governing parties should be more satisfied with legislative performance than those in the opposition. We would also expect members in the majority to engage in more, or at least different, activities than would those in the minority. The key question in understanding the role of each legislator in the process of general resource allocation is to learn about the nature of his efforts to influence the outcome of the problem which he has cited as the most important one. Table 7.5 gives a summary of such activities.

We first examine how legislators have utilized the formal channels open to them for participating in decision making. These include: authoring or sponsoring bills, speaking on the floor, working for a bill in committee, and offering amendments. Our data indicate that speaking on the floor appears to be the most frequent activity in Kenya and Turkey while working for bills in committee is the most common in Korea. Although many Turkish deputies cite authoring or sponsoring bills, frequently this does not reflect an important form of activity. On many occasions, party or government leaders encourage their deputies to sponsor bills. In such cases, the deputy is responding to the wishes of the leadership rather than initiating an action on his own. On the more significant indicator of a legislator's participation in decision making, that of offering amendments, initiative is lacking uniformly in all three countries.

A greater percentage of Kenyan legislators spoke on the floor than did Turkish or Korean legislators. This is not surprising in light of our earlier observation that more Kenyans identified the parliament of that country as the center of decision making. It seems somewhat puzzling, on the other hand, that a fifth of the Turkish legislators interviewed emphasized speaking on the floor on major issues. Not a single Turkish deputy said that he could not do anything or just vote for bills when they come up; this suggests a general reluctance on the part of Turkish deputies to recognize their limits as parliamentary actors.

TABLE 7.5.
**What the Legislator Has Done (First Mentioned by MPs)**
**(percentages)**

|  | Kenya | Korea | Turkey |
|---|---|---|---|
| Authored or sponsored bills | — | 1.7 | 18.3 |
| Spoken on the floor | 32.1 | 9.2 | 19.2 |
| Sought support outside legislature | 3.6 | 1.7 | 6.7 |
| Worked for bill in a committee | — | 22.7 | 6.7 |
| Offered an amendment | — | 0.8 | — |
| Convinced colleague in private | 7.1 | 20.2 | 7.7 |
| Nothing, or voted on bill when it came | 21.4 | 21.8 | — |
| Other | 3.6 | — | 14.1 |
| No answer, don't know | 32.2 | 21.9 | 31.7 |
| *N* = | (28) | (119) | (104) |

We turn now to an examination of different levels of activity within each national legislature, to test our assumptions about the effects of leadership position and party. As we would expect, the Kenyan frontbenchers reported greater activity, primarily speeches on the floor, than did backbenchers, many of whom said that they did nothing except vote.

In Korea we did not find substantial differences between elected members of the government and the opposition parties with regard to the total level of activity, but there were differences with regard to types of activity. Members of both parties spoke on the floor to a limited degree. Members of government parties were much more active in committees, a finding that supports the conclusions that the committees were used by the government to process legislation but that opposition members found them to be of little use in voicing their points of view. More Korean opposition members were active in committees than on the floor, however. Their most frequent activity was influencing colleagues in private. Presumably, some of these efforts were directed at members of the majority party, who may have been more influenced by such efforts than by more publicized criticisms of government policy and legislation.

The most notable contrast in legislating activity in Korea was between elected members and appointed members. Appointed members were likely (almost 60 percent) to do nothing but vote on bills. They appeared to be an obedient and somewhat passive group, with little function except to follow their leaders.

Finally, a comparison of party leaders and the rank and file showed that leaders, as would be expected, were more likely to speak on the floor, work in committees, and convince colleagues in private.

In Turkey, members of the government parties, as expected, were more likely to sponsor bills and speak on the floor than those in the opposition party. Neither group spent much time on committee work. The differences between the opposition and governing parties were smaller than those found in Korea.

## SATISFACTION WITH LEGISLATIVE OUTCOMES

Legislators in the three countries were asked how satisfied they were with the legislative outcome on those issues that they considered to be most important. Levels of satisfaction obviously may be affected by a number of factors. A legislator may be satisfied because his party has prevailed on an issue, because he thinks the outcome will benefit his district or the groups he represents, or because he feels some personal sense of accomplishment. Answers to questions concerning satisfaction are impressionistic, of course, but they are one way of measuring legislators' perceptions of outcomes of issues they consider important and that normally involve some aspect of general resource allocation.

There are no striking differences in table 7.6 among the three countries in levels of satisfaction. Meaningful comparisons are difficult because only in Kenya did some MPs respond "somewhat satisfied," and because in Turkey legislators often responded that the problems they had identified remained unresolved—probably because much of the interviewing was done at a time when the governing coalition was on the brink of dissolution.

In Kenya we found that slightly more frontbench than backbench members were dissatisfied, but the difference was too small to be significant. Satisfaction differed by tribe in Kenya; members of the dominant Kikuyu tribe expressed higher levels of satisfaction than did those from the Luo tribe, the second largest.

In Korea, satisfaction with legislative output was clearly dichotomized along government-opposition lines, as we would expect in a legislature where the government has had little difficulty in achieving its goals. These partisan differences were even greater when the views of party leaders were examined; 75 percent of the leaders of the Democratic Republican Party expressed satisfaction, while 80 percent of the leaders of the opposition parties said they were dissatisfied.

In Turkey almost two-thirds of the members of government parties believed that the problems they had identified remained unsolved. And, opposition members were the most dissatisfied. The members of the unstable majority coalition noted that the government's inability to produce major pieces of legislation resulted in many issues remaining unresolved.

## CONCLUSION

What role do legislators play in the process of general resource allocation? Our examination of three countries suggests that the roles of different legis-

**TABLE 7.6.**
**How Satisfied Legislator Is with Legislative Outcome**
**(percentages)**

|  | Kenya | Korea | Turkey |
|---|---|---|---|
| Satisfied | 21.4 | 37.0 | 12.5 |
| Somewhat satisfied | 28.6 | — | — |
| Not satisfied | 21.4 | 38.7 | 18.3 |
| Problem not solved | — | 7.6 | 33.7 |
| No answer, don't know, inapplicable | 28.6 | 16.8 | 35.6 |
| N | (28) | (119) | (104) |

latures in decision making are in many ways similar. More frequently than not, legislative problems and solutions are spawned outside of the representational body. But legislatures are not merely institutions where only a seal of approval is placed on government policies; they are also places where disapproval or criticism is voiced. While our data do not permit us to measure whether such criticism is of consequence, it is plausible that governments try to preempt opposition by giving consideration to the possible reactions their proposals will face in the legislature. Leadership of parliamentary parties often serves as an important link in this process. Issues may be taken up in the caucus of the parliamentary parties as the Turkish example shows. Or, as is the case in Korea, the government may feel obliged to respond to problems which are initially introduced by opposition parties.

This examination of the role of legislators and legislatures in the process of general resource allocation is suggestive of the ways in which both the institution and its members may help manage tension and introduce change. That many legislators have opportunities to speak on the floor, that both individual members and parties may bring up issues for discussion and criticize the government, and that some proposals do in fact originate in the legislature are all examples of the ways in which the political system may acquire increasing capacity to cope with tension and to manage change through legislative institutions and representatives.

# Chapter 8

# SPECIFIC RESOURCE ALLOCATION:
# THE LEGISLATORS' ROLE

This chapter examines the role of legislators in the process of specific resource allocation. By specific allocation we mean administrative decisions involving the commitment of public funds or services to a specific project or district. Legislators try to influence this process, for they regard it as one of their principal representative duties to secure goods and services for their constituents. In fact, it is vitally important for a legislator to be effective in this role because his constituents are likely to judge him on the basis of how well he performs this service role.

Legislators' efforts to obtain public goods and services for their constituencies contribute in a significant way to the development of linkages between the political center and the peripheries. Such activities of legislators lead invariably to the creation of a close communications channel between the national government and the people at the periphery, promote active exchanges of resources and support between the center and the grassroots, and help develop a sense of community among those who feel left out of the mainstream of national political life. Thus, legislators' participation in specific resource allocation has important integrative effects in the developing political systems.

There are several reasons why legislators are concerned with the process of specific resource allocation. First, since legislators are identified as representatives of geographical areas, electors of those areas tend to come to them for assistance. Electors may come as individuals or as representatives of particular groups within the electoral district. Although the legislator may see it as part of his duty to give assistance to citizens who have asked for it, he is also strongly motivated by the fact that he is, in most cases, dependent on constituents for reelection.

Legislators are in a unique position to participate in the process of specific resource allocation. While opportunities in the process of legislative decision making are limited, opportunities for performing constituency services abound. Bureaucrats are generally sensitive to the requests of deputies because they need the good will of legislators to secure budgetary allocations and other benefits for civil servants. To cite an example from Turkey, it was alleged that the rector of a certain university in the capital could walk into the Grand National Assembly with a bill, and walk out the other door with a law. The secret of this success was that all the university hospitals allowed deputies to bring in constituents who needed medical attention not available in the provinces.

The intervention of legislators on behalf of constituents can bring personal benefits as well as votes. The construction of a road may raise the value of real estate a deputy might own in his province: irrigation programs may benefit his own farmland. Declaring industrial enterprises worthy of development credit may mean higher returns for legislators who happen also to be shareholders, or jobs for those who are not reelected. Again, an example from Kenya is instructive. Kenyan legislators often organize rural development projects to which they also make monetary contributions. After a certain percentage of the total cost has been collected in the locality, the deputy goes to the government and asks it to match the funds collected or make up the difference, which the government often does. In one case, local development projects organized by a deputy were contracted to a construction company which he owned.

## IMPORTANCE OF CONSTITUENCY
## SERVICE

We asked legislators in Kenya, Korea, and Turkey what types of problems and activities occupied most of their time, and to judge the importance of their constituency service. A majority of legislators in Kenya, Korea, and Turkey devoted most of their time to problems related to their districts.

We also asked members more detailed questions about which activities took up most of their time. These data were reported in chapter 5 (table 5.2), and enabled us to classify legislators as internals and externals. We found that in both Kenya and Korea constituency services had priority over lawmaking and policy-related activities. In Kenya 59 percent of the members ranked "obtaining resources for my district" as first or second in importance, and 44 percent gave similar ranking to "interceding with civil servants on behalf of constituents." In Korea the comparable figures were 43 percent and 60 percent. In Turkey these activities were ranked a little lower than lawmaking and policy activities. An analysis of these data (table 5.4) resulted in a classification of 58 percent of the MPs in Kenya, 44 percent of those in Korea, and 24 percent of those in Turkey as externals.

## LEGISLATOR-CONSTITUENT COMMUNICATIONS

Demands for services from constituents may be made in a number of ways, such as writing letters to a representative, visiting him in the capital, or trying to petition him when he is visiting the district. The legislator may promote such contacts when visiting his district in order to gain visibility, establish a good reputation, or gain electoral support. Constituency demands may also be referred to legislators by local notables or the leaders of local party branches. (Since we are concerned with constituents, we will from this point on include only elected members of the Korean legislature, excluding appointed members from the analysis.)

In chapter 6 we reported data for each country on the frequency of legislators' visits to the constituency, the types of groups that visited members, and the topics that were discussed during these visits. We summarize the findings from that poll briefly here.

We found that nearly all Kenyan MPs visited their constituency at least three or four times a month; three-quarters of the Turkish legislators visited at least once or twice a month; and almost half of the Korean legislators visited their districts less often than once a month, but only a few of them visited more than once or twice a month.

Kenyan legislators generally reported that they met constituents both individually and in groups. Almost two-thirds of the Korean members met constituents individually rather than in groups. And most Turkish members preferred group meetings. When asked to specify types of persons or groups they most regularly met in the district, both Korean and Turkish legislators cited local party officials, while Kenyan leaders were more likely to mention civil servants.

Members were asked what kinds of interaction they had with constituents. Kenyan and Korean members most often said they talked to constituents about their problems, while those in Turkey were more likely to inform constituents about new laws and seek their opinions about legislation. Those in Kenya talked about district rather than national questions. Those in Korea also discussed district matters, but spent more time discussing partisan questions. Those in Turkey gave more attention to national issues, and less time to district and partisan questions. These priorities reflect the cross-national differences we have reported elsewhere, particularly in the chapters on representation.

When the legislature is in session, legislators spend most of their time in the capital. There are many claims on the member's time when he is in the capital. He must attend meetings of the legislature and, if a committee member, meetings of the committee. There are also partisan activities that take up his time. He pursues activities that are designed to serve the interest of his district or his constituents, and may receive personal visits and/or correspondence from constituents, most of whom seek some kind of service.

Table 8.1 shows that legislators receive a sizable amount of correspondence and host many visitors. It is highly likely that the legislator constitutes a target for citizens who want to enlist his support for their business with government offices. Kenyan legislators appeared to receive fewer letters and slightly fewer visitors while in the capital than their Korean and Turkish counterparts. This is not unusual since Kenyan constituents have much greater access to their legislators in their district. Moreover, the Kenyan constituencies are smaller than those in other countries, and Kenya has a lower rate of literacy, thus fewer constituents who write.

The typical letter or visitor asks deputies for assistance in personal matters (83 percent in Kenya, 50 percent in Korea, and 78 percent in Turkey). In Turkey, since shifts of civil servants to different posts are decided by the ministries, many requests are concerned with the appointment of a bureaucrat to a particular position. In both Turkey and Kenya, constituents ask their deputies to help them find jobs.

It seems reasonable to expect constituents to go to the deputy who represents their own district (which means a larger number of deputies in Turkey with its multimember districts). Yet, because many deputies have reported that they receive communications and visitors who are nonconstituents, it is plausible to infer that citizens can, to some degree, choose the legislator whose assistance they receive. Constituents who are asking for a legislator's intervention to achieve a personal or a public end would be inclined to go not only to a deputy with whom they are familiar but also to one who would be in a position to produce results.

TABLE 8.1.
Letters and Visitors per Week Received by Legislators
(percentages)

| Range | Letters | | | Visitors | | |
|---|---|---|---|---|---|---|
| | Kenya | Korea | Turkey | Kenya | Korea | Turkey |
| 1–3 | 37.0 | 4.3 | 10.7 | 12.0 | 1.2 | 4.0 |
| 4–10 | 22.2 | 15.7 | 27.2 | 16.0 | 12.0 | 21.0 |
| 11–30 | 14.8 | 43.4 | 38.8 | 24.0 | 31.3 | 28.0 |
| 31–50 | 18.5 | 14.5 | 8.7 | 12.0 | 19.3 | 22.0 |
| 51 or more | 7.4 | 20.5 | 14.6 | 32.0 | 33.7 | 25.0 |
| None | 0.0 | 1.2 | 0.0 | 4.0 | 2.4 | 0.0 |
| N = | (27) | (83) | (103) | (25) | (83) | (100) |

## THE LEGISLATOR AND DISTRICT PROBLEMS

There are two types of problems related to legislators' allocation of specific resources. The first concerns only individuals. For example, a constituent may want his son to be admitted to a military school and ask the deputy (or one of the deputies from his district) to intercede on his behalf. This is a demand for a personal service. Many requests made of legislators are of this nature and consume a significant amount of their time. To illustrate, we quote a Turkish deputy:

> They [constituents with personal grievances] come all the time. They may call you any time of the day or the night from the bus or the train station, tell you their problem and expect you to get on it immediately. They often don't know the capital, how to get around, how to do business. They want you to go and meet them, take them around and feed them. If their business cannot be taken care of in a day, you may have to find a bed for them. When all is done, you have to see them off and, on many an occasion buy their return ticket.

While legislators may expend considerable resources in performing personal services for their constituents, they are also concerned with problems of a broader scope. Villages may need roads, water, or school buildings. Towns may need hospitals. Districts or provinces may seek industrial investment. Particular segments of the population, such as interest groups, may have other demands. Collectively, these requests may be called community demands.

## PERCEPTION OF COMMUNITY PROBLEMS

A legislator's perceptions of his community problems influence both the type of resource allocation activities he will undertake, and where he will intervene. Similar problems were considered prominent by constituents, local notables, and legislators in Kenya, Korea, and Turkey. Most problems cited refer to some aspect of economic development or economic life as listed in table 8.2.

Constituents and notables frequently cited social needs such as schools, roads, and water supplies. Economic, commercial, and industrial problems include inflation, unemployment, and demands for industrialization.

Kenya deviates from Korea and Turkey in its emphasis on agricultural problems. Although agriculture accounts for a major portion of the GNP in all three countries, Korea and Turkey have engaged in rapid industrialization attempts, a policy supported by large segments of their populations. Our judgments from field experience in these countries also suggest to us that many peasants see industrialization, rather than improvements in agriculture, as the best avenue for their economic betterment.

For the most part, legislators agreed with constituents and notables about

TABLE 8.2.
Perceptions of Most Important Community Problems (percentages)

| Constituents problem area | Kenya | | | Korea | | | Turkey | | |
|---|---|---|---|---|---|---|---|---|---|
| | MPs | Constituents | Notables | MPs | Constituents | Notables | MPs | Constituents | Notables |
| Political, partisan, or administrative | 3.6 | 1.7 | 3.1 | 9.6 | 1.2 | 3.8 | 4.8 | 1.3 | 2.1 |
| Sociocultural | 0.0 | 0.7 | 0.4 | 2.4 | 4.4 | 10.3 | 6.7 | 2.7 | 2.6 |
| Industrial-commercial | 17.9 | 17.5 | 15.2 | 31.3 | 11.3 | 18.2 | 44.2 | 1.6 | 9.7 |
| Agricultural | 7.1 | 22.4 | 20.1 | 12.0 | 7.7 | 10.7 | 5.8 | 4.3 | 9.2 |
| Educational | 17.9 | 8.2 | 7.8 | 1.2 | 2.0 | 6.0 | 5.8 | 1.9 | 5.7 |
| Welfare related | 0 | 8.4 | 10.4 | 13.3 | 5.8 | 5.6 | 4.8 | 6.7 | 4.7 |
| Social overhead | 50.0 | 23.7 | 30.0 | 25.3 | 29.4 | 33.5 | 18.3 | 50.6 | 43.1 |
| Other | 3.6 | 0.6 | 2.6 | 4.8 | 5.1 | 6.2 | 7.7 | 4.3 | 4.8 |
| Unspecific (Kenya) | 0.0 | 8.8 | 10.4 | — | — | — | — | — | — |
| No problems | 0.0 | 1.1 | 0.4 | 0.0 | 0.0 | 0.0 | 0.0 | 0.0 | 0.0 |
| No answer, don't know | 0.0 | 6.5 | 2.6 | 0.0 | 33.1 | 5.7 | 0.0 | 26.7 | 18.1 |
| N = | (28) | (4,128) | (453) | (83) | (2,274) | (468) | (104) | (2,000) | (279) |

the most important community problems, but there were some interesting differences of emphasis. While Turkish MPs gave less priority than did constituents and notables to social needs, Kenyan MPs gave higher priority than did other groups to these needs. Except in Kenya, MPs gave greater priority to industrial and commercial needs than did others in their district. Kenyan MPs were less interested in agricultural matters and more interested in education than were constituents and notables in that country. Legislators, because they represented many communities, cited problems at the district and regional level (data not shown), in contrast to constituents and local notables who pointed to more specific problems. This may help explain why (except in Kenya) legislators appear to give more attention to industrial and commercial problems and less to social problems than do constituents and notables.

## SOURCES OF INFORMATION

The ways in which personal and community demands are communicated to the legislator are similar. Both may be communicated to the legislator when he visits his district or by letters or visitors when he is in the capital. Some need not be communicated at all, because the legislator may already be aware of them. Let us begin by examining how district problems get communicated to the legislators.

It is apparent from table 8.3 that district problems, in most cases, were known to the legislators. Most were not related through specific channels, but rather were issues the legislator and the voters were familiar with. Only in Korea were the local notables and community leaders identified in some number as a source from which the legislator had learned about local problems. While the reasons for this are not clear, it is probable that Korean legislators had fewer contacts with their constituencies, as some of our earlier

**TABLE 8.3.**

**Legislators' Sources of Information on District Problems (First Problem Mentioned) (percentages)**

|  | Kenya | Korea | Turkey |
|---|---|---|---|
| Nobody I knew | 8.3 | 7.4 | 53.5 |
| Voters in general | 75.0 | 51.9 | 33.7 |
| Leaders of social organizations | 12.5 | 2.5 | 3.0 |
| Local officials | 4.2 | 4.9 | 1.0 |
| Local notables | 0.0 | 17.3 | 1.0 |
| Village leaders | 0.0 | 8.6 | 3.0 |
| Party officials | 0.0 | 7.4 | 5.0 |
| N = | (24) | (81) | (101) |

observations also indicated, and relied more frequently on their political machines and their contacts with traditional holders of local political power for information.

## LEGISLATORS' ACTIVITIES

A legislator will do different things, and intervene at different places in order to solve district problems. In Kenya we have data on what legislators have done to help solve district problems. While the data may not be typical of other countries, it provides useful information for Kenya.

Of the twenty-five Kenyan MPs responding, over one-third had organized self-help programs or raised money for the district; one-fourth had contacted a ministry, a provincial or district commissioner, or were themselves ministers who could provide direct help. A few said they had spoken in the National Assembly; one-fourth listed nothing they had done.

It was not unusual to see Korean or Turkish legislators in the halls of government offices inquiring about when various projects in their districts would start or trying to convince officials that their district should be given priority in government investment. It was also possible to hear legislators speaking on the floor for their districts, but this was not done with great frequency because it was ineffective. As one Turkish deputy explained, "If you occupy the floor to talk about your district problems, your colleagues will say 'he is sending his regards to his electorate.'"

Many legislators in all three countries felt that they were somewhat effective in solving district problems. Almost two-thirds of MPs in Kenya said they had been very effective, and another 20 percent said they had been somewhat effective. In Turkey, almost one-third claimed to be very effective and an equal number somewhat effective. While only one-sixth of the Korean MPs said they were very effective, nearly half said somewhat effective.

Few Kenyan legislators claimed to have been ineffective in solving the problem they have named as most important in their districts, while more Korean and Turkish legislators reported that they had been ineffective at this task. The greater satisfaction expressed by Kenyan MPs may reflect the higher flexibility of the Kenyan political system, but it should also be mentioned that the Kenyan legislators, on an average, had been serving for longer periods of time at the time of the interviews than had other MPs. The Turkish and Korean surveys were conducted six to ten months after elections in those countries, whereas the Kenyan survey was carried out shortly before Kenya's elections. Thus, Kenyan legislators had had more time to become familiar with the legislative process and the methods of getting resources for their district. This advantage no doubt increased their effectiveness.

What qualities distinguished legislators who claimed to have been effective from those who said they had been ineffective? Were backbenchers less effective than frontbenchers? Did the members of the government parties feel more effective than the members of the opposition?

Both in Turkey and Kenya, MPs from rural districts claimed to have been more effective than their colleagues from urban areas. Those from mixed districts fell between the two (gammas = 0.32 and 0.59, respectively). It is probable that the types of constituency service requests that originate in rural districts are more modest and as such may be easier to fulfill. It is equally probable that more government services reach the urban areas, thus diminishing the likelihood of requests for minor services in urban areas, and increasing the likelihood of more serious requests. A Turkish deputy from a province near Istanbul, conversing with a colleague from Eastern Turkey, expressed this occurrence well: "You know, I am quite lucky to be from *X*. Your people all come to you for any problems they have. Mine, well, they mostly don't get past Istanbul. It is like having a dam that holds a river back."

In Korea and Turkey, party was an influential factor in determining legislators' ability to solve district problems. Members of the government party expressed greater effectiveness in solving district problems, both in Korea and Turkey (gammas = 0.52 and 0.18). This relationship was weaker in Turkey, suggesting that in a more competitive system, members of opposition parties may have satisfactory opportunities to perform services for their districts.

Those legislators who held government or party positions prior to becoming representatives professed greater effectiveness in getting things done for their district in Turkey (gamma = 0.39). The same relationship was not evident in Kenya or Korea, mainly because in these countries there were very few legislators who had not held a government or a party position before.

In summary, those legislators who represented rural districts, who held a party or government job prior to election, and who were members of the government party, were more likely to say they were successful in their efforts to provide services to their districts and to help solve district problems.

## WHO GETS WHAT AND HOW

So far, we have examined the legislators' constituency service role. In this section we focus on a related question: who actually benefits from these services? Both constituents' access to and contact with an MP are crucial preconditions to receiving such benefits, and so we begin with an analysis of these. We will also present data on the kind of services that legislators provide for their constituents and districts.

Our data show that individual voters had differential access to their MPs. Some voters saw their legislators more frequently than did others, talked with MPs about community or personal problems more regularly, and obtained more services. Comparing constituents and local notables, we discover a marked difference between the two groups in their contact with an MP. Local notables in all three countries interacted much more frequently with their MPs than did constituents (table 8.4). Such interaction was highest in Kenya, and lowest in Korea. In Turkey constituents rarely saw their deputies, but local notables including provincial and subprovincial party chiefs and local interest group leaders maintained regular contacts with their MPs.

The differences in contact among the three nations cannot be explained by distance alone since we know that Korean MPs can reach their districts just as easily as can MPs in other countries. Although it is true that each MP in both Korea and Turkey represents a larger constituency than does a Kenyan MP, it still does not provide an adequate explanation because the Turkish constituents had more extensive contact with their MPs than did Korean constituents. A more plausible explanation may be found in the peculiar nature of politics in Kenya. In comparison to the other two countries Kenya is the least industrialized, with the largest number of rural election districts. In these rural districts, as we have discussed earlier, a form of linkage institution that we call the patron-client system has evolved. Weak party organization and the lack of active voluntary interest groups in Kenya have contributed to the gradual emergence of this patron-client system as a principal political organization in many rural districts. Legislators play key roles in this organization, for they use it as their election machines. For rural voters it offers vital access to government. Competition for scarce government resources is therefore waged through such organizations, the results of which are the unusually frequent contacts between constituents and their MPs in Kenya.

More local notables than constituents had talked to their MPs in all three countries, which is not surprising given the fact the notables were all community leaders. Also, local notables had discussed problems of a public

TABLE 8.4.
How Many Times Legislator Seen in Last Six Months (percentages)

| | Kenya | | Korea | | Turkey | |
|---|---|---|---|---|---|---|
| | Constituent | Notable | Constituent | Notable | Constituent | Notable |
| One time | 12.6 | 15.2 | 5.3 | 14.1 | 8.8 | 15.7 |
| Two times | 13.2 | 8.2 | 6.7 | 13.0 | 2.4 | 8.0 |
| Three times | 6.7 | 8.6 | 0.8 | 6.8 | 1.9 | 11.5 |
| Four or more times | 16.8 | 56.7 | 1.3 | 9.4 | 2.3 | 28.2 |
| None, no answer, don't know | 50.7 | 21.4 | 85.9 | 56.6 | 84.6 | 36.6 |
| N = | (4,128) | (453) | (2,274) | (468) | (2,007) | (287) |

nature more frequently with their MPs than constituents did. Most constituents talked to their MPs about personal problems or requests, when they had an opportunity to see their legislators (tables 8.5 and 8.6). It seems evident that the notables acted often as the spokesmen for their villages when they dealt with elected officials such as their MPs.

The contrasts between the countries were interesting. More constituents and local notables reported talking to legislators in Turkey than in Kenya or Korea. This is contrary to our expectation that more Kenyans should have talked to their MPs because more of them claimed to have seen their legislators within the six months preceding the survey than did the voters in the other two countries. Apparently, visibility of the legislator in his district in Kenya does not always translate into conversations with him, whereas in Turkey citizens and elites are likely to seek to see their legislators in order to communicate community problems to him.

Again in Turkey, conversations with deputies appeared to deal almost exclusively with community problems, in sharp contrast to the situation in Kenya and Korea where requests are often personal in nature. The existence of strong party organizations which tend to the personal problems of citizens probably lessens the need of Turks to ask deputies for personal favors, but there is also a cultural bias operating against receiving personal favors from public persons. Many respondents in Turkey, when asked whether a legislator

TABLE 8.5.
Have You Ever Talked to an MP About Any Problem (percentages)

| | Kenya | | Korea | | Turkey | |
|---|---|---|---|---|---|---|
| | Constituents | Notables | Constituents | Notables | Constituents | Notables |
| Yes | 7.2 | 47.4 | 5.4 | 45.6 | 10.7 | 64.8 |
| No | 92.8 | 52.6 | 94.6 | 54.4 | 89.3 | 35.2 |
| N = | (3,381) | (342) | (1,724) | (377) | (1,950) | (287) |

TABLE 8.6.
What Problem Have You Talked About With Legislator (percentages)

| | Kenya | | Korea | | Turkey | |
|---|---|---|---|---|---|---|
| | Constituents | Notables | Constituents | Notables | Constituents | Notables |
| Personal problems | 59.1 | 37.7 | 54.2 | 58.8 | 13.2 | 3.5 |
| Public problems | 39.7 | 61.1 | 32.5 | 39.9 | 66.5 | 67.8 |
| Both | 0.0 | 0.0 | 13.3 | 1.3 | 20.3 | 28.7 |
| N = | (3,381) | (342) | (1,724) | (377) | (1,950) | (287) |

had done something for them personally, responded with expressions like "Heaven Forbid!" or "Thanks be to Allah, I have never had to do that!" While reluctance of Turks to admit that they received personal favors may cause them to exaggerate the public nature of the demands they make on legislators, this does not alter the basic emphasis they place on public matters when talking to their deputies.

Only Korean local notables talked about personal problems to legislators as often or more often than did constituents. Such a difference lends further support to our earlier observation that Korean political parties at the local level tend to be personal political machines of legislators. Exchanges of personal favors for electoral support constitute the basis of a patron-client relationship.

Needless to say, talking to a legislator does not in itself insure a favorable outcome. The legislator may not have enough time, influence, or information to produce a favorable result for each request that is made to him. Further, he is unlikely to attach equal importance to all the demands he receives for constituency service, but rather is apt to develop a set of priorities concerning which problems and which constituents will get his attention. In Turkey, for example, if a constituent asks an MP for assistance in finding a job, he is likely to receive a personal card expressing the MP's support and directions to a government office or a State Economic Enterprise, where his chances of finding a job are not high. However, if a request comes from someone whose support at election time is important, an MP will pay closer attention to it and work harder to produce results. On community or subdistrict problems, electoral supporters, friends, relatives, and hometown people may receive favorable consideration by a legislator.

## PERCEPTIONS OF SERVICE

Legislators perform services for individual constituents as well as for the community. They spend a great deal of their time attending to personal requests from constituents. However, a legislator can provide such services only for a small number of his constituents. The data presented in table 8.7 show that very small percentages (0.9% in Korea and 4.5% in Kenya) of constituents in the three countries received personal favors from MPs.

Local notables did better than constituents in receiving personal services from MPs. The disparity in services received was the largest between constituents and local notables in Kenya, and the smallest in Turkey. Kenyan constituents received more assistance from their MPs than did the constituents in Korea and Turkey. Also, Kenyan notables did significantly better in this respect than did either Korean or Turkish notables. The saliency of patron-client organizations in constituencies seems to be a key factor explaining the larger amount of personal services rendered by Kenyan legislators.

Looking at the types of services that constituents have received, we found varying patterns in each country. In Kenya legislators were involved most frequently in securing government loans or finding employment for their constituents. In Korea MPs most often performed ceremonial services such as attending a wedding, a funeral, or a clan meeting. In Turkey deputies spent a large part of their time trying to find jobs for their constituents or interceding with government agencies on behalf of individual voters.

In addition to personal services, legislators also provide services which benefit the community as a whole. Most of the public projects they help bring to the district are of this type. We asked our respondents if they were aware of community services that their MPs had performed in order to ascertain the amount of such services provided by MPs in each constituency. Kenyan constituents showed the highest awareness of such services, much more than did constituents in Korea or Turkey. There is, in fact, evidence to say that the Kenyan MPs were actually far more active in providing this kind of services than were MPs in the other two countries. The difference in awareness between constituents and local notables was also significant in all three countries: local notables were more aware of MPs' effort to provide community services.

The type of community services that MPs tried to provide varied from country to country. In Kenya MPs worked hard to raise funds, both from government and private sources, to help local self-help projects (Harambee). They provided active assistance in creating local cooperatives and in construction projects such as roads, communication lines, primary schools, water and irrigation works. In Korea MPs played some limited role in the construction of public facilities. In Turkey MPs focused their efforts upon industrial and commercial projects such as getting factories built or new businesses opened in the district.

The type of community services legislators are expected to perform is closely related to the economic structure and goals of a society. Kenya is basically a rural and agricultural society. The problems perceived, the solutions offered, and the services provided in Kenya tended to reflect this. In Korea and Turkey, both more developed than Kenya, problems and solutions

TABLE 8.7.

Has Your Legislator Done Something For You? (percentages)

| | Kenya | | Korea | | Turkey | |
|---|---|---|---|---|---|---|
| | Constituents | Notables | Constituents | Notables | Constituents | Notables |
| Yes | 4.5 | 10.4 | 0.9 | 5.1 | 3.0 | 3.6 |
| No | 95.5 | 89.6 | 99.1 | 94.9 | 97.0 | 96.4 |
| $N =$ | (3,549) | (413) | (1,768) | (390) | (1,948) | (280) |

cited were usually related to industry and commerce. Once industrialization becomes a widespread phenomenon, even the more rural and agricultural segments of the population might begin to perceive their problems in commercial and industrial terms and, rather than expecting agricultural betterment, seek economic betterment through industrial growth.

## SERVICES TO INDIVIDUALS

The end result of the process of specific resource allocation is the benefit of an individual or community. While any citizen may request individual favors from a representative, we have already noted that, in fact, only a small percentage of the population actually does so. Among those who make requests, some obtain a satisfactory result while others fail to receive any benefit. Who are the beneficiaries of a legislator's activities? To answer this question, we examined the social background and political characteristics of constituents and local notables to identify those who appeared to be likely candidates to enjoy personal services.

Data analysis indicated that social background variables do not predict who among the constituents and local notables might be the recipients of such services. Political variables, on the other hand, were better, if somewhat modest, predictors of benefits received.

The effects of political variables on the services received were quite evident in Kenya. Those constituents who knew their MPs personally from before the election and those who helped their MPs in election campaigns obtained a greater amount of services than other constituents. Campaign work would certainly obligate a winner to return the favor, usually in the form of constituency service, and that appears to be the situation in many rural districts in Kenya. Personal acquaintance with an MP was also a good predictor of services received in both Kenya and Turkey. However, the same variable failed to predict the services received among the Turkish local notables. This may be a result of the extremely high percentage of the Turkish notables who personally knew their MPs well (82.3%), a case of invariance in the independent variable.

In Korea two political variables showed some effects on the services received by constituents: the level of political interest and the experience of contacting officials. Those constituents who exhibited a high political interest reported having received more benefits than others did. Likewise, those who had experience in contacting and lobbying government officials obtained more services from their MPs than those who did not have such experience.

Our analysis fails to suggest a general conclusion regarding the determinants of personal services received by constituents. Although some political variables such as political interest, campaign work, acquaintance with an MP, and lobbying experience, showed some predictive powers in one or other country, none proved to be a consistent predictor across all three nations.

## SERVICES TO COMMUNITIES

Legislators provide a varying amount of community services, a type of services distinguishable from those provided for individual constituents. Some districts receive more benefits of this kind than other districts, largely due to the aggressive actions taken by their representatives. What factors might account for the varying levels of community services received by each constituency? We have no data to measure directly the amount of such benefits actually distributed in each district, but we do have some information from which we can assess roughly the amount of community services received by each district. We asked both the constituents and local notables if they could identify any community services that they attributed to the activities of their MPs. Although we cannot always assume a perfect correlation between the public's perceptions of community services and the actual amount of such services obtained by a district, the two variables must nevertheless be correlated to some extent.

We have examined the correlations between a set of fourteen variables, all relating to district characteristics, and the constituents' perception of community services received. While we do not present the full results of this analysis here, it is useful to list some of these variables: percentage of urban population in each district, annual rates of in- and out-migration, age distribution of district population, the literacy rate, ethnic composition, level of electoral competition, voter turnout rates, distance from the nation's capital, and the level of communications and transportation development. The unit of analysis employed in this section is the data aggregated to the district level.

The results of analysis produced no clear patterns across the three nations. Only two variables, the degree of electoral competition and age distribution in districts, showed modest positive associations with the constituents' perception of community services received. The correlations were the strongest in Kenya, and the weakest in Korea. It may be possible to interpret these results, with some caution, that those MPs serving competitive districts must provide services more actively than other MPs who represent safer districts or, alternatively they must advertise more of what they are doing in order to remain a viable candidate in the next election. The effects of competition on community services were relatively weak in Turkey. This was because multi-member districts were used in Turkey, which diminishes both the visibility and role of individual deputies and enhances the role of political parties, in contrast to the system of a single-member district which would have the opposite effects. The average age of district population was moderately correlated with constituents' perception of services received in all three countries, but the meaning of this is not altogether clear to us. All that can be said at this point of analysis is that electoral districts with older populations had done better in obtaining community services than other districts.

We discovered a few interesting facts in the analysis of the Kenyan data, although these cannot be generalized to the other two countries. First, rural districts received more community services than did urban ones. Second, electoral districts with stable populations, i.e., small in- or out-migration, obtained more community services. Third, the districts with a better developed transportation system, measured by paved road per square miles, benefited more from community services than did the districts with a poor transportation network. Finally, the distance between a district and Nairobi, the capital city, also made a significant difference: districts closer to the capital received generally a greater amount of services. These findings suggest that there are identifiable factors that affect the allocation of community services in each country, but there are no such factors common to all nations.

The question of who gets what and how is important to an understanding of political representation. This is also a question most difficult, if not impossible, to research. We have approached it from the viewpoints of all major participants in the resource allocation process: MPs, constituents, and local notables. We have tried to show the interactions among these participants and how such interactions shaped the outcomes, i.e., who shares such benefits and who does not. Furthermore, we have tried to identify the correlates of personal and community services provided by MPs in their districts. The analysis produced no such correlates applicable to all three countries.

**Part IV**

**PUBLIC SUPPORT FOR THE LEGISLATURE**

# Chapter 9

# LEVELS AND SOURCES OF LEGISLATIVE SUPPORT

Popular support is critically important to the persistence and the effective functioning of a legislative body. Without it the legislature cannot perform its functions in any effective manner. David Easton has formulated the concept of support as a key variable that explains the stability of a political system or subsystem.[1] Legislatures, like institutions of all kinds, require support to persist over time. The degree of support that a legislature receives indicates how firmly that institution is rooted in the mind of citizens and elites. Hence, both the durability and effectiveness of a legislature depend in a significant way on the amount of support manifested by the public and the elite strata. Patterson and his associates have offered a theoretical rationale for studying support: "Legislatures require support to persist, to deal effectively with public and organized group demands, and to make necessary political decisions. . . . But since legislatures, more than most public and private groups and more than the bureaucratic or judicial branches of the government, are representative political institutions, the generation of public support is an important prerequisite for successful decision making on public policy."[2]

In many countries, particularly in the non-Western world, legislatures are relatively fragile institutions. They have neither a firm foundation of representative tradition nor a widespread public attachment to a representative body. Often they are relegated to the periphery of power, playing a subservient role to the powerful executive, the military junta, the dominant political party, or a charismatic leader. They have frequently been abolished, suspended, or forced to relinquish their constitutional powers. But legislatures have also been resurrected on numerous occasions, demonstrating their remarkable resilience in the modern world.

We have noted in the first chapter that students of political development, notably Huntington, have emphasized the central importance of institutional differentiation. Legislatures in developing countries are not only fragile and vulnerable to attack, but are still in the process of becoming autonomous entities. The institutionalization of the legislature requires not only the development of internal norms and structures, but the growth of external support —from other national political elites, local elites, and ordinary citizens. Legislatures lack the power that can be commanded by military leaders or the visibility and charismatic qualities of chief executives. Moreover, in developing societies, it may be very difficult for legislative leaders to make citizens aware of the fact that the legislature is a distinct institution.

The relationship between public support for the legislature and support for the political system as a whole is important but it is difficult to measure. If there are sharp conflicts or intense rivalries between the legislature and other political institutions, those citizens who are aware of these differences may support one institution but not the others. Where these conflicts are either unimportant or unrecognized by many citizens, support for the legislature may generate greater support for the political system as a whole because of the ability of the legislature to lend legitimacy to the actions of the government. If support for the legislature not only is strong but contributes to regime support, political or military leaders may recognize that it is risky to abolish or suspend that body.

In many countries of Asia and Africa where legislatures have neither a long history nor a firmly established tradition, the foundation of mass support for such institutions, is, as a general rule, highly insecure. And, to use Easton's terminology, the "reservoir of good will" among the public is likely to be shallow. This is what makes the support of citizens and elites particularly important to the development of a strong legislature in new states. Without some strong attachment to the legislature on the part of the general public and certain more influential groups, it is likely that the legislature will remain a weak body, usually under the shadow of a predominant executive. Therefore, the question of support for the legislature as a distinct institution is an important one. The capacity of the legislature to survive or to gain political strength in the future, especially in the face of possible efforts by the executive branch to weaken or eliminate it, may depend in part on the level of support it receives from the public.

## CONCEPTUAL FRAMEWORK: THE
## SOURCES OF SUPPORT

A variety of factors may influence the amount of support that citizens give to the legislature. It also seems likely that the factors which explain support in one country may not always explain support in another. In an effort to bring as many relevant variables as possible into our crossnational study, we begin with a general conceptual mapping of the key variables we have identified and their relationships to legislative support. Such variables and their relationships are depicted in schematic form in figure 9.1. The level of support for the legislative institution is the dependent variable which we seek to explain. The independent variables include five distinct categories: personal characteristics, the frequency of contact with MPs from one's district, cognitive variables, evaluative attitudes, and finally, district level variables such as socioeconomic conditions and MPs' activism in the districts.

*Personal characteristics.* We expect to find that those citizens who have the advantages of a higher social status would manifest higher levels of support for the legislature.[3] This includes such factors as higher education and higher prestige occupations. Younger citizens with the advantages of a greater opportunity for better education and a greater exposure to modern values should be more supportive of the legislature than are their older counterparts. In many developing countries women have traditionally been

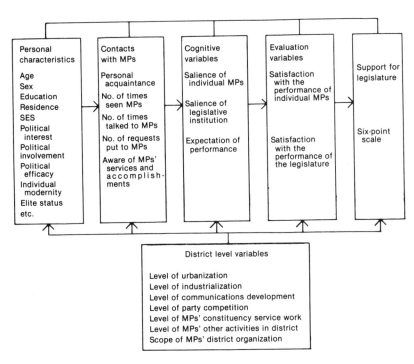

**FIGURE 9.1.**
**A Conceptual Framework of the Diverse Sources of Legislative Support**

assigned a lower social status than men, resulting in poorer education and lower political consciousness. Urban residents should be more supportive because of their greater access to the mass media and better information about politics; they might also have a higher feeling of political efficacy; all of these factors should contribute to legislative support.

Studies have shown that legislative support is higher among citizens who are knowledgeable about and involved in politics.[4] This leads us to hypothesize that legislative support should be higher among constituents with more interest in political affairs, among those who are actively involved in politics, and among those with higher political efficacy.

It seems plausible that some broader measure of knowledge and political awareness, not necessarily limited to purely political matters, might be related to legislative support. One such measure is the OM−12 scale, designed by Inkeles and his associates to indicate an individual's modern beliefs and attitudes.[5] We expect greater legislative support among those constituents with a higher level of individual modernity. We also expect local elites not only to have more knowledge of politics but also to have a greater stake in the political system, and thus be more supportive of the legislature.

*Scope of contacts with MPs.* Those constituents who have the greatest contact with MPs and the highest awareness of what MPs have done for their district are expected to be more supportive of the legislature. We asked constituents questions about whether they were acquainted with their MPs; how often they had seen them or talked to them; whether they could recall what the MPs had done for the district; and whether the MPs had helped them personally in any way. We anticipate that greater contact would lead to greater salience of both individual MPs and the legislative institution, and also to a greater satisfaction with legislators' performance, particularly in regard to constituent assistance.

*Cognitive variables.* The extent to which constituents are aware of and familiar with various aspects of the legislature is what we call salience. There is institutional salience, related to the actions of the legislature as a collectivity; and there is individual salience, related to the roles and actions of individual legislators. We hypothesize that higher salience would produce greater support for the legislature and would also affect constituents' evaluation of the performance of the legislature and its members. The exact relationship between salience and evaluation is difficult to predict because those constituents most familiar with the legislature (and aware of its failings) might evaluate it less favorably.

*Evaluative attitudes.* Positive evaluations of the performance of the legislature and its individual members are important sources of legislative support.

As in the case of salience, evaluative attitudes can be directed toward either the legislative institution or its members. We do not assume that these two types of evaluations would be the same, and the distinction between them is important in hypothesizing about the connection between satisfaction and legislative support.

In most developing nations where the legislature is neither powerful nor highly visible, citizens are unlikely to have clear impressions of what the legislature does as a collective body. But these same citizens may have reasonably intimate knowledge about the actions of MPs from their own districts, as they are often the most visible figures in their communities. The relative importance of our two satisfaction variables might also vary with political strata. Those in the upper stratum and more politically aware and active are likely to base their support for the legislature on their satisfaction with its performance as an institution. Those in the lower stratum with less political knowledge might base support on their satisfaction with the performance of the individual MPs.[6]

*District level variables.* We expect that there would be variations in levels of support between districts, not only because of variations in socioeconomic conditions, but also because of the variety of activities and services that legislators provide for the district. We also expect satisfaction with the performance of individual MPs, as well as legislative support, to vary by district. Some legislators work harder to build an electoral organization in the district that reaches the grassroots level, and this should lead to variations in individual salience from one district to another. We expect higher levels of salience, satisfaction, and support to result not only from direct dealings with MPs but also from the spillover effect of MP activities and organization in the district.

*Interrelationships among variables.* The relationships depicted in figure 9.1 are not intended to be a causal model of legislative support, but rather, a conceptual framework. Obviously, other variables not included may also affect support. Moreover, there might be other possible relationships among the variables which we have not specified. The conceptual framework we have presented will nevertheless help us clarify the possible relationships and their directions among the variables that we think important and for which we have data from our crossnational survey. Although we do not propose to test all causal relationships implied by our conceptual framework, we will try to test some of them in our analysis, going beyond simple bivariate analyses.

## THE CONCEPT OF LEGISLATIVE
## SUPPORT AND ITS MEASUREMENT

### DEFINING SUPPORT

David Easton has explicated his concept of support by an exemplification, instead of a clear formal stipulation. He has asserted that " A supports B, either when A acts on behalf of B or *when he orients himself favorably toward B*" (emphasis added).[7] Perhaps he thought that the term "support" is too generic to require a formal definition. Or perhaps he believed that the meaning of the term is intuitively clear. Whatever the case, it remains that Easton has left us without a formal definition of his central concept. Even if we take his exemplifications such as the sentence italicized above, it still leaves the concept open to many varied interpretations.[8]

In his discussion of support, Easton has distinguished between two different kinds of support: diffuse and specific.[9] Support of a diffuse sort entails deep-seated sentiment or attachment to a political object. This kind of support, Easton argues, does not depend on the specific output of a political object and therefore is relatively persistent over time.

By contrast, specific support is based on short-term satisfaction with the performance or specific outputs of an institution. From the perspective of the survival of an institution or the system as a whole, Easton further argues that the diffuse support is far more important because it "enables a system to weather the many storms when outputs cannot be balanced off against inputs of demands."[10] Empirical studies of support for various political institutions have employed this distinction in the past and many have concentrated, with good reason, on the diffuse support.[11]

Although conceptually pregnant as it may seem in its abstraction, the distinction will reveal, upon closer scrutiny, several insuperable difficulties for its application in empirical studies. Diffuse and specific support are still ambiguous analytic concepts which, as Gerhard Loewenberg has pointed out, present us with formidable measurement problems.[12] Is it really possible to disentangle the supportive attitudes that we observe and separate empirically that part of support based on a person's satisfaction with specific outputs and another part which is independent of the effects of such outputs? We think not.

For this and other reasons we have rejected the distinction between diffuse and specific support for the purposes of our study.[13] We conceive of support as an attitude that is learned over a period of time. If a person has developed a strongly supportive attitude for an institution as a result of early socialization, his or her attitude is less likely to be changed by disapproval of recent actions taken by that institution. Nevertheless, the attitude of any individual is likely to be a result of his or her beliefs and perceptions, ranging from the individual's earliest political memory to the newspaper headlines of the day.

We will define legislative support in terms of the value or worth that constituents attribute to the legislature. Do they consider it a worthy institution? To what extent do they value it as a key political institution? More to the point, are they willing to eliminate this institution? If not, what are they prepared to do to maintain it? Legislative support, as we define it, refers therefore to the attitudes of individual citizens reflective of their degree of willingness to uphold the legislature.

## MEASURING SUPPORT

Our operational measure of legislative support is derived from several comparable survey questions employed in Kenya, Korea, and Turkey. Each of these questions was designed to determine whether constituents consider it both necessary and desirable to maintain a legislative body, whether they regard the legislature as one of the best things to be established since independence, whether they believe their country would be worse off if the legislature were abolished (or reduced in size), and whether they believe that it has played an important and useful role. In table 9.1 we list the support questions and the constituents' responses in the three countries.

The data suggest several conclusions. First, the level of legislative support is generally high in all countries, perhaps surprisingly high for an institution that is neither highly institutionalized nor very powerful. In Korea and Turkey over four-fifths of those interviewed indicated that the legislature was a necessary institution. Similarly, at least three-fifths of the constituents in all three countries believed that they were better off because they had a legislature and that it has played a significant and useful role. Second, because only a small percentage of the constituents gave negative answers, the legislature is certainly not a target of public hostility in Kenya, Korea, or Turkey. The main line of division was between those who gave positive answers and those who had no opinions. Third, of the three countries, the Turkish constituents indicated the strongest support for their legislature, a result that might be expected given the long history of the legislature and its relatively strong political influence in the Turkish political system.

For the purposes of measuring support, we have eliminated those respondents who answered "don't know" to all of the questions on support. For the remaining respondents, all of whom have expressed views on some or all of the support questions, we have lumped together the negative and "don't know" responses. This overcomes the problem of a small number of negative responses.

It also seems reasonable to analyze legislative support in positive terms,

## TABLE 9.1.
### Responses to Support Questions in Kenya, Korea, and Turkey (percentages)

| Support Items | Korea | | | Turkey | | | Kenya | | |
|---|---|---|---|---|---|---|---|---|---|
| | Supportive | Negative | No answer, don't know | Supportive | Negative | No answer, don't know | Supportive | Negative | No answer, don't know |
| Do we really need a legislature? | 81 | 3 | 16 | 93 | 2 | 5 | not asked | | |
| What difference has it made to this country? | 67 | 8 | 25 | 83 | 3 | 14 | 61 | 13 | 26 |
| Are we better off because we have a legislature? | 63 | 9 | 28 | 80 | 8 | 12 | 64 | 8 | 28 |
| Is the legislature one of the best things established since independence? | 42 | 13 | 45 | 90 | 2 | 8 | 71 | 8 | 21 |
| Could we do just as well with half as many MPs? ("No" scored as support.) | 20 | 30 | 50 | 51 | 34 | 15 | not asked | | |

and to compare the number of positive responses given by various individuals and groups. Those who answered "don't know" in response to some of the questions could be distinguished from those who were willing to assert positively that the legislature was a necessary institution and one that benefited society.

In an effort to obtain a single summary measure of legislative support, we employed the Guttman scaling technique and succeeded in constructing a scale based on five identical items for Korea and Turkey. The results of the scaling operation showed acceptable Coefficients of Reproducibility and of Scalability in Korea; 0.90 and 0.64 respectively. Similar results were obtain in Turkey (CR = 0.91 and CS = 0.60). We could not use the same procedure for Kenya simply because two of the five support items were not asked in the Kenyan survey.[14] Instead, we formed a simple three item additive index with scores ranging from a low of 0 to a high of 3. The scale positions and the distribution of the constituents on this scale are reported in table 9.2. In the analysis that follows we will use these scales and index as our operational measure of the level of support for the legislature.

## SOCIAL AND POLITICAL LOCATIONS OF LEGISLATIVE SUPPORT

### SOCIAL STRATA

Our task here is to identify the loci of legislative support in Kenya, Korea,

TABLE 9.2.
Level of Legislative Support Based on Scale Positions
in Kenya, Korea, and Turkey (percentages)

| Scale scores | | Korea N = 2015 | Kenya N = 1958 | Index scores | | Turkey N = 3748 |
|---|---|---|---|---|---|---|
| low | 0 | 17.6 | 2.0 | low | 0 | 5.8 |
| | 1 | 13.0 | 4.5 | | 1 | 18.5 |
| | 2 | 25.9 | 17.8 | high | 2 | 32.7 |
| | 3 | 30.1 | 46.1 | | 3 | 43.0 |
| high | 4 | 1.2 | 3.9 | | | 100.0 |
| | 5 | 12.2 | 25.7 | | | |
| | | 100.0 | 100.0 | | | |

and Turkey. We will examine bivariate relationships rather briefly, because in subsequent chapters we will look at multivariate correlations of support. Several studies conducted in different nations have shown that support for an institution such as the legislature is lodged heavily in higher social strata.[15]

In an effort to determine social location of support we have examined several variables: sex, age, education, residence, and class. The results indicate that men are markedly more supportive of the legislature than are women in all three countries. (Gammas are 0.15 for Kenya, 0.33 for Korea, and 0.34 for Turkey.) Of course, in most societies, and in these three countries in particular, politics has been and continues to be primarily the domain of men. With a more active interest in political affairs, it is not surprising that men are more supportive.

We expected to find younger generations to be more supportive because of their higher education and the fact that they had grown up in the more modern period. But in all three countries, we found generally weak relationships between age and legislative support (the highest relationship being in Kenya where the Kendall's *tau* was only −0.06).

As we expected, we found those with higher education to be consistently more supportive of the legislature in all three countries, but the relationship was curvilinear. In general, constituents with middle or high school education were the most supportive; college graduates ranked slightly behind them; and those with little or no education ranked lowest in support. The data seemed to indicate threshold point, beyond which the positive effects of education on support diminished. Thus, college graduates, with greater political knowledge and interest, may insist on a higher standard of performance for the legislature and therefore may easily become disillusioned with it.

We expected higher levels of support from urban areas because urban residents were not only better educated but were closer to the center of politics and more politically aware than their rural counterparts. Contrary to expectations, urban constituents in Kenya were slightly less supportive than were their rural counterparts; relationships in the other countries were too weak to draw any conclusion.

We divided constituents into four groups on the basis of class in order to measure the effect of class on support. The evidence was both consistent and clear. Members of the upper and middle classes were considerably more supportive of the legislature than were members of lower classes. In Kenya, for example, nearly one-half of those in the upper classes gave the strongest support rating possible to the legislature, less than one-fourth in the lower classes did so. A similar pattern emerged in Korea. (The Kendall's *taus* for Kenya and Korea are −0.13 and −0.14.) In Turkey the tendency was less clear; but strongest support was found among constituents from middle and working class backgrounds. Support from the Turkish working class may have resulted from approval of pro-labor legislation passed by the Turkish legislature, while support from the upper classes may have been weakened by elitist attitudes among those groups.

## POLITICAL STRATA

We expected support to be uneven across political strata. Boynton and his collaborators have suggested that "support tends to come most strongly from the politically knowledgeable and participant segments of the population."[16] In nations in Asia and Africa, the base of political stratum is usually narrow with much of their citizenry remaining politically uninvolved. There is even greater likelihood that legislative support is disproportionately concentrated in a small but politically active stratum.

We used two measures of political stratification: efficacy and citizen participation. Efficacy indicates not only the self-perception of one's role in the political process, but also the degree of self-assertiveness of an individual citizen. A 4-point index of efficacy was constructed from three standard items that we included in the survey.[17] The specific items used were: (1) people like me don't have any say about what the government does; (2) government officials usually do not care a great deal about what people like me think; and (3) sometimes politics and government seem so complicated that a person like me can't really understand what's going on. Although on occasion the content directions of some questions were reversed (especially in Kenya because of the sensitivity of the regime there to these items), we later recoded them to be in the same direction before the construction of our index.

Constituents with efficacious feelings were more supportive of the legislature than those without efficacious feelings in each of the three countries. In Kenya, nearly 50 percent of the most efficacious strata gave the highest possible support to the legislature, in contrast to only 38 percent of the least efficacious group (Kendall's *tau* = 0.10). The pattern was much the same in Korea and Turkey, with the strength of efficacy-support relationships reaching 0.19 and 0.10 respectively. There is evidence, therefore, to conclude that the legislature has its strongest advocates among the most politically assertive constituents.

The second measure of political stratification we used was degree of citizen participation. To indicate the extent of such an involvement we have constructed a simple 6-point index based on five survey items: (1) persuading other people to vote for a given candidate, (2) attending election rallies, (3) campaigning actively for candidates, (4) talking to government officials about local issues, and (5) talking to government officials about national issues. Responses to these queries served as the basis for the construction of the activism index.[18] Although there were some important variations in the level of political activism in the three countries, our expectation was upheld consistently in all of our research sites: the politically active stratum was distinctly more supportive than the inactive stratum in every country (Kendall's *tau* varied from 0.10 to 0.11).


## MODERNITY AND SUPPORT

Rapid modernization is taking place in Kenya, Korea, and Turkey just as in other countries of Asia and Africa. Different segments of these societies are being affected at different rates by modernization, causing a significant sociocultural gap between the most modern sectors, often consisting of well-educated, urban, middle-class citizens, and the vast sectors of tradition-bound rural populations. The varying impact of modernization leads to the creation of a bifurcated structure of political culture in some of these countries, one sector almost as modern as its counterparts in the industrialized west, and another barely beyond that of an agrarian society. In Seoul, Istanbul, and Nairobi, and especially among their more affluent and well-educated members, we find beliefs and attitudes almost identical to those held by citizens in industrialized nations. As we move from major urban centers to rural areas, beliefs and attitudes change rapidly.[19]

We have employed a measure to classify various population groups according to their levels of modernization. This measure has been designed and used successfully by Inkeles and his research team in six developing countries.[20] The specific scale that we have employed in our study is what Inkeles calls the OM−12 (the overall modernity scale), which represents a briefest distillate from 119 survey items included in his project. We have made some minor modifications to the scale so as to make it relevant to our research countries. Our summary index of individual modernity was created from eleven questions. Scores ranged from a low of 0 to a high of 0.11.[21]

In rapidly developing societies like Kenya, Korea, and Turkey stratification systems are closely enmeshed with modernization. As a general rule, those constituents who come from the most modernized sectors of society and therefore hold the most modern beliefs and attitudes are also likely to occupy higher ranks in social and political stratification systems. Indeed, this is the case in all of our three countries. Members of higher social and political strata in Kenya, Korea, and Turkey embrace distinctly more modern beliefs and values than others of lower strata. In table 9.3 we display the relationship between individual modernity and stratification variables. Almost without exception, our measure of modernity, the Inkeles OM−12 scale, shows strong correlations with all of our stratification variables. In all three countries, the most modern individuals are found disproportionately among the young, among males, among the better educated, among urban residents, and also among those with prestigious occupations and high SES status. Further, those citizens who are politically active and feel efficacious have markedly more modern beliefs and attitudes than those who are inactive or do not feel efficacious. Given such close connections between modernity and our stratification variables, it seems appropriate to use the modernity measure as a shorthand surrogate for the social and political location of a constitutent.

We have found modest correlations between support and a number of personal characteristics that are indicative of social or political stratification. We have also found (see table 9.3) that most of these correlate positively with our measure of individual modernity. This suggests that modernity may be used as a convenient summary variable for the attitudes associated with high levels of stratification and determining what relationships exist between individual modernity and supportive attitudes.

Although one should exercise caution in making direct crossnational comparisons, it does seem apparent that constitutents in both Turkey and Korea are generally more modern in their beliefs and attitudes than are the citizens in Kenya. In spite of this variation, and in spite of other important sociopolitical differences among the three countries, there is a consistent and strongly positive correlation between the level of individual modernity and the level of legislative support in all countries.

In Kenya the modern sectors are distinctly more supportive of the legislature than are the less modern sectors (Kendall's *tau* = 0.22). The same is true of modern constituents in Korea and Turkey. In Korea, the relationship is even stronger than in Kenya (Kendall's *tau* = 0.26). It is less strong in Turkey but still above the significant level (Kendall's *tau* = 0.10). Thus, the evidence suggests that the legislature draws its strongest support from the modern sectors of society.

TABLE 9.3.

Relationships between Modernity and Stratification Variables

(Kendall's *tau*)

| | Level of Individual Modernity | | |
|---|---|---|---|
| Variables | Kenya | Korea | Turkey |
| Social stratification | | | |
| Age (young-old) | -0.22[a] | -0.19[a] | -0.09[a] |
| Sex (male-female) | -0.25[a] | -0.33[a] | -0.13[a] |
| Education (years of schooling) | 0.34[a] | 0.43[a] | 0.33[a] |
| Occupation (7-pt. prestige ranking) | 0.22[a] | 0.26[a] | 0.23[a] |
| Class status (high-low) | -0.20[a] | -0.33[a] | -0.28[a] |
| Place of residence (rural-urban) | 0.11[a] | 0.03 | 0.19[a] |
| Political stratification | | | |
| Political activism (6-pt. index) | 0.19[a] | 0.24[a] | 0.24[a] |
| Political efficacy (4-pt. index) | 0.12[a] | 0.36[a] | 0.16[a] |

a. Significant at the level of 0.001.

## THE SUPPORT OF LOCAL ELITES

Table 9.4 compares the levels of legislative support from constituents (already reported in table 9.2) to those from local elites.[22] In both Korea and Kenya the local elites were much more supportive of the legislature than were average constituents. In Turkey, however, differences between the two groups were significantly smaller. An examination of the answers to specific questions on support shows that in all three countries the elites were more likely to give positive answers and less likely to say they did not know than were constituents. However, a relatively small proportion of both constituents and elites gave negative answers. In other words, elites in all three countries were likely to respond favorably to questions that implied support. And, in Korea and Turkey, elites were more likely than constituents to believe that the country could do just as well with half as many MPs (scored as a negative answer on the support scale).

One reason for the higher levels of elite support, at least in Korea and Kenya, is that elites represent higher levels of social and political stratification than do constituents, and so, as we have shown previously, are more likely to support the legislature. There is much less variation in personal variables among elites than among constituents, and consequently we find that for elites the correlations between support and the individual variables reported in tables 9.3 and 9.4 are negligible. In Korea, however, there is a very modest correlation between support and political efficacy (0.14) and support and activism (0.10). The relationship between support and modernism is very low among elites in Kenya (0.12) and Korea (0.10) and is nonexistent in Turkey. In analyzing support levels among elites, therefore, we have no need to be concerned with individual characteristics, but can treat the elites in each country as a group.

**TABLE 9.4.**
**Elite Status and Legislative Support (percentages)**

| Support Levels | Elite Status | | | | | |
| | Kenya | | Korea | | Turkey | |
| | Local notables (N = 448) | Mass citizens (N = 3,748) | Local notables (N = 465) | Mass citizens (N = 2,015) | Local notables (N = 286) | Mass citizens (N = 1,955) |
| --- | --- | --- | --- | --- | --- | --- |
| High | 62 | 43 | 30 | 13 | 25 | 30 |
| Medium | 31 | 33 | 57 | 56 | 72 | 63 |
| Low | 7 | 24 | 13 | 31 | 3 | 7 |
| | 100 | 100 | 100 | 100 | 100 | 100 |

# Chapter 10

## SALIENCE, SATISFACTION, AND SUPPORT

The first purpose of this chapter is to summarize what we have learned about constituents' knowledge concerning their representatives and their legislatures, and about their levels of satisfaction with the performance of MPs and legislative institutions. The second purpose is to determine what kinds of respondents have various levels of knowledge and satisfaction. The final purpose is to explore the relationships that exist between these variables and support for the legislature. We will try to determine whether constituents for whom the legislature is more salient are more supportive and satisfied with its performance, and whether salience of, and satisfaction with, the legislature is directly linked to legislative support.

### THE SALIENCE OF LEGISLATIVE
### INSTITUTIONS AND MEMBERS

How much do the people of Kenya, Korea, and Turkey know about their representative and legislative institutions? Studies in the United States show relatively low levels of citizen familiarity with some basic facts about Congress and members of congress.[1] One might expect to find even less knowledge about the legislatures in the countries of our study, where legislative institutions have much briefer histories, less power, and less visibility in the media. Moreover, levels of education are lower and communications media less extensive in these countries.

Within any country we would expect to find that legislative salience is greater for persons with social and political advantages. Salience is important because it is the sole basis on which citizens can make informed judgments about the legislature. Without the active support of the well-informed segments of society, a legislature cannot function as a significant political institution. And well-informed citizens are not likely to give their support unless they are reasonably satisfied with the performance of the legislature and its members.

## LEVELS OF SALIENCE

We have already reported data in chapter 6 that show how familiar constituents are with the legislature and with their own representatives, and the findings can be summarized briefly here. Turkish constituents were more familiar with the legislature and its history and were better able to distinguish it from other institutions than were citizens from Korea and Kenya (table 6.1). This was probably not only because the Turkish legislature has a longer history than the legislature in the other two countries but also because it plays a more central role in Turkish government and politics. The strong executives in both Korea and Kenya tend to overshadow the legislative bodies, and this presumably has an impact on public perceptions.

When we asked about individual MPs, we found that Kenyan constituents were better informed about their legislators than were constituents in the other two countries (table 6.2). An astonishing 84 percent of the Kenyan constituents could name their legislator, compared to 69 percent in Korea, and 53 percent in Turkey who could name at least one of their representatives. The single-member district system in Kenya and the relatively large amount of service work performed by Kenyan MPs may help to explain this. However, Kenyan constituents were less likely than those in the other two countries to be able to distinguish the function of MPs from that of civil servants.

For our purposes in this chapter, it is desirable to combine several measures of familiarity or knowledge into two indexes of salience. An analysis of the responses shows that the questions can logically be divided into two groups. First are four questions that measure familiarity with the legislative institution; the answers can be combined into an index of institutional salience. Answers to the other three questions, dealing with familiarity with and perceptions of individual members, form an index of the salience of individual MPs.[2] Because there is a low correlation in each country between the indexes of individual and institutional salience, and because the two indexes have quite different relationships to other variables, we will treat them separately.

## SOME CORRELATES OF SALIENCE

We have hypothesized that those constituents with social and political advantages would regard the legislature and its members as more salient than would other constituents. Table 10.1 shows the relationships between a number of independent variables and our two measures of salience. In all three countries, sex, education, occupation, and social class show strong positive correlations with the salience of the legislative institution. Constituents who are male, better educated, and who have high prestige occupations and high socioeconomic status are markedly more familiar with the legislature than are other constituents.

The correlation between these variables and salience of individual MPs is not consistent in all three countries. In Korea alone, all of the variables show significant correlations to salience, ranging from a low of 0.17 to a high of 0.34. In Turkey, only two variables, sex and education, show moderately strong correlations. None of these variables is correlated with the salience of individual MPs in Kenya. Thus, we cannot draw a conclusion that applies consistently to all three countries.

Remarkably strong and consistent relationships exist between individual modernity and our two measures of salience. Without exception, the modernity variable correlates strongly with both salience of the legislature and salience of individual MPs in all three countries (Kendall's *taus* = 0.27 to 0.51). However, the strength of the relationship between modernity and salience of the legislature is consistently stronger than that between modernity and salience of individual MPs.

TABLE 10.1.
Correlates of Institutional and Individual Salience
in Kenya, Korea, and Turkey (Kendall's *taus*)

| Independent variables | Salience of legislative institution | | | Salience of individual MPs | | |
|---|---|---|---|---|---|---|
| | Kenya | Korea | Turkey | Kenya | Korea | Turkey |
| Background | | | | | | |
| Sex | 0.26[a] | 0.30[a] | 0.49[a] | 0.06 | 0.34[a] | 0.45[a] |
| Education | 0.32[a] | 0.39[a] | 0.34[a] | 0.10[a] | 0.24[a] | 0.22[a] |
| Occupation | 0.22[a] | 0.21[a] | 0.20[a] | 0.08[a] | 0.17[a] | 0.08[a] |
| Social class | 0.23[a] | 0.19[a] | 0.22[a] | 0.09[a] | 0.19[a] | 0.13[a] |
| Individual modernity | | | | | | |
| OM–12 scale | 0.44[a] | 0.51[a] | 0.35[a] | 0.27[a] | 0.45[a] | 0.24[a] |
| Political activity | | | | | | |
| Talked to others about voting for candidate | 0.16[a] | 0.12[a] | 0.28[a] | 0.11[a] | 0.16[a] | 0.23[a] |
| Attended election rallies | 0.18[a] | 0.11[a] | 0.31[a] | 0.13[a] | 0.17[a] | 0.28[a] |
| Worked in campaign | 0.07 | 0.06 | 0.13[a] | 0.07 | 0.13[a] | 0.23[a] |
| Political interest | | | | | | |
| Discussed politics with friends | 0.14[a] | 0.19[a] | 0.21[a] | 0.06 | 0.14[a] | 0.21[a] |
| Contact with MPs | | | | | | |
| Saw MP in district | 0.19[a] | 0.15[a] | 0.08[a] | 0.28[a] | 0.12[a] | 0.15[a] |
| Talked to MP personally | 0.09[a] | 0.06 | 0.15[a] | 0.06 | 0.07 | 0.16[a] |

a. Significant at the level of 0.001.

We have also examined the relationships between salience and three groups of variables that indicate the political advantages of the constituent: political activity, political interest, and constituent contact with MPs. The results of our analysis show neither strong positive relationships between salience and the three groups of variables nor consistent patterns across different countries (table 10.1). The activity variables show fairly strong correlations with both types of salience in Turkey (most between 0.23 and 0.31), but substantially weaker correlations in the other two countries. One reason for low correlation is that most constituents voted but relatively few engaged in the other types of political activities that are examined. The interest variable shows some positive correlation with individual and particularly institutional salience, notably in Turkey and Korea, but the correlations are not strong. There is some correlation, particularly for individual salience, with one measure of MP contact: seeing the MP in the district. The correlation with the other measure of MP contact—talking to MPs—is weaker, partly because so few constituents have done so.

What emerges from the data is the general impression that the salience of legislative institutions requires some measure of social and political awareness, while salience of individual MPs requires less. In order to have some knowledge of the legislature, one must have higher social position and more involvement in politics, while many of those in the lower social strata with little political participation seem to know something about their MPs and what they have done for the district, but seem to know very little about the legislature itself.

## SALIENCE AND LEGISLATIVE SUPPORT

Does salience lead to support of the legislature? More specifically, does familiarity with the institution and with the individual MPs produce higher levels of support for the institution? We have seen that higher status, and more particularly a high level of modernity, are associated with higher support. Is this because these high status, more modern citizens are more familiar with the legislature and its members? Or is it possible that familiarity breeds contempt, and undermines support? Later in this chapter, we will examine the causal links from salience to satisfaction and then to support. First, we examine the direct link between salience and support.

Table 10.2 shows that in Korea and Turkey there was a moderately strong positive correlation between support and institutional salience and slightly lower correlation between support and MP salience. In Kenya both correlations were lower. Thus, the link between salience and support seemed visible, but hardly powerful.

We should recognize that correlation between salience and support may result in part from the technique we have used in constructing the support index. Because we are interested in positive manifestations of support, and because relatively few respondents gave negative answers, we have combined negative responses with "don't knows" in constructing the support scale. We would expect those with lower salience levels to fail to answer support questions more often than those with higher salience. It must be kept in mind, however, that those who failed to answer any of the questions that constitute the support scale have been eliminated from the analysis. All of those in the study expressed a positive or negative opinion in response to at least some of the support questions.

## SALIENCE AMONG LOCAL ELITES

We would expect local elites to be more familiar than the average citizen with both the legislative institution and with the individual MPs. Elites rank high in those personal qualities that we have found to be associated with salience (table 10.1). Moreover, they have much greater opportunity for personal contact with MPs, and consequently should be familiar with them. In fact, we found the level of elite salience, by most of our measures, to be very high. Almost every elite respondent knew the name of one or more of his representatives, and in Kenya and Turkey from 85 to 95 percent of them expressed opinions about how well their MPs were doing their jobs and about the honesty of most legislators. Consequently, in those two countries

**TABLE 10.2.**
Salience and Legislative Support among Constituents (percentages)

| | Level of legislative support | | | | | | | | |
|---|---|---|---|---|---|---|---|---|---|
| | **Kenya** | | | **Korea** | | | **Turkey** | | |
| | Low | Medium | High | Low | Medium | High | Low | Medium | High |
| Level of MP Salience | | | | | | | | | |
| 0 | 40 | 40 | 20 | 57 | 40 | 3 | 22 | 58 | 20 |
| 1 | 35 | 31 | 34 | 38 | 56 | 6 | 7 | 68 | 25 |
| 2 | 27 | 32 | 42 | 31 | 55 | 13 | 4 | 66 | 31 |
| 3 | 19 | 34 | 48 | 16 | 61 | 24 | 3 | 59 | 38 |
| | | tau = 0.11[a] | | | tau = 0.21[a] | | | tau = 0.17[a] | |
| Level of legislative salience | | | | | | | | | |
| 0 | 33 | 35 | 32 | 46 | 48 | 6 | 25 | 61 | 14 |
| 1 | 23 | 30 | 47 | 29 | 59 | 12 | 10 | 64 | 26 |
| 2 | 19 | 35 | 46 | 21 | 62 | 18 | 3 | 66 | 31 |
| 3 | 14 | 29 | 57 | 21 | 60 | 19 | 2 | 62 | 37 |
| 4 | 9 | 35 | 57 | 14 | 52 | 34 | 1 | 66 | 33 |
| | | tau = 0.14[a] | | | tau = 0.22[a] | | | tau = 0.20[a] | |

a. Significant at the level of 0.001.

most elite respondents scored very high on the individual salience score. Korean elites have lower scores because many of them were unwilling to express opinions about the performance and honesty of MPs. Turkish elites ranked very high in institutional questions; Korean elites were a little less accurate, particularly in distinguishing the legislature from other institutions; Kenyan elites ranked lower, partly for the same reason. With the exception of MP salience in Korea, the salience of elites on both scales in all three countries was substantially higher than that of average constituents.

Because the level of MP salience was so high among elites, particularly in Kenya and Turkey, there was little reason to be concerned with variables that affected it or to expect that variations in salience would affect support for the legislature.

There was greater variance in levels of elite familiarity with the legislative institution. Higher institutional salience was related to higher education and more political activity in Kenya and Turkey, and in all three countries it was related to higher levels of political efficacy, individual modernity, and more contact with MPs (all these correlations ranging from 0.13 to 0.28). We can make some distinctions between the more active, politically involved, and modern elites and those who are less so, and these distinctions have something to do with institutional support in Korea and Kenya and nothing to do with it in Turkey.

## CONSTITUENT SATISFACTION WITH THE LEGISLATURE

How satisfied are constituents with the performance of the legislature and with the performance of individual MPs? Easton suggested that the level of citizens' support for a political institution depends partly upon citizen satisfaction with specific outputs of the legislature.[3] The performance of both the legislature and individual MPs may be considered to be specific outputs. Using this conceptual framework as a starting point, we will summarize what we know about levels of satisfaction, and then explore the sources of that satisfaction.

### DIMENSIONS AND LEVELS OF SATISFACTION

Constituent satisfaction defies easy measurement. Instead of asking questions about specific laws or actions of the legislature, which most respondents could not reasonably be expected to answer, we asked a very general question about the legislature: Had it performed reasonably well?

To measure the image of the legislator, we asked respondents whether each of several characteristics, such as honesty and hard work, was important

for legislators to possess and whether they thought most or only a few legislators had this characteristic. Because there was considerable consensus about
the qualities that were most important, we focused on these in measuring the
image of legislators. It is very possible that many respondents have a clearer
impression of the performance of legislators from their own districts than
they do of the legislature as a whole. We asked respondents to evaluate the
importance of seven jobs that legislators might perform, and asked how well
their assemblyman was doing in each of these areas, paying particular attention to the jobs generally perceived as most important. We also used an
index evaluating the MP's performance of these jobs.

*Performance of the institution.* The question about how well the legislature
is performing has the advantage of being a simple, concise measure of performance satisfaction, but is so general that it is hard to interpret the meaning
of differences found from one country to another. Both Turkish and Kenyan
respondents reported very high levels of satisfaction. In Turkey, 78 percent
of the constituents said the legislature performed well and only 8 percent
said it did not. In Kenya 70 percent said the legislature performed well and 9
percent said it did not. In Korea, only 36 percent said the legislature performed well, 24 percent said it did not, and an even larger group were unwilling or unable to make an evaluation. Perhaps because the Assembly in
Korea has lost power to the president, or perhaps because it has become
entangled in partisan controversies, little more than one-third of the constituents articulated a positive evaluation of its general performance.

*Perceptions of MPs' characteristics.* Respondents in the three countries
were presented with a list of seven characteristics and asked whether each
was important for an assemblyman to possess. The results of this poll were
reported in an earlier chapter (table 6.3), but will be briefly summarized
here. Constituents in all three countries ranked honesty at or very close to
the top of the list, and also attached great importance to hard work, an
understanding of the common people, and a good education, in that order.
Three other characteristics assumed less importance: that an MP be an important man in his community, that he be successful in his occupation, and
that he be a long-term resident of the district.

How well did legislators measure up to these expectations? As we reported
in table 6.7, members in all three countries were judged to be least successful
with respect to the qualifications that were most important, such as honesty,
hard work, and understanding of the common people.

*Performance of individual MPs.* When we turn to the constituents' expectations concerning their own legislators, we find some differences in the
general importance they attach to these jobs. The highest priority jobs tend

to be described as very important more often in Kenya, and less important in Korea, and of very little importance in Turkey. Despite these differences, there was remarkable agreement among the three sets of constituents concerning the relative importance of tasks performed by MPs. These data were described in table 6.4 and can be very briefly summarized here.

Constituents in all three countries emphasized those aspects of an MP's job that were directly concerned with articulating the needs of people in the district, getting projects and benefits for the district, staying in touch with the district, and helping people with their problems. In all countries the single most frequently emphasized activity was telling the government what constituents wanted.

We should be cautious in interpreting these data. Respondents were not asked to list the MP's jobs they considered important, and most could probably not have done so. Instead, they were given a list of jobs and asked to judge the importance of each. While many respondents ranked either all of the jobs or none of them as important, there were substantial differences in each country between the proportions ranking as important various jobs (from 55 to 84 percent in Kenya, from 25 to 52 percent in Korea, and from 18 to 46 percent in Turkey).

The next question was how well constituents thought legislators performed these jobs. These data, already reported in table 6.8, showed that levels of satisfaction were highest in Kenya. In Turkey and, particularly, in Korea, many respondents believe that their legislators were doing a poor job in getting projects for and visiting the district. In both countries legislators scored best on two less valued functions: participating in the debate and passage of bills, and explaining governmental policies to the people. In short, the level of satisfaction was low in Turkey and Korea.

## WHO IS SATISFIED WITH THE LEGISLATURE?

In order to determine which respondents are most satisfied, we have looked at answers to the question about whether the legislature is performing well and also at the index of satisfaction with MP performance derived from the seven survey questions described earlier.

We will summarize the correlates of performance satisfaction only briefly because these relationships will be included in the subsequent multivariate analysis. Generally, personal characteristics had little effect on either measure of satisfaction, although males, better educated constituents, and those with higher class status were generally more satisfied. In Turkey urban residents were considerably more satisfied with individual MP performance than were rural residents. Individual modernity had a slightly stronger, more consistent positive correlation to both measures of satisfaction. Efficacy and activism had very modest correlations to performance satisfaction. Contact with the

MP had some effect on satisfaction (particularly with individual MP performance) in Kenya, but much less effect in the other two countries. In Turkey, of course, the use of multimember districts reduced the likelihood that there would be correlations between contact and performance satisfaction, particularly since respondents were not asked to specify which MP they had contacted or which one they were evaluating.

There was a consistently positive relationship between both types of salience and both types of satisfaction. The correlation beween institutional salience and both measures of performance was moderate, as was the correlation between individual salience and institutional performance satisfaction. The relationship between individual salience and satisfaction with MP performance was very strong (Kendall's *tau* ranging from 0.52 to 0.65 in the three countries). Those who knew most about their own MPs were most likely to be satisfied with their legislators' performance.

## SATISFACTION AND SUPPORT

We have hypothesized that there will be a positive relationship between the level of support for the legislature and satisfaction with performance of both the institution and the MP. In fact, the correlation between support and satisfaction with institutional performance was positive in all three countries. (Kendall's *tau* is 0.20 in Kenya, 0.21 in Korea, and 0.09 in Turkey. The figure would be higher in Kenya except for the small number expressing dissatisfaction.) The question on institutional satisfaction was very general, asked in the middle of a series of questions on support, and some respondents may not have distinguished the questions as clearly in practice as we did in our theoretical formulations. We will pursue the question of relationships among salience, satisfaction, and support in more detail later.

Our most detailed measure of performance is the one that summarizes the evaluation of the MP's performance of seven different jobs. A large proportion of Turkish and Kenyan respondents provided answers to these questions. Less than half did so in Korea. There was a positive relationship between this measure of MP job satisfaction and legislative support but it was weak (Kendall's *tau* ranged from 0.09 to 0.17). Despite our expectation, most citizens apparently did not see any particular connection between the actions of their MPs and their own evaluations of the activities of the legislature in the national capital.

## ELITES' SATISFACTION WITH LEGISLATIVE PERFORMANCE

It is important to measure and analyze levels of elite satisfaction with legislative performance for several reasons. We would expect elites to be considerably more familiar with, and therefore able to judge, the accomplishments of the legislature, the qualifications of members generally, and the performance of their own MPs. It is also possible that elites, better informed and more perceptive than average citizens, will have different expectations and judgments about the legislature than do other citizens.

In both Kenya and Korea, elites are much more favorably impressed with the legislature's performance than are average citizens. In Kenya, 93 percent of the elites said that the legislature was performing well and only 3 percent said that it was not (compared to 70 percent positive and 9 percent negative responses among average citizens). In Korea, the margin of satisfaction was 53 to 32 among elites (and 36 to 24 among citizens). (In both countries far fewer elites than citizens gave no response.) In Turkey, however, there was more criticism from elites than from citizens; elites give a 74 to 22 favorable judgment to the legislature, compared to 78 to 8 among citizens.

In table 6.3, we showed that elites agree with constitutents about what qualities legislators should have. Honesty and hard work were consistently ranked highest, with understanding of the common people and good education close behind. In Kenya and Korea, the elites agreed with the constituents in their judgment about how well MPs met those qualifications. In Turkey the elites were more favorably impressed by the qualification of MPs than were average citizens, and made greater distinctions among the various qualities on the list.

In table 6.4, we compared the priorities ascribed by constituents and elites to the various jobs of MPs, and found few differences. Although the elites tended to attribute more importance to lawmaking and explaining government policies than constituents did, both groups generally gave highest priority to jobs related to the district. In table 6.8, we showed that Kenyan and Korean elites gave a somewhat more favorable evaluation of jobs being done by MPs than did citizens—particularly with regard to lawmaking functions. Turkish elites, however, were consistently critical of their MPs, and roughly half of them evaluated job performance on a number of specific tasks as poor.

Can we pinpoint the independent variables that are associated with higher satisfaction among elites? None of the social or political variables was correlated with satisfaction with legislative performance in all three countries, nor were contact with MPs or either of the salience indices.

Several independent variables were correlated, however, with the scale of MP job satisfaction. The correlation between contact with the MP and evaluation of the MP's job performance was 0.23, 0.14, and 0.24 in Kenya, Korea, and Turkey, respectively. Those for MP salience and job evaluation were very high: 0.57, 0.44, and 0.42 in the three countries. It is significant that the elites, who were most familiar and had most contact with the MPs, and were most willing to make judgments about them, were also much more favorably impressed by their job performance.

In Korea, the correlation between elite support and elites' satisfaction with the legislature and also between elite support and satisfaction with individual MPs' performance was a modest 0.21. In Turkey, there was a 0.14 correlation between support and satisfaction with the legislature, but insignificant correlation between MP job performance and support. In Kenya, the levels of elite satisfaction and support were both too high for there to be much variance to explain with correlations. In none of these countries could elite support for the legislature be explained by satisfaction with performance to the extent that it could be so explained among constituents.

# Chapter 11

# MULTIVARIATE ANALYSIS OF LEGISLATIVE SUPPORT

Constituent support for the legislative institution arises from many diverse sources. In our conceptual framework (outlined in figure 9.1) we have listed some of the variables that we believe have the greatest direct or indirect effects on support, and we have suggested how these variables are related. In chapter 9 we measured the effects of personal variables on support. In chapter 10 we measured the salience of and satisfaction with the legislature, and we identified variables related to salience and satisfaction and the effects of these two factors on support. Obviously, if we are correct in assuming that a number of variables directly and indirectly affect the levels of support for the legislature, we need to use multivariate techniques in measuring their effects in order to get a better understanding of legislative support and its causes.

We will begin by employing multiple regression analysis. The next step is to use path analysis in an attempt to develop a parsimonious model of the causes of legislative support. Then we will seek to determine whether the causes of support can be explained differently for particular subgroups in the three countries, comparing modern and traditional constituents and mass constituents and elites. Throughout this analysis we will be primarily concerned with identifying patterns related to support that are common to all three countries. We will also look briefly at the differences among the three countries in the factors influencing support, and at variations from district to district within the three countries.

## MULTIPLE REGRESSION ANALYSIS

The first step in evaluating the importance of these variables is to employ a multiple regression analysis. The selection of specific variables to be entered into the regression equation is based on our conceptual framework and on the results of our bivariate analyses in chapters 9 and 10. We will use nine variables in the analysis. These include the index of modernity (which we have found correlates highly with several background variables); indices of political efficacy and activism used in previous chapters; the four indices of salience and satisfaction; the expectation-performance differential for the job performance of MPs; and the differential between expected and perceived qualifications of MPs.

In table 11.1 we report the results of the regression analysis. The table shows the zero-order correlations; the unstandardized regression coefficients (*B*), which help us to determine the impact of a given variable on legislative support; the standardized Betas, which indicate the predictive power of each independent variable; and the multiple correlations to show the combined explanatory power of the independent variables.

The nine independent variables were collectively capable of explaining a sizable amount of variance in legislative support in all three countries. In Kenya, nearly one-half of the variance in constituent support could be accounted for by these variables ($R = 0.68$, $R^2 = 0.46$). The proportion of

**TABLE 11.1.**
**The Results of Regression Analysis on**
**Legislative Support in Kenya, Korea, and Turkey**

| Independent variables | Kenya | | | Korea | | | Turkey | | |
|---|---|---|---|---|---|---|---|---|---|
| | *r* | *B* | Beta | *r* | *B* | Beta | *r* | *B* | Beta |
| Modernity: OM—12 scale | 0.37 | 0.08 | 0.18 | 0.44 | 0.15 | 0.20 | 0.15 | 0.59 | 0.01 |
| Political efficacy: 4-pt. index | 0.14 | 0.04 | 0.03 | 0.33 | 0.12 | 0.08 | -0.13 | 0.29 | 0.02 |
| Political activism: 6-pt. index | 0.19 | 0.04 | 0.05 | 0.20 | 0.02 | 0.01 | 0.14 | -0.47 | -0.01 |
| Salience of individual MPs | 0.22 | 0.09 | 0.07 | 0.38 | 0.15 | 0.09 | 0.24 | 0.12 | 0.09 |
| Salience of the legis-lative institution | 0.30 | 0.11 | 0.11 | 0.38 | 0.20 | 0.16 | 0.32 | 0.20 | 0.21 |
| Expectation-perform-ance differential | -0.03 | -0.02 | -0.06 | -0.08 | -0.06 | -0.04 | -0.14 | -0.01 | -0.01 |
| Qualification differential | -0.01 | -0.01 | -0.03 | -0.13 | -0.02 | -0.02 | -0.09 | -0.02 | -0.03 |
| Satisfaction with the performance of MPs | 0.21 | 0.01 | 0.01 | 0.31 | 0.07 | 0.08 | 0.17 | 0.16 | 0.03 |
| Satisfaction with the performance of legislature | 0.63 | 1.26 | 0.54 | 0.43 | 1.03 | 0.31 | 0.32 | 0.82 | 0.26 |
| | | $R = 0.68$ | | | $R = 0.61$ | | | $R = 0.42$ | |
| | | $R^2 = 0.46$ | | | $R^2 = 0.37$ | | | $R^2 = 0.18$ | |

*Note:* For the purpose of emphasis the Betas for the variables that appear important in all three countries are underlined.

variance explained was smaller in the other two countries: 37 percent in Korea and only 18 percent in Turkey. Despite the differences, it is noteworthy that the same set of variables had so much explanatory power in countries that are so diverse.

The degree of constituent satisfaction with the performance of the legislative institution had the strongest independent effect on support in all three countries. In Kenya this variable showed a Beta value of 0.54, with other independent variables all showing very modest Betas. The pattern was similar in the other two countries. The Beta value for satisfaction with legislative performance was 0.31 in Korea and 0.26 in Turkey, in both cases the highest value found among the variables that were included in this analysis. In all three countries the salience of the legislative institution was also important, with either the second or third highest Beta value among the independent variables. In all three countries both the salience of the legislative institution and satisfaction with its performance contributed heavily to the level of legislative support. On the other hand, in none of the countries did either the salience of the individual MP or satisfaction with his performance have much of an impact. Also, the two measures of differential had virtually no consistent impact in the three countries on legislative support.

There is one other variable that was of substantial importance: the index of individual modernity, which was used in lieu of several social and political stratification variables with which it was rather highly correlated. Modernity had a predictive capacity of some magnitude in both Kenya (Beta 0.18) and Korea (Beta 0.20), but not at all in Turkey (Beta 0.01). We concluded from this that in Kenya and Korea constituents with more modern attitudes and values were supportive of the legislature, and that this modernity had an effect on support beyond the effect that was mediated through salience and satisfaction with performance. We will present a more detailed study of the differences between modern and traditional constituents later in this chapter.

Among a large number of variables that we thought would have some influence on the constituent support for the legislature, we were able to identify two key determinants that are common to all three countries: the degree of satisfaction with institutional performance and the salience with which constituents regarded the legislative institution.

## MODELS OF LEGISLATIVE SUPPORT:
## PATH ANALYSIS

In order to carry this analysis a step further we will examine causal linkages among the variables that exert either direct or indirect effects upon legislative support. To begin with, we already know that in all three countries

the cognitive and evaluative variables, i.e., the perceived salience of the legislature and satisfaction with legislative performance, had the greatest direct
effect on support. How much of the variance in support was due to the direct
effects of these cognitive and evaluative variables and how much of it could
be explained by the indirect effects of other variables that operated through
them? Path analysis was particularly useful in determining the simple and
compound paths between the variables included in a causal model.[1] The
path coefficients that indicated strengths of linkages could be obtained by
regressing all antecedent variables on each of the endogenous variables included in the path model. Thus, the path coefficients were in effect the standardized regression coefficients produced by a series of regression analyses.

Although not explicitly specified in our conceptual framework (see chapter
9), there was an implicit causal ordering of the independent variables in it.
We postulated that personal factors such as age and education, and other
political orientation variables such as the sense of efficacy and the level of
activism, would affect the degree of constituents' contact with their MPs and
that these contact variables would in turn affect the various aspects of constituent cognitions about the legislature and its members.

Further, such cognitions were postulated to act upon the evaluative attitudes of the constituents regarding the performance of the legislative institution as well as its individual members. It was posited that these evaluative
attitudes, that is, the extent to which the constituents are satisfied with the

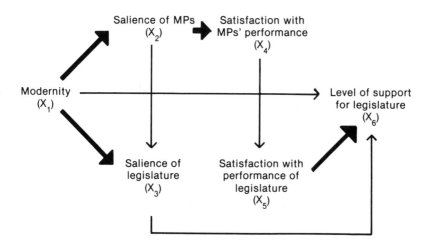

*Note:* A heavy line indicates a path coefficient greater than 0.20 in all three countries. A light
line indicates a path coefficient greater than 0.10 but less than 0.20 in at least two countries. No
line is drawn where path coefficients are not significant in two or more countries.

**FIGURE 11.1. Minimal Path Model for Three-country Data**

legislative performance, would have direct effects upon their support for the legislature. This initial model was revised as we moved through both simple and multivariate analyses, because some of the postulated links proved to be very weak. The revised path model, with all weak links removed, is more parsimonious in terms of the number of variables included, and yet, retains a substantial explanatory power.

Figure 11.1 describes the general pattern of the linkages in the three countries for a parsimonious, or minimal, path model involving only five independent variables. The full results of path analysis in each country are also reported in table 11.2. Furthermore, in figure 11.2, for the purpose of illustration, we depict the path linkages in Korea, a pattern very much typical of the other two countries. It should be stressed that the performance of our minimal model is quite impressive. The five variables explain collectively 33 percent of the total variance in Kenya, 26 percent in Korea, and 18 percent in Turkey.

We identified two principal chains of influence on constituent support for the legislature in all three countries (see figure 11.1). The first chain consisted of the steps from individual modernity to the perceived salience of individual MPs, from the salience of MPs to the constituent satisfaction with MPs' performance, from the satisfaction with MPs' performance to the satisfaction with the performance of the legislative institution, and finally, from the satis-

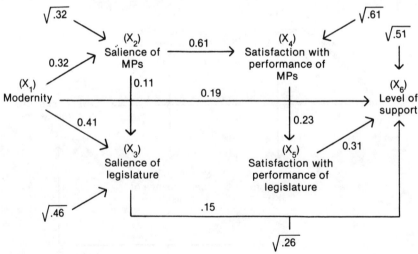

Total number of cases = 2014
Multiple R = 0.51
$R^2$ = 0.26

FIGURE 11.2. Six-variable Path Model: A Typical Case (Korea)

faction with the legislature to support. The second chain of influence passed from individual modernity to the salience of individual MPs and the legislature as a collective body, and from the salience of MPs and the legislature to the salience of the legislative institution, and finally, from the salience of the institution to the constituent support for the legislature. (The final link in this last chain was weak in Turkey.)

There was a modest direct link between individual modernity and support for the legislature (see figure 11.1). However, this link was observed only in Korea and Kenya. The stength of the linkage between modernity and legislative support was 0.19 (path coefficient) in Korea and 0.17 in Kenya, indicating that in these two countries individual modernity had a direct effect on support for the legislature. The absence of such a direct effect in Turkey suggested the impact of modernity on support there was mediated through both cognitive and evaluative variables. Perhaps the lack of any direct effect for modernity results from the fact that Turkey was the most modernized of the three countries studied.

In chapter 9, we developed a conceptual framework of the sources of legislative support (figure 9.1). A revision of that figure, based on our multivariate analysis, and particularly on our path model, would look like figure 11.3. In most respects the models are very similar. We have eliminated the

TABLE 11.2.
**Minimal (6-Variable) Path Model: Path Coefficients (Betas) for Support in Kenya, Korea, and Turkey ($X_1$ = Individual Modernity Score)**

| Dependent variables | Country | $B_1$ | $B_2$ | $B_3$ | $B_4$ | $B_5$ |
|---|---|---|---|---|---|---|
| $X_2$ Salience of MPs | Kenya | 0.20 | | | | |
| | Korea | 0.32 | | | | |
| | Turkey | 0.24 | | | | |
| $X_3$ Salience of the legislature | Kenya | 0.38 | 0.11 | | | |
| | Korea | 0.41 | 0.11 | | | |
| | Turkey | 0.34 | 0.31 | | | |
| $X_4$ Satisfaction with MPs' performance | Kenya | −0.04 | 0.77 | −0.05 | | |
| | Korea | 0.01 | 0.61 | −0.02 | | |
| | Turkey | 0.07 | 0.64 | −0.11 | | |
| $X_5$ Satisfaction with performance of the legislature | Kenya | 0.12 | 0.05 | 0.02 | 0.17 | |
| | Korea | 0.03 | 0.02 | 0.02 | 0.23 | |
| | Turkey | 0.02 | 0.06 | 0.10 | 0.10 | |
| $X_6$ Support for the legislature | Kenya | 0.17 | 0.02 | 0.08 | 0.05 | 0.48 |
| | Korea | 0.19 | 0.07 | 0.15 | 0.09 | 0.31 |
| | Turkey | 0.01 | 0.09 | 0.21 | 0.03 | 0.26 |

*Note*: Multiple correlations for support in each country are:
Kenya (*N* = 3,747): *R* = 0.57 and $R^2$ = 0.33
Korea (*N* = 2,014): *R* = 0.51 and $R^2$ = 0.26
Turkey (*N* = 1,954): *R* = 0.42 and $R^2$ = 0.18

contacts with MPs because they seem to have no major effect on salience, satisfaction, or support, probably because (except in Kenya) very few constituents have even a minimum amount of contact with MPs. We experimented with a more elaborate path model including qualification differentials and expectation-performance differentials, but abandoned it because it added very little to the predictive power of the model. (Note that the district variables, shown in figure 9.1, are discussed later in this chapter.)

A careful examination of figure 11.1 and table 11.2 leads to several conclusions. The first is that there was remarkable similarity among the three countries in the strength of linkages; most linkages in the model were either relatively high in all three countries or very low in all three. The greatest variations generally occurred in some of the linkages with moderate strength, such as that between institutional salience and support for the legislature.

It should be kept in mind that our modernity index, which measures a variety of attitudes and values, was used in this model because it has a rather high correlation with numerous background variables and correlates better with salience and with support than do any of those variables. In that sense, it is a summary variable, distinguishing high status, better educated, more "modern" constituents from others.

It is clear that modernity directly affected the salience of individual legislators and of the legislative institution; the relationship was strong and consistent in all three countries. But the only other direct linkage of modernity with the dependent variable was a modest link to support in Kenya and Korea.

The salience of MPs had a very strong impact on satisfaction with the performance of MPs. But salience of the legislature had virtually no effect on satisfaction with that institution's performance; it did, however, have a direct effect on legislative support. The path coefficient was 0.21 in Turkey, 0.15 in Korea, and 0.08 in Kenya.

Although there was a strong linkage from modernity to MP salience, and satisfaction with MP performance, there was virtually no direct connection

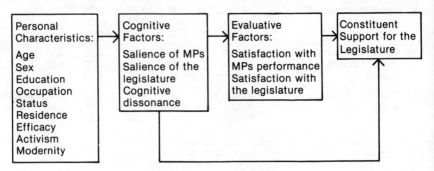

FIGURE 11.3. A General Causal Model of Constituent Support for the Legislature

between the latter and legislative support. The path model did not support the hypothesis that support depended directly on the performance of individual legislators. Instead, the model demonstrated that support depended very heavily on satisfaction with performance by the legislature. In some respects that is an important finding, but it leaves some unanswered questions. We know that satisfaction with the performance of the legislative institution was measured only by a single question, but we want to know which variables caused such satisfaction. Path coefficients did not supply a very clear or comprehensive answer; the only linkage of any importance was that running from satisfaction with the MPs' performance to satisfaction with performance of the legislature. That linkage varied from a low path coefficient of 0.10 in Turkey to a moderate 0.17 in Kenya and 0.23 in Korea.

We hypothesized that many constituents would be more familiar with the work of individual MPs than with the work of the legislature, and that, as a consequence, those who were most satisfied with what their own MPs were accomplishing would be most supportive of the legislature. The path model, and the accompanying path coefficients, do not fully support that hypothesis. Perhaps the legislature is such a distant institution that many constituents probably do not make a clear connection between what their MP is doing in the district and the need to maintain and support the legislature. The path model suggests another answer, one that is somewhat more complicated. It appears that there was a weak relationship (much stronger in Turkey) between MP and institutional salience; and a modest relationship (particularly in Kenya and Korea) between satisfaction with individual MP performance and satisfaction with institutional performance. It seems reasonable that the salience of and satisfaction with the legislative institution might have derived in part from knowledge of and satisfaction with an individual MP rather than the other way around. This would explain why the arrows in figure 11.1 go from the MP to the institution, and would suggest that the role of the MP in building legislative support was of some importance. Those constitutents who knew something about the MP were likely to know something about the legislature and thus to support it more (a correlation that was strongest in Turkey). Likewise, those constitutents who were most satisfied with an MP's performance were most likely to be satisfied with the legislative institution's performance and thus supported it more. This was more true in Korea and Kenya than in Turkey.

## SECTORAL VARIANCE IN
## DETERMINANTS OF SUPPORT

Our analysis of the determinants of legislative support, up to this point, has been based on the implicit assumption that the perceptions and attitudes about the legislature held by diverse groups are affected by the same types of forces. That assumption is open to question, however. We have discovered that modernity affects the salience of, and to some degree the support for, the legislature. It is also very possible that modernity affects the relationships among salience, satisfaction, and support.

We know that modern constituents are more familiar with the legislature and the activities of MPs than are nonmodern constituents. We would expect modern constituents to base their support—or lack of it—for the legislature on more specific perceptions about it, including their satisfaction with its performance. For the more traditional respondents, we would expect less informed and perceptive and more traditional bases of support. We would also expect to find somewhat similar differences between the elites, who are best informed about the legislature and its members, and constituents. To test these assumptions, we will compare first the most modern and the most traditional respondents, and second the local elite and citizen respondents.

## MODERN AND TRADITIONAL PATTERNS OF SUPPORT

To compare the sources of support in the modern and traditional sectors, we divided constituents in the three countries into two groups on the basis of individual modernity scores. Those who had modernity scores of less than 3 were classified as members of the traditional sector, and those with modernity scores greater than 8 were classified as members of the modern sector.[2] We did not include constituents who were neither very modern nor very traditional in their attitudes because we were primarily interested in discerning the differences between the most modern and the most traditional sectors in these societies.

In the modern sector, where political knowledge and interest were most heavily concentrated, we expected to find the following contrasts with the more traditional sectors: (1) Modern constituents' support for the legislature would derive from more complex bases because of their political sophistication. (2) Modern constituents' perceptions of the salience of individual MPs and the legislature and their satisfaction with the performance of MPs and the institution would not be closely interrelated due to their ability to differentiate different components of the legislative process. (3) Modern citizens would base their levels of support more heavily on satisfaction with the performance of the legislature. In contrast, traditionalists either do not relate performance satisfaction to support at all, or base support solely on their perception of individual MPs, who are more visible than the distant legislature.

In figure 11.4 we display the results of the analysis of the Kenyan data; we conducted similar analyses for the other countries which produced similar results (data not shown). We generally found substantial differences in many of the path coefficients between traditional and modern constituents, but there were relatively few in which the pattern was the same for all three countries. In fact, in only one of the ten sets of path coefficients calculated were there consistent differences between modern and traditional constituents in all three countries: the relationship between salience of the legislature and satisfaction with its performance. In four other cases, one or two countries had higher path coefficients for traditional respondents, with little differences in the other countries. In the other five cases some countries had higher path coefficients for traditional and some for modern respondents. These differences make generalization difficult. In Turkey almost all of the path coefficients were higher for traditional constituents; in Kenya most were higher or about the same for traditional constituents; in Korea there was no consistent pattern.

Despite these differences, in all three countries the four independent variables in the model explained more variance in support among traditional than

(A) Among modern Kenyan Constituents   N = 636   R = 0.53

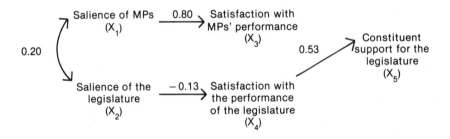

(B) Among traditional Kenyan constituents   N = 866   R = 0.56

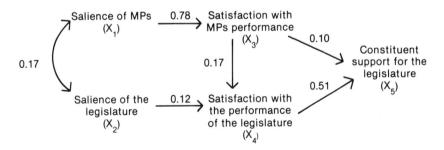

*Note:* Only path coefficients greater than 0.10 are reported in the figure.

**FIGURE 11.4. Sectorial Variations in Legislative Support
between Modern and Traditional Sectors in Kenya (path coefficients)**

among modern respondents. The contrast was greatest in Turkey (37 percent of the variance explained for traditional respondents and 10 percent for modern ones). The comparable figures were 27 percent and 18 percent in Korea and 32 percent and 28 percent in Kenya. These findings support our hypothesis that the structure of sources of support is more complex and varied for modern constituents, and thus less predictable by a simple model.

We speculated that traditional citizens would be less likely to distinguish between their salience of MPs and the legislature and between their satisfaction with MPs and with the legislature. This was true in Turkey and in Kenya for the measures of satisfaction, but was not true in Korea. Consequently, we cannot generalize about such relationships.

We also speculated that modern constituents would base their support more heavily on satisfaction with the legislature than would traditional respondents. This was not the case; the reverse was true in Korea and Turkey, and in Kenya there was little difference between the groups. In Korea and Turkey, modern respondents did base their support for the legislature more heavily on satisfaction with MP performance, the reverse was true in Kenya, but in none of the three countries was the difference very great.

Clearly we were incorrect in speculating that satisfaction with the performance of MPs would have more influence on support than satisfaction with the legislature for traditional respondents. In all countries and for both types of respondents, the links between support and satisfaction with legislative performance were very high, and stronger than the links between support and satisfaction with individual MPs.

The most consistent patterns of differences between traditional and modern constituents involved the effects of legislative salience on other variables. These findings are not easily explained and do not fit our explanations. In Kenya and Korea there was a negative path coefficient (−0.10 and −0.18 respectively) between legislative salience and satisfaction with MPs' performance for traditional respondents, but virtually no relationship for modern respondents. There is no good theoretical reason for this occurrence.

In all three countries, there was a positive path coefficient for traditional constituents between legislative salience and satisfaction with legislative performance. The coefficients ranged from 0.10 to 0.19. This relationship was not duplicated for modern constituents, perhaps because few traditional respondents knew much about the legislature. In short, differences in salience have the most impact on satisfaction with and support for the legislature for traditional citizens in all countries, particularly Turkey and Korea.

## LOCAL ELITES AND MASS CITIZENS

We would expect a greater complexity in the structure of legislative support among the local notables than among constituents. One aspect of this complexity would be the number of independent variables required to account for local notables' support of the legislature. And indeed, we found that in all three countries the five variables included in the path model accounted for less of the variance in legislative support from local notables than from constituents.

The data in table 11.3 show multiple correlations of 0.36, 0.37, and 0.19 for the local notables in Kenya, Korea, and Turkey, respectively. Each of these is markedly lower than the multiple correlations reported for constituents (see table 11.2). This suggests that local notables, because of their greater political involvement and more sophisticated view of the legislature, were unlikely to base their support on just a few simple factors. Their support for the legislature seemed to derive from more complex sources than did the support given to the legislature by constituents.

A comparison of tables 11.3 and 11.2 shows that most of the path coefficients for constituents were larger than the path coefficients for local notables. For example, linkages between modernity and both types of salience were much weaker among local notables than among constituents—presumably because there was less variation among the notables in both modernity and salience levels.

**TABLE 11.3.**
**Path Coefficients for Legislative Support in Local Elite Strata**
**in Kenya, Korea, and Turkey ($X_1$ = Individual Modernity Score)**

| Dependent variables | Country | $B_1$ | $B_2$ | $B_3$ | $B_4$ | $B_5$ |
|---|---|---|---|---|---|---|
| $X_2$ Salience of MPs | Kenya | 0.09 | | | | |
| | Korea | 0.10 | | | | |
| | Turkey | 0.14 | | | | |
| $X_3$ Salience of the | Kenya | 0.26 | 0.09 | | | |
| legislature | Korea | 0.28 | 0.04 | | | |
| | Turkey | 0.27 | 0.14 | | | |
| $X_4$ Satisfaction with MPs' | Kenya | −0.08 | 0.71 | 0.04 | | |
| performance | Korea | 0.09 | 0.60 | −0.01 | | |
| | Turkey | 0.05 | 0.65 | 0.01 | | |
| $X_5$ Satisfaction with | Kenya | 0.05 | 0.06 | 0.11 | 0.04 | |
| performance of the | Korea | −0.02 | 0.30 | 0.07 | 0.09 | |
| legislature | Turkey | −0.12 | −0.02 | 0.04 | 0.08 | |
| $X_6$ Constituent support | Kenya | 0.13 | −0.06 | 0.07 | 0.17 | 0.27 |
| for legislature | Korea | 0.13 | 0.03 | 0.12 | 0.18 | 0.15 |
| | Turkey | −0.02 | 0.09 | 0.11 | −0.06 | 0.14 |

*Note:* Multiple correlations for support in each country are as follows:
Kenya ($N$ = 477): $R$ = 0.36 and $R^2$ = 0.13
Korea ($N$ = 464): $R$ = 0.37 and $R^2$ = 0.14
Turkey ($N$ = 278): $R$ = 0.19 and $R^2$ = 0.04

However, path coefficients between salience of MPs and satisfaction with MPs' performance were very high for both constituents and elites. Legislative salience had less effect on elite support, particularly in Turkey, where the relationship was highest for constituents. The linkage between satisfaction with the MP and satisfaction with the legislature was much weaker among elites. Finally, the strong linkage between satisfaction with the legislature and support for it among constituents (ranging from 0.16 to 0.48) fell to a modest 0.14 to 0.27 in the case of elites. In short, elites' support of the legislature was based less on our measures of salience and satisfaction than was the support of constituents.

## NATIONAL VARIATIONS IN THE
## DETERMINANTS OF SUPPORT

Are there any important differences in the structure of legislative support in the three countries? In figure 11.5 we present path diagrams of legislative support for the three countries. What emerges in the data, despite all of the country variations noted earlier, is an unmistakably striking similarity in the patterns of path linkages in all three countries, a subject which we have already treated in some detail. There are nevertheless some notable differences in terms of the sources of legislative support that merit further consideration. The first of these differences, rather obvious in the data, has something to do with the performance of our path model in the three countries. The model showed the best performance in Kenya, accounting for 33 percent of the variance in legislative support. It was less efficient in the other countries, explaining 26 percent of the variance in Korea and only 18 percent in Turkey.

This difference may be due to the different political sophistication levels of the populations in the three countries. In Turkey, which has attained the highest socioeconomic development of the three, and which has a parliamentary history extending more than half a century, citizens have acquired a good deal of political sophistication, especially in comparison to those in Kenya whose history of political independence spans less than two decades.

Politically aware and sophisticated citizens are likely to extend or withdraw their support for political institutions for reasons which are both complex and carefully thought out. Those who are poorly informed and have little political experience are likely to give support, if they do it at all, for much simpler reasons. They may extend their support for the legislature because their MPs have perhaps brought some direct and tangible personal benefits to them, or may develop habitually deferential attitudes toward any institution of authority, a general tendency often observed in highly traditional societies.

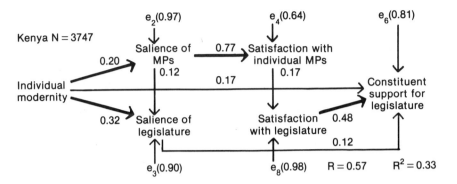

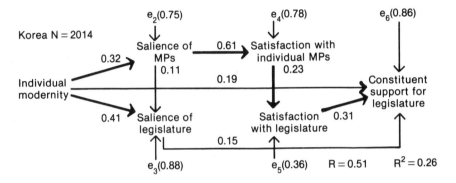

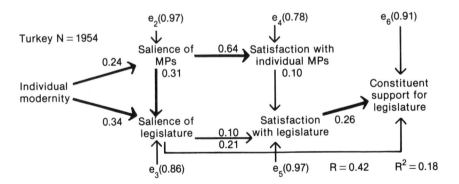

Note: Only path coefficients greater than 0.10 are reported.

FIGURE 11.5. Path Model for Legislative Support
Based on Six Variables in Kenya, Korea, and Turkey

Another difference relates to the relative effect of individual modernity on support. We have used the modernity variable here as a summary indicator of various positions that one occupies in social and political stratification systems. The individual modernity factor showed a direct effect of some magnitude in both Korea and Kenya. The direct path linkages between modernity and legislative support in these two countries were 0.19 and 0.17, respectively, compared to 0.01 in Turkey. This suggests that the level of modernity has only an indirect effect on support in Turkey. What might account for this variation? We believe that the relative importance of the modernity variable is determined by the particular stage of modernization in which a society is currently located. As a society becomes more advanced, more of its citizens will acquire a degree of individual modernity, and that variable will have less utility in explaining support.

The effect of constituent satisfaction with MP performance on their satisfaction with the institutional performance was smallest in Turkey (0.10). In Kenya and Korea the effects were substantially larger (0.17 and 0.23, respectively). These differences also appear to be rooted in the different stages of modernization in which the three countries were located at the time of our survey. Further, they indicate that many Turkish citizens were able to distinguish the performance of individual MPs from the performance of the legislature. This capacity to make a clear distinction may explain the weak path linkage between the two variables in Turkey.

It is noteworthy that the linkage between satisfaction with the legislature and support for that institution was much higher in Kenya than in the other two countries. There was, however, no important direct link between satisfaction with MPs' performance and support for the legislature.

In this section we have attempted to identify country variations in the structure of legislative support. What variations existed between Kenya, Korea, and Turkey were largely accounted for by the different levels of political sophistication which characterized the populations of those countries at the time of our survey. Furthermore, the levels of political sophistication appeared to be a product of both the socioeconomic and the political modernization of a country. Although we have stressed the differences between countries here, we should nevertheless not overlook the striking similarities in the basic structure of legislative support across the three nations with different histories, cultures, and parliamentary experiences.

## DISTRICT VARIATIONS IN SUPPORT

We turn now to an examination of the differences in levels of legislative salience, satisfaction, and support in legislative districts. If such differences did exist, could they be explained by characteristics of the districts or activities of the MPs in those districts? We hypothesized that in districts where legislators were more active and concerned with constituency needs, constituents would be more familiar with representatives (higher salience), would be more satisfied with their performance, and would be more supportive of the legislature.

The importance of interdistrict analysis lies in its potential for measuring the impact individual MPs can have on the attitudes of constituents toward the legislative system. We asked constituents whether they had seen or talked to their MP recently. We asked MPs how often they visited their constituency, whom they contacted there, what they talked about, and what priority they attached to serving constituency needs. We have summarized our findings about these questions in earlier chapters, and we can rank MPs from more to less active in, and concerned about, their constituency.

We expected that activities of MPs would affect perceptions and attitudes in their districts both directly and indirectly. Some constituents might deal directly with the MP, making requests of him and listening to reports of his accomplishments. Others might lack direct contact with the MP, but gain a favorable impression of him from others. In short, we expected a spillover effect; in districts with more active MPs we expected to find higher levels of salience and satisfaction with performance of both the MP and the legislature. We looked at the attitudes and perceptions of both elites and constituents, although there were so few elites interviewed in each district that statistical analysis of their responses was unreliable.

We can summarize briefly the findings concerning district variations before looking at each country in more detail. There were differences, sometimes considerable, from one district to another on the variables of salience, satisfaction, and support. There were also differences among some of the variables that we might expect to be explanatory. But we did not find the same districts consistently high in salience, satisfaction, and support, nor in the variables that were supposed to be explanatory. Even more discouraging to any clear and simple explanation of interdistrict variations was the fact that constituents and elites in a district very often disagreed on their perceptions of MPs and on their levels of salience, satisfaction, and support.

## KENYA

Although levels of MP salience and familiarity with the MP's name were very high among Kenyan constituents, there were a few districts in which both measures were low, and several others that showed moderate MP salience. There was a rough correlation between measure of contact with the MP and MP salience, particularly at the top and bottom of the ranks. In a few districts, the MP was highly visible and well known; in a few he was seldom seen and little was known about him.

Elite responses regarding MP salience and contact with MPs had no relationship at all to constituent responses. This suggests that some MPs spent more time with elites when visiting the district, and others had more contact with constituents.

We asked MPs a number of questions about their activities in the district, but there was not enough variation in their answers to provide important clues to differences in constituent responses. In-depth interviewing of the MPs, however, provided more clues to their impact on the district. The MPs in three districts—Laikipia, Embu, and Githunguri—were ranked high in salience and in measures of contact by both constituents and elites, and also were given very high job performance evaluations by both groups. All three MPs were excellent examples of service-oriented legislators. They devoted a great deal of time to their districts, helping to organize local development projects, and demonstrating unusual skill in taking care of needs of their districts.

Among the MPs who received low performance ratings was a national labor union leader who paid little attention to his district. Another MP got higher evaluations from elites than from constituents because he was closely tied to the power elite but was less well known to constituents. In the district incorporating the capital city of Nairobi, the local MP was not well known, probably because many residents of the city came from other districts.

In Kenya, the most visible and salient MPs were ranked high in satisfaction with job performance. But there was a wide range in the evaluation of MPs by both elites and constituents which could not be attributed to differences in salience or contact. The MP in Kenya has a chance to be an organizer and entrepreneur in his district. Some MPs in our study took advantage of this opportunity and were evaluated favorably. Others did not work very hard, were judged harshly by constituents and elites, and often were defeated or did not seek reelection.

We hypothesized that when an MP was salient and perceived to be performing well, his constituents would have a more favorable impression of the legislature and be more supportive of it. In Kenya this was not the case. For neither constituents nor elites did we find consistent relationships between high MP performance evaluation on the one hand, and high institutional performance evaluation or high support for the legislature on the other.

## KOREA

Interdistrict analysis in Korea was complicated by the fact that each district elected two legislators. Some respondents were familiar with both, others with only one, and others with neither. When we asked questions about salience, satisfaction, and contact, we did not ask respondents to specify which MP they were referring to. Where our data show that one MP was more active in the district than the other, it was impossible to tell which of the two had the greater effect on respondents. Therefore, we did not expect to find any strong relationship between MP reports of activity and the perceptions of constituents and elites.

There was some variation among districts in the salience of MPs and in the proportion of constituents who could name one or both MPs. Elite responses on these items were quite different from those of constituents in all districts. With the exception of three districts that ranked high in salience, knowledge of MP's name, and contact, we could not explain salience by frequency of contact. We did not find that MPs were consistently better known and more visible in rural districts, as we had expected to. Nor did we find any clear relationship between the reported activities and priorities of MPs and the meausure of contact, visibility, and salience given them by constituents and elites.

Constituents and elites did not consistently agree in their evaluation of MP's job performance. Among constituents, we found at the top and bottom of the scale some relationship between salience and evaluation. There were not very large interdistrict variations in the levels of legislative support among constituents. However, what modest differences there were did run roughly parallel to satisfaction with MP job evaluation, at least at the top and bottom of the scale.

There was also some relationship between constituents' evaluation of the legislature's performance and support for it. A similar pattern emerged for elites: small interdistrict differences in support that roughly parallelled differences in evaluation of MP job performance. Despite the problems caused by there being two MPs from each district, we have some reason to believe that a more positive evaluation of the MP was associated with higher support for the legislature.[3]

## TURKEY

District level analysis in Turkey was seriously handicapped by the fact that legislators were elected at large in each province, and so numbers in our sample provinces ranged from 3 to 38. While we might expect that in a large province with many legislators most constituents would have less direct contact and less familiarity with any legislator, this is not inevitable. Legislators may concentrate their efforts within particular sections of the province, perhaps where they live, and become well known in those areas. Our questionnaire did not ask respondents to identify MPs they recognized; in a large province a few prominent MPs might be well known and all the rest totally unknown.

In Turkey, there was substantial interdistrict variation in the proportion of constituents who knew the MP and scored high in MP salience. Relatively few Turkish constituents had seen one or more MPs lately, but in districts where a substantial number had done so, the level of salience was relatively high. Elites, on the other hand, had much more contact with MPs, and this contact was highest in districts where direct constituent-MP contact was lowest.

Among constituents, knowledge of the MP's name, salience, and contact with the MP were all higher in provinces that were primarily rural and that had fewer MPs. The larger, more urban the province, the more distant MPs were from constituents. Istanbul and Ankara ranked near the bottom of the contact and salience scales. Although Istanbul had 38 MPs (or because it had that many), less than one-fourth of the constituents knew the name of an MP and only 6 percent had seen a representative in recent months. These were the lowest percentages for these items recorded in any of the provinces.

The low levels of contact and salience among constituents in large urban provinces suggested that few of the MPs in these areas devoted much of their time and effort to providing services for, and maintaining contacts with, their constituents. They appeared to work through the local elites, who were familiar with them.

If rural constituents knew more about their MPs and had more contact with them, we might expect them to be more satisfied with MP performance than would constituents in urban provinces. This was not the case. Roughly half of the Turkish constituents gave a reasonably high evaluation of MPs; but the variations in evaluation did not correlate positively to variations in salience. In fact, the highest levels of satisfaction with MP performance were found in Istanbul and Ankara, where MPs were least known. Perhaps constituents in large urban areas were more easily satisfied because they expect fewer services and less personal attention from their MPs. This view is supported by the fact that in Istanbul and Ankara (though not in all urban provinces) fewer constituents ranked MP's district duties as very important. In rural districts we found all MP duties to be ranked high in importance.

Support for the legislature among Turkish constituents was modest, with some moderate district variations not related in any consistent way to contact, salience, or satisfaction, or urban-rural differences. Elite support was somewhat lower, with district variations that had no obvious explanation. We concluded that in Turkey the most significant differences were between urban and rural areas: the more rural the district, the more expected of MPs and the greater their visibility and salience.

## SUMMARY

In this chapter, we have tried to examine the principal sources of public support for the legislative institution. Despite the vast differences that obviously existed in the three political systems under examination, our findings were strikingly similar across the three nations. Two important variables emerged in the multivariate analysis: constituent satisfaction with performance of the legislature and salience of the legislative institution. It was constituent satisfaction with the legislative institution rather than satisfaction with the job of the individual MP that proved to be crucial to support. Similarly, it was salience of the institution rather than salience of the individual MP that had the greatest effect on support.

Our path analysis produced remarkably consistent patterns in the three countries. There were two primary path linkages to constituent support for the legislature. The first ran from individual modernity to salience of MPs, to satisfaction with individual MPs' performance, to satisfaction with institutional performance, to support. The second also started with individual modernity and ran to salience of the institution and then directly to support.

For a variety of reasons we expected to find sectoral variations in the causal structure of legislative support.[4] In all three nations modernization had penetrated different segments of society to varying degrees, and we expected to find somewhat different causal structures of legislative support for modern and traditional citizens. Our analysis indicated that support among modern citizens in all three countries derived from much more complex sources than did support among traditional citizens. Our four-variable model could predict a greater amount of variance in support among the more traditional citizens than among modern ones.

There was no consistent support for our speculation that modern citizens would rely on satisfaction with the institution and traditional citizens would rely on appraisal of the individual MP for their support of the legislature. However, in both Kenya and Turkey the linkages between the two measures of performance satisfaction were greater for traditional than for modern respondents. In general, the lack of strong consistent patterns in the three countries for these relationships suggests the need for caution in our interpretations.

The analysis also revealed some differences between elites and average constituents. Local elites were consistently more supportive of the legislature, and more modern in their beliefs and attitudes. We expected that the local elites, with greater political sophistication and involvement in politics, would base their support on a greater variety of sources. This proved to be the case in all three countries. The explanatory capacity of our path model was consistently smaller for the support from local elites than for support from constituents. A different, more complex model is needed to explain variations in elites' support of legislative institutions.

# Part V

# SUMMARY AND CONCLUSIONS

# Chapter 12

# THE LEGISLATURE AND POLITICAL DEVELOPMENT

## COMPARATIVE PERSPECTIVE IN LEGISLATIVE RESEARCH

The principal objective of our study was to draw some general conclusions about the linkage functions of legislatures. We analyzed the data collected in Kenya, Korea, and Turkey with a view toward developing a theory that was valid crossnationally not only for the countries in our studies, but for other countries as well.

We make no claim that the nations we studied were in any precise sense a sample of all those in the non-Western world. Nevertheless, where we found consistent empirical support for our hypotheses in all three countries, there is, we believe, good reason to suggest that these hypotheses are applicable elsewhere. This belief is based on two considerations. First, many of the hypotheses tested in the study were developed from the findings of previous studies in other countries. Second, any confirmatory evidence from nations as disparate in sociopolitical character as Kenya, Korea, and Turkey may provide an additional basis for broader applicability.

Rather than a study of individual countries, we sought to conduct a comparative study of the type described by Przeworski and Teune:

"Comparative" studies were defined as those in which the influence of larger systems upon the characteristics of units within them is examined at some stage of analysis. Consequently comparative studies involve at least two levels of analysis. In this sense not all of the studies conducted across systems or nations are comparative, but all studies that are comparative are cross-systemic. If national social, political, or economic systems constitute one of the levels of analysis, the study is a cross-national comparative study. If, however, the analysis is conducted exclusively at the level of nations, then according to this definition it is not comparative.[1]

Moreover, the authors further note that "systems differ not when the frequency of particular characteristics differ, but when the patterns of the relationships among variables differ."[2] We have sought to examine and explain these differing patterns, and not merely differences in frequencies.

It was desirable for comparative purposes not merely to describe the differences among Kenya, Korea, and Turkey, but to show which characteristics in each of these systems explained the differences. This was difficult to do with any confidence since only three nations were studied and they differed in many respects.

The differences that we found among Kenya, Korea, and Turkey may be attributable to many variations, particularly those that Przeworski and Teune called differences in "settings."[3] The three countries displayed differences in the following characteristics: the level of economic and social development, the nature of the ruling regime, the patterns of political culture, the party and electoral systems, and the character and history of the legislature. It was difficult and often impossible to determine which one or ones explained the differences we found. As Przeworski and Teune suggest, "most system-level variables will equally well account for the same differences of within-system relationships.[4]

There are many pitfalls involved in attempting to use more than a single level of analysis. It is important to distinguish clearly between those relationships that exist within countries and those that exist between them. One might, for example, be seeking to make generalizations about the relationship between modernity and the salience of legislators, or between modernity and support for the legislature. We found that an index of individual modernity was a good summary variable for a number of socioeconomic variables, and that individuals scoring high on the modernity index were both more familiar with legislators and more supportive of the legislature. We also found that the reasons for their support of the legislature differed from those of less modern individuals. But it was not true that constituents in the more modern parts of a country, or in the most modern, developed countries know more about their representatives than do traditional citizens.

Similarly, we found that legislators from less developed parts of countries were more likely to be externals, but that the frequency of external MPs from country to country varied only imperfectly with the level of national development. This suggests that variables other than development contribute to legislative role.

In the United States, which has a much higher level of development, most legislators perform both internal and external roles. This illustrates a problem raised by Przeworski and Teune: relations that may be linear within a small range of observations (in this case a range in the level of development) may be curvilinear when a larger range of observations is employed.[5] In other words, it is risky to make generalizations about differences between systems based on observations of only three systems.

There is another fundamental problem associated with our hypotheses about political developments. We believe that legislators may play a critical role in representation and resource allocations, contributing to the creation of public support for the regime and linkages between the center and the periphery. This process would be dynamic rather than static. A full test of this hypothesis would require comparisons over a long period of time of systems in which legislators played a variety of roles with varying degrees of success. As we were unable to do this, we conducted surveys at a single point in time. Although this enabled us to identify some differences in the way representation and resource allocation occurred in the three countries, we were unable to measure the success of these functions in any systematic way. Moreover, though political development is clearly a dynamic process, we could not trace it over time.

Our study relied on surveys of legislators, local elites, and constituents, rather than on written records of bills passed, committee hearings, debates, or question periods. The problems inherent in survey research are familiar ones, and in chapter 2 we outlined the steps we took to avoid these problems. Although great care was taken when constructing and translating our survey instruments to maintain crossnational equivalence in context, we cannot be sure that we were completely successful. In the more rural parts of these countries, we were interviewing constituents who were unfamiliar with the concept of public opinion polls, some of whom may have been intimidated by the procedure and unwilling to provide frank answers. We took steps to minimize these problems but obviously could not completely eliminate them.[6]

Specialists in comparative research are particularly concerned about the problems of establishing equivalence in measurement.[7] We are familiar with these problems, and sought to deal with them as carefully as possible throughout the course of the project. As noted in chapter 2, we developed common survey instruments—with only slight variations in a few questions—through joint efforts of experts from the three countries.

There are obvious difficulties in measuring urban/rural aspects of districts, or in measuring education simply by counting the number of years of schooling. However, since we were not so much interested in comparing the knowledge and attitudes of persons in each country indicated by their education as in determining whether levels of education have the same effects on knowledge and attitudes in each country, it was not really necessary to find measures of education or other characteristics that were equivalent in the three countries.

It was even more difficult to find common measures for such concepts as modernity, participation, salience, and representation. Fortunately, we were able to use an index of modernity that was developed for and tested in crossnational research.[8] We used the same questions in each country to measure political participation, but recognized that participation in political campaigns or voting in elections probably had different meanings in the three countries.

Some of the problems of equivalence were inherent in our research. We did not assume that such concepts as representation and support meant the same thing in each country. Actually, one of the goals of our research was to find out what MPs, elites, and constituents believed were the essential ingredients of the representative process. We were able to show which jobs of the legislator were considered most important by various groups we interviewed, and were impressed by the similarity of viewpoints. For example, constituents in each country said that telling the government what constituents want was the most important job of the MP, but constituents in the three countries may have had different things in mind when they responded positively to that phrase. Similarly, when MPs were asked what their most important job was, the answers that were coded as representing the voters or other groups may have had different meanings to legislators in different countries, or even among legislators in the same country.

Mass surveys require almost complete reliance on structured questions because the interviews are conducted and coded by many individuals and because it is important to be able to make comparisons within and among countries. Thus, we were not able to probe the attitudes and perceptions of legislators in any detail in order to find out more about how and why they differed in their performance of representative functions. Nor were we able to find out much about how legislators perceived their districts or about the factors which may have affected the way they represented their districts.

Moreover, our research design did not permit us to observe the MP in his district.[9] We could compare his role perceptions and his reported activity in the district with the perceptions and reactions of his constituents, but we had no detailed account of what the MP actually did in his district when he visited.

The analysis of resource allocation would have been much stronger if we could have measured what the MP actually accomplished: how many new schools, improved roads, the jobs he gained for his constituents, and how often and with what success he intervened in disputes between individual constituents and bureaucrats. Similarly, we had no information about the existence and effectiveness of other channels that might have been available to constituents in specific districts: local officials, party leaders, or bureaucrats.

Finally, there was a vexing problem in analyzing the role of the legislator in the multimember districts of Turkey, particularly in the provinces that had a large number of members. We did not ask constituents or elites to specify the particular legislator whose name they knew, or whom they had seen or talked to. Nor did we ask them to be specific in evaluating the performance of their districts' MPs. Consequently, it was very difficult to evaluate the effectiveness or representational linkages in Turkey. This was not a mechanical breakdown in our interviewing procedure; it would not have been realistic to expect constituents to identify and discuss a large number of MPs in the interview. Instead, it illustrates a more basic methodological problem—that of analyzing and comparing the process of representation in multimember and single-member districts.

## LINKAGE FUNCTIONS OF LEGISLATURES

Our principal research interest was directed to the role of legislative institutions in the political system, a perspective which required us to look closely at the external linkages of a legislative body. We have selected three aspects of such linkages for analysis: representation, resource allocation, and public support for the legislature. What emerged from our crossnational comparative study is briefly summarized below.

### REPRESENTATIONS

Studies of the characteristics of legislators in other countries have consistently shown that members are better educated and are drawn from higher occupational, income, and social levels than those of the average person. The legislators of Kenya, Korea, and Turkey obviously fit this pattern. Although we did not examine trends over time, there was little evidence of a broadening of the base from which MPs were drawn in these countries—a trend that has been found in some non-Western countries in recent years.[10]

We found relatively high levels of turnover—particularly in Kenya and Turkey. In Kenya the turnover resulted in part from the frequent electoral defeat of MPs, often for failure to serve constituency needs. In Turkey, the turnover was partly voluntary, but was also caused by the failure of some MPs to win party renomination and by the emergence of new parties and factions in recent years.

Representation has many dimensions, and it is useful for our purposes to use the categories delineated by Eulau and Karps:

1. policy responsiveness, involving issues of public policy, generally related to the passage of legislation;
2. allocation responsiveness, "the representative's efforts to obtain benefits for his constituency through pork-barrel exchanges in the appropriations process or through administrative interventions";

3. service responsiveness, "the efforts of the representative to secure particu-
   larized benefits for individuals or groups in his constituency";
4. symbolic responsiveness, "public gestures of a sort that create a sense
   of trust and support in the relationship between representative and
   represented."[11]

In our surveys of legislators, we found considerable awareness of the importance of symbolic responsiveness, though it was difficult to tell how often
MPs practiced the public gestures Eulau and Karps talk about. We found
that some members, whom we labeled internals, devoted more of their time
to policy responsiveness, while others, the externals, were more concerned
with allocation and service responsiveness. This difference in priorities can
be explained by a number of factors. Some are personal, such as age and
experience. But the more important differences relate to the character of the
constituency and its needs, as well as the nature of the regime, the operation
of the legislature, and electoral necessities.

The level of social and economic development in a society, and within a
constituency, affect the issues confronting the legislature. We found that the
Turkish legislator, particularly one representing an urban constituency, was
more likely to represent—through his party—certain classes and groups that
were seeking particular policies and programs. The Kenyan MP represented
a geographic entity that was seeking certain direct benefits from the government. Moreover, in Kenya the domination of the executive over the policymaking process led members to work behind the scenes to gain benefits from
executive agencies while they worked within their districts to develop projects
eligible for aid.

The importance attached to allocation and service responsiveness by MPs
in our study—particularly in Kenya but to some extent in Korea and Turkey
—was comparable to what has been found in studies of a number of non-
Western legislatures. Mohapatra found that in the Indian state of Orissa,
four-fifths of the members of the state legislature believed that the role of
ombudsman was a proper one, and an even larger proportion actually practiced it.[12] In the Indian state of Rajasthan, Narain and Puri found that legislators reported that problems of local development were the ones most often
stressed by constituents, those most often emphasized in legislators' campaigns, and those to which they devoted the largest share of their time.[13]
Maheshwari reported that a sample of MPs in the Indian national parliament
said that a high proportion of the problems brought to them by constituents were individual in character, and that these members believed that
trying to deal with these requests was a matter of high priority.[14] Several
studies of Malaysian and Singaporean legislators have documented the strong
constituency orientation of most legislators and have described in some
detail the procedures they use to maintain allocation, service, and symbolic
responsiveness.[15]

Two surveys of legislators have been conducted in recent years using many of the questions that we devised for our study; they were in Malaysia and in Papua New Guinea. Musolf and Springer found that the activities which occupied most of Malaysian MPs' time were resolving local conflicts (29 percent), explaining government policy to voters (25 percent), interceding with civil servants (21 percent), and seeking resources for the district (15 percent); only a few emphasized debate and expressing the views of constituents. Most members said that they would like to spend more time on getting resources for the district and expressing the views of the district on policy. The high priority given to resolving local conflicts probably reflects the ethnic conflicts between Malays and Chinese that have plagued that country.[16]

A study by Gadbois, Jewell, and Sylvester in Papua New Guinea shows that legislators are much more likely to emphasize purposive roles related to representing their constituents and getting projects for them than they are to stress policymaking (17 to 52 percent of first-mentioned roles). More than three-fourths of the legislators in this study said they devoted more time to problems in the electorate than to national problems. Most legislators claimed to spend a great deal of time in their electorate, and most believed that their constituents expected them to provide benefits for the district as a whole as well as for individual constituents.[17]

Several studies suggest that constituency services are also important to legislators in Western countries, although there is more attention given to policy matters in Western legislatures than in non-Western legislatures. Several studies in recent years have stressed the service responsibilities of British MPs.[18] Kornberg and Mishler, in their study of the Canadian parliament, suggest that while most MPs have a strong interest in policy matters, a high proportion believe that it is important to deal with the problems of individual constituents and in fact is essential for winning reelection.[19] Clarke has found that Canadian provincial legislators devote a substantial amount of their time to constituency service, and has measured the variables that lead to differences in the amount of time spent.[20] Scholars of the United States Congress in recent years have emphasized that, despite their heavy involvement in policy, almost all members devote time and attention, and a large proportion of their staff resources, to service and allocation responsibilities; the growing importance of these activities is responsible, some say, for the increasing success of House members in winning reelection.[21]

Britain, Canada, and the United States, of course, all have national legislators elected from single-member districts, and that probably accounts for the importance of both service and allocation responsiveness among these legislators. Loewenberg has reported on a study of MPs in Belgium, Italy, and Switzerland, countries in which multimember districts are used. When asked to define their constituency, most MPs answered in terms of interest groups, social classes, or political groups, and relatively few emphasized a geographic constituency, even when asked specifically about that category.

Loewenberg also found some differences among the countries and within them in symbolic, service, and policy responsiveness.[22]

Symbolic responsiveness may be the most important aspect of representation. It is likely that the demand of the constituency for resources and the demands of constituents for services will exceed the ability of the legislator to provide them, in most districts at least. The success of the legislator as an individual, and his contribution to the linkage function, may depend on his skill in symbolic responsiveness. To represent his district well, the MP must not only come from the district and understand its needs, but must develop and maintain contacts, spend time in the district, and be visible and accessible.

Our data show that most legislators recognize this in principle and claim to devote time and skills to their district. The way they do this job—the people they see and the things they discuss—differs in particular cases. The techniques of representation that work well in one political culture, or in certain types of districts, may not be effective elsewhere. We know that legislators follow different patterns of activity in their districts, but we cannot tell with our data how much of their diversity reflects local preference and how much reflects variations in personal styles and devotion to the job.

Our research design enabled us to measure the congruence between MPs' roles and the expectations of their constituents. We could determine whether legislators shared the goals and focused on the problems considered important by constituents. We used the term "legislative culture" to describe constituent cognitions, role expectations, and evaluations concerning the legislature and its members. We did not, of course, expect to find perfect congruence, but the fundamental differences we did find suggest that the system of representation was not working well.

We began with cognitions, and found a rather high level of constituent familiarity with their legislators. This was highest in Kenya, where many MPs appeared to be important local leaders, and lowest in Turkey, where the legislators in multimember districts were more responsive to parties and organized groups than to individual constituents. We found, particularly in Turkey and Korea, more widespread knowledge about legislative institutions than we might have expected. The legislature and its members were salient enough to make it possible for us to query the constituents about the qualities that legislators should have and the jobs that they should do. We found remarkable consensus in the three countries that honesty, hard work, and an understanding of the common people were most important. These qualifications overshadowed educational achievement, occupational success, and long residence in the district.

We found considerable agreement that the most important jobs of the MP were those directly related to his constituency: expressing the people's views, getting resources and projects for the district, and visiting the district. Generally, the legislators recognized the importance of these activities, but not surprisingly, many of them gave greater priority to policymaking activities than their constituents did. Kenyan MPs seemed to be most in tune with their constituents; they spent the most time on district activities and would like to have spent even more time on them. Turkish MPs spent less time on district activities but said that they would have liked to devote more time to these duties. Korean MPs, who spent somewhat more time on district matters, wanted to become more involved in policymaking, a preference that is close to that of the local elites in that country. Regarding the focus of representation, Kenyan legislators agreed with constituents and elites that top priority should be given to constituent views. Korean MPs, however, gave much greater priority to party than did constituents and elites, while Turkish MPs emphasized their personal convictions much more than other groups did.

If we consider role congruence between legislators and the local elites and constituents in their districts as a measure of symbolic responsiveness, we can conclude that Kenyan MPs were more responsive than those in Korea and Turkey. In Kenya, there seemed to be a widely shared perception that the legislator's major responsibility was to gain resources for his district and help his constituents. Korean legislators were more loyal to their party, and much more interested in policymaking (however limited their actual input) than their constituents wished. But local elites in Korea agreed with the priorities of their legislators. The differences in role expectations between Turkish MPs and constituents probably resulted from the fact that Turkish MPs were directly responsive to partisan and interest groups and only indirectly responsive to constituents, although both elites and constituents emphasized party loyalty more than MPs did. It may be that the demands made on legislators are more varied in Korea and Turkey than in Kenya, and that this is one reason why there was less congruence concerning role expectations in those countries. We would expect that the greater diversity of demands in Korea and Turkey is a result of the higher level of socioeconomic development in these countries.

## RESOURCE ALLOCATION

In all three countries in our study, the executive branch dominated the process of general resource allocation. The executive introduced most successful legislation, including the budget, and MPs reported that the executive and party leaders (including opposition leaders in Korea) initiated most legislative proposals. The committee systems in Kenya, Korea, and Turkey provided few opportunities for ordinary legislators to influence general resource allocation, although in Turkey there were some chances to affect specific allocations. Strong party discipline in Turkey and in the majority party in Korea placed further limits on the ability of rank and file legislators to influence policy. Legislators generally reported that most key decisions were made in the cabinet or by government leaders. Most MPs also reported that their own legislative activities were rather modest, limited to some speech-making on the floor or some committee work. Even those MPs—mostly in Turkey and Korea—who claimed to have a strong interest and an active role in legislative matters did not appear to have much impact on the general allocation of resources.

When we looked at specific resource allocation, the MPs' role appeared to be larger. We found that constituents expected legislators to participate in specific resource allocation, and that many members considered it important and devoted a large portion of their time to it. Although we did not have data on the attitudes of bureaucrats, it appeared that many of them were responsive to pressures from legislators. While MPs devoted attention both to the needs of individuals and the problems of their districts, we were primarily concerned with the latter in our study of resource allocation. Obviously, the ability of legislators to gain specific benefits for their districts affected both economic and political development.

Our data suggest that there was considerable agreement between constituents and their legislators about the most important problems in the districts, most of which related to gaining resources for such projects as roads, schools, health facilities, and promotion of local industry and agriculture. There were many ways in which legislators generated resources for their districts. These included fund raising and initiation of projects in the district. They also included a variety of efforts, both publicized and behind the scenes, in the capital to get funds allocated to the district. Apparently, the most effective efforts were carried out through bargaining with government ministers and civil servants, although at times the push for resources was made in speeches and questions on the floor. Some two-thirds of the MPs in Korea and Turkey, and more in Kenya, believed that they had been effective in getting resources for their districts. It was, however, difficult to tell whether these self-evaluations were realistic.

Relatively few constituents (except local elites) reported having been in contact with a legislator or reported that an MP had done something for them. Except in Kenya, fewer than half of the constituents could mention anything specific that the MP had done for the district. This awareness tended to be higher in rural districts where the visibility of the MP was greatest, and the existence of other political actors and institutions, especially interest groups and various government agencies, was limited.

It was no easy task to evaluate the effectiveness of legislators in specific resource allocation or the impact of such activities on economic and political development. We knew the importance attached to this function by constituents and MPs, but we could not measure, either quantitatively or qualitatively, the consequences of these activities for individuals or communities in the district.

What are the consequences for economic development if legislators are able to affect the specific allocation of resources? Obviously, one effect is to allocate more funds to those districts represented by legislators who are politically powerful, industrious, and skillful. Because the executive controls the resources sought by legislators, it can maintain support for its legislative program, and perhaps can coopt members of opposition parties. These are political techniques not unfamiliar in Western legislative bodies. Obviously, one consequence of this process is that resources may be allocated, not to the districts with the greatest need, or to those that can utilize them most effectively, but to districts whose representatives are most influential and skillful.

Districts already rich or more developed than others are likely to benefit disproportionately where the opportunities for legislators to influence the process of specific resource allocation are greatest. Where this occurs, the activities of legislators may contribute to unbalanced and uneven development between regions, and to increased competition between regions for scarce resources. These activities by legislators may also undermine the effectiveness of national planning for the effective distribution of resources. The negative consequences of active involvement by legislators in the process of specific resource allocation were already perceptible in Kenya at the time of our study, where the proportion of MPs concerned with this aspect of representation was particularly high. On the other hand, it can be argued that local political leaders, and legislators, understand local needs better than central planners do. Legislators may be in a unique position to encourage the initiation of local projects, and even to raise funds for local projects, that are compatible with national programs.

These arguments about the advantages and disadvantages of legislators' involvement in specific resource allocations are not new. Our data shed some light on the ways in which MPs affect economic development. But, there is very little useful information from studies in other countries on the role of legislators in specific resource allocation.[23] We were more concerned with the effects on political development, and argued that where legislators play an effective role in specific resource allocation they may affect local attitudes and increase public support for the government and its policies. We turn next to this question of support.

## LEGISLATIVE SUPPORT

We have hypothesized that legislators, by performing effectively as a linkage between the national government and local communities, can help to build public support not only for the legislature but for other political institutions in the regime. They may help to develop public support for the policies of the government, thus enhancing its capacity for governing. Ideally, we should have data on public support for the entire regime, including the executive leadership, but we judged that questions of this kind were too sensitive to ask and were not likely to produce consistently honest answers. We did, however, ask several questions designed to tap support for the legislature, and were able to measure such support on a scale and correlate support with other variables. We anticipated that knowledge, and a favorable evaluation, of the legislature would lead to its support. Moreover, we thought that many constituents would be more familiar with individual MPs than with the legislature, and that favorable evaluations of the representatives would lead to support of the legislature.

We found what seem to us to be impressive overall levels of support. We also found that most respondents were favorably impressed with the legislature's performance. This satisfaction correlated strongly with support, although it is not clear that all respondents distinguished between the two concepts. We found that most respondents were favorably impressed with the performance in those parts of the MP's job that they were most familiar with and considered most important: those related to constituency service. We found considerable variation in the degree of familiarity and satisfaction with MPs from one district to another, suggesting that respondents were in fact reacting to variations in visibility and performance by the legislators. We did not find as much relationship between satisfaction with the MP's job performance and legislative support as we had anticipated, nor did these two covary from district to district as much as we had expected.

We used a variety of approaches, including multiple regression and path analysis, in an effort to uncover the sources of legislative support. The results showed complex bases of support across nations and across social groups, rather than single uniform and consistent patterns across nations and across different social strata. We discovered modest causal linkages from salience of MPs and/or satisfaction with MPs' performance to salience of the legislative institution and satisfaction with institutional performance, and finally, to legislative support. Moreover, we uncovered fairly strong causal links running from modernity, an efficient summary variable for a large number of socio-economic attributes of an individual, to the salience and satisfaction variables.

A more detailed analysis revealed that support rested on different foundations for different types of respondents. The more traditional constituents supported the legislature, probably along with other political institutions, out of a sense of basic loyalty or a deeply ingrained deferential attitude to the authority system. On the other hand, those who were modern in their perspectives and attitudes were directly affected, in extending or withholding their support, by their evaluation of the job done by the legislature or by individual legislators. In this respect, support grew out of fundamentally different kinds of bases for different types of constituents. Interestingly, we found a weak relationship between the evaluation of the legislator's job and support for the legislature. We anticipated, on theoretical grounds, a strong connection between evaluation and support: we thought that a favorable evaluation would lead to a higher satisfaction with an MP's job performance, and that a high satisfaction would lead to a higher support. Our evidence failed to support this anticipation. This may be due to the failure among many of our respondents to form an integrated conception of the whole legislative system. Many did not recognize any relationship between the accomplishments of their own MP and the utility and contributions of the legislature as a political institution; this was especially true among members of the less modernized sectors of society. It may be expected that as these developing societies attain a higher level of political maturity, citizens will acquire a more integrated conception of the legislature.

On balance, we concluded that the level of knowledge, approval, and support for the legislative institutions was quite high, given the limited role that legislatures have played in these countries, particularly in Kenya and Korea. Also noteworthy was the perceived role of the legislator. While many respondents had little firsthand contact with MPs and many did not know much about their MPs' functions, we found surprisingly high name recognition of MPs, a strong belief in the principle of representation, a clear desire that MPs should serve constituency needs, and some willingness to pass judgment on the accomplishments of MPs. In Kenya and Korea, at least, there was clearly a potential for MPs to serve a major linkage role, and many of them seemed to be filling it with some success. In Turkey the pattern was more complicated; the linkage role was clearer in rural provinces, while in urban ones the MP worked through the party and various social and economic groups.

## NEXT STEPS IN COMPARATIVE
## LEGISLATIVE RESEARCH

Our crossnational research effort, as one of the few studies of this kind to date, must of necessity be considered exploratory. We have provided some tentative answers to the questions, but at the same time have confronted several puzzling aspects of crossnational data that require further investigation.

From the viewpoint of research strategy, it would be valuable if research projects in other countries could include parallel surveys with key actors in the legislative process, such as MPs, their constituents, local notables, government bureaucrats, leaders of interest groups, and party politicians. Such a strategy is essential if we are to understand the legislature in its interactive context. Studies that focus upon MPs, constituents, or any other activist groups alone can provide only a partial picture of the linkage functions of the legislature. One drawback of this suggestion is the almost prohibitively high research cost involved. The problem could be solved, however, by means of carefully coordinated collaborative research among scholars of different countries.

A more modest, and therefore more practical, step may involve the use of similar questions by individual scholars in their surveys of legislators or of constituents. As noted earlier, very similar survey instruments were employed for studies of legislators in Malaysia and Papua New Guinea. We have found that there is great value in using not only the same research instruments, but also common conceptual and methodological approaches in studying these nations. We have also found that such coordination and collaboration require time, patience, and substantial resources, but the experience is highly rewarding because it makes possible the cumulative development of knowledge.

Another methodological approach that deserves greater attention is the indepth study of legislators' activities in their districts, along the lines that Fenno followed in the United States[24] or that Ong employed on a small scale in Malaysia.[25] Such a study could be combined with surveys of constituents and elites in those districts, or perhaps surveys of individuals who have had contact with the legislators. In addition, it would be valuable to study the consequences of legislators' activities: what benefits are actually gained for individuals and what projects are obtained for the district?

We recognize the impact that variations in national political culture have on legislative systems, but in our study of three countries we were more impressed by the similarities we found than by the differences. The underlying problems of representative government are universal, and need to be studied in a wide variety of settings.

Some of the differences in representation that we found seemed to be related to the differences between single- and multimember districting, but it is difficult to draw conclusions because so little is known about the effects of districting. Most studies of representation have been done in legislatures with single-member districts; consequently, we know very little about how legislators perform the representative function in nations with large, multimember districts.[26]

There is a growing awareness and knowledge of the allocation and service roles played by legislators in many countries. The consequences of these roles for both economic and political development need to be followed by much more systematic analysis. In order to understand the importance of symbolic representation, we need to learn more about what constituents expect from their representatives and how this influences what the legislator does.

In the area of resource allocation, the list of research needs encompasses almost every facet of the topic because we know so little. What types of resources are being allocated? What criteria do legislators use in responding to demands, and what tactics do they use in seeking to get resources for their districts? How do administrators perceive the activities of legislators, and what criteria do they use in determining their response? What differences do legislative activities make? What are the consequences of resource allocation for economic development? Are resources allocated in a significantly different pattern from what would occur if there were no legislators or if legislators were not involved in the allocation process?

Similarly, in the area of political support, very little is known with certainty. A continuing challenge for researchers is to develop more sensitive questions for measuring supportive attitudes. It is equally difficult to find ways of measuring supportive behavior. In those parts of the world where legislatures have been abolished or suspended, those who oppose the government and demand reform usually focus attention on the need for restoring the legislature. We need to learn more about why there is such persistent support for a latent or nonexistent institution, why the legislature is so often perceived as a vehicle for reform. The research problems related to public support are inherently difficult, and in those nations where they are more interesting—because support is weak or changing or because there is more support for some political institutions than for others—it is difficult, and sometimes impossible, to ask blunt questions and get honest answers from the public about support.

The fundamental questions addressed in this volume are under what conditions and in what ways does a legislature contribute to resolving conflict, developing national integration, bridging the gap between the center and the periphery, and enhancing both the capability of the government and the equal treatment of citizens. We have found that the answers to these questions are elusive and not readily provided by a study conducted at one point in time among three nations, however comparative in spirit and in methodology. The basic question—what difference does the legislature make—is the most important question that can be asked about legislative institutions, and the most difficult to answer. Both because it is important and because it is difficult, the question deserves the continuing attention of legislative scholars devoted to comparative research.

# NOTES

## FOREWORD

1. V. O. Key, Jr., *Southern Politics* (New York: Alfred A. Knopf, 1949).

2. Oliver Garceau and Corrine Silverman, "A Pressure Group and the Pressured," *American Political Science Review* 48 (1954): 672–79; Donald R. Matthews, *U.S. Senators and Their World* (New York: Random House, 1960); John C. Wahlke et al., *The Legislative System* (New York: John Wiley & Sons, Inc., 1962).

3. William H. Hunt, *Careers and Perspectives of French Politicians*, Ph. D. Dissertation, Vanderbilt University, 1966.

4. Giovanni Sartori, *Il Parlamento Italiano, 1946–1963* (Naples: Edizioni Scientifiche Italiane, 1963); Dario Canton, *El Parlamento Argentino en epochas de cambio: 1890, 1916 y 1946* (Buenos Aires: Editorial de Instituto, 1966); Frederic De Buyst, *La Fonction Parlementaire en Belgique: Mecanismes d'Access et Images* (Brussels: Centre de Recherche et d'Information, 1966); Peter Gerlich and Helmut Kramer, *Abgeordnete in Parteiendemokratie* (Vienna: Verlag fur Geschichte und Politik, 1969); Matti Oskanen, *Kansanedustajan Rooli* (Helsinki: Oy Gandeamus ab, Justannusosasto, 1972); Roland Cayrol, Jean-Luc Parodi, and Colette Ysmal, *Le Depute Francais* (Paris: Armand Colin, 1973); and Chong Lim Kim, "Consensus on Legislative Roles Among Japanese Prefectural Assemblymen," in *Legislatures in Comparative Perspective*, Allan Kornberg, ed. (New York: David McKay, 1973).

5. Heinz Eulau and Kenneth Prewitt, *Labyrinths of Democracy* (Indianapolis: The Bobbs-Merrill Company, 1973); and Robert D. Putnam, *The Beliefs of Politicians* (New Haven: Yale University Press, 1973).

6. Hunt, *Careers and Perspectives of French Politicians*.

7. Warren E. Miller and Donald E. Stokes, "Constituency Influences in Congress," *American Political Science Review* 57 (1963): 45–56.

8. Samuel C. Patterson, Ronald D. Hedlund, and G. Robert Boynton, *Representatives and Represented: Bases of Public Support for the American Legislatures* (New York: John Wiley & Sons, Inc., 1975).

9. Garceau and Silverman, "A Pressure Group and the Pressured"; Matthews, *U.S. Senators and Their World*; Wahlke et al., *The Legislative System*.

10. Putnam, *The Beliefs of Politicians*; and Eulau and Prewitt, *Labyrinths of Democracy*.

11. Wahlke et al., *The Legislative System*; Patterson, Hedlund, and Boynton, *Representatives and Represented: Bases of Public Support for the American Legislatures*; and Matthews, *U.S. Senators and Their World*.

12. David Easton, *The Political System* (New York: Alfred Knopf, 1953) and *A Systems Analysis of Political Life* (New York: John Wiley & Sons, Inc., 1965).

13. Patterson, Hedlund, and Boynton, *Representatives and Represented: Bases of Public Support*.

## 1. LEGISLATURES, LEGISLATORS, AND POLITICAL DEVELOPMENT

1. In commenting on a working paper for this study, Immanuel Wallerstein, the noted student of political change in Africa and the author of *The Modern World System* (New York: Academic Press, 1974), suggested to one of the coauthors that legislative behavior in the context of developing countries is merely "epiphenomena, the study of which will yield limited results."

2. For a notable exception to the way legislative behavior has normally been treated by students of the legislative process, see *Legislatures and Development*, edited by Lloyd Musolf and Joel Smith (Durham; Duke University Press 1979).

3. The principal members of this group during the early and middle 1960s, when the approach was formulated, included Gabriel Almond, Leonard Binder, James S. Coleman, Joseph LaPalombara, Lucian Pye, and Myron Weiner. Samuel Huntington became a member of the group at the end of the decade, but after it had produced a series of seven volumes beginning with *Communications and Political Development* in 1963 and culminating in *Crises and Sequences in Political Development* in 1971 (all volumes in the series were published by Princeton University Press).

4. Samuel P. Huntington, *Political Order in Changing Societies* (New Haven: Yale University Press, 1968).

5. For an early articulation of the "mainstream" approach, see Gabriel Almond's introductory chapter to *The Politics of Developing Areas*, Gabriel Almond and James S. Coleman, eds. (Princeton: Princeton University Press, 1958), 3–6.

6. James S. Coleman, "The Development Syndrome" in *Crises and Sequences in Political Development*, Leonard Binder et al., eds. (Princeton: Princeton University Press, 1971), 78–79.

7. This does not mean that some aspects of the legislative process, such as the recruitment of individual legislators, are unaffected by the class structure of these societies, for as discussed in chapter 4, they very much are. Rather, as Richard Sklar has critically noted, class analysis of the political economies of developing states and an application of the dependency model to these polities are two different things. While the former is partly relevant to this study, the latter is not. See Richard L. Sklar, "The Nature of Class Domination in Africa," *Journal of Modern African Studies* 17:4 (1979): 531–52.

8. For perhaps the best presentation of this thesis, see Theodore J. Lowi, *The End of Liberalism* (New York: Norton, 1979).

9. For two of the most prominent discussions of center-periphery relations—one which considers these relations within the context of individual nation states, the other in terms of the relationship between states—see Edward Shils, "Centre and Periphery," *The Logic of Personal Knowledge* (Glencoe: Free Press, 1961), 117–30, and Andre Gunder Frank, *Capitalism and Underdevelopment*.

10. Hanna Pitkin, *The Concept of Representation* (Berkeley: University of California Press, 1967), 235.

11. David Easton, *A Systems Analysis of Political Life* (New York: Wiley, 1965); and his "A Re-Assessment of the Concept of Political Support," *British Journal of Political Science* 5 (1975): 435–57.

12. Easton, "A Re-Assessment of the Concept of Political Support," 437.

13. Ibid., 444–46.


## 2. RESEARCH DESIGN AND ORGANIZATION

1. Adam Przeworski and Henry Teune, *The Logic of Comparative Social Inquiry* (New York: John Wiley, 1970), 39.

2. The civil servant data was comprised of 225 interviews in Korea and 232 in Turkey. In both countries our sample of civil servants was stratified by the major government agencies as well as by rank distribution. The sample included civil servants with a rank of section chief or higher. Functionally, the civil servants included in our survey were all senior bureaucrats occupying important positions in key government agencies—sixteen ministries and other agencies in Korea and ten ministries in Turkey. A similar survey of administrators in Kenya was judged to be impractical, likely to meet resistance from administrators, and perhaps likely to jeopardize other parts of the survey. Preliminary results from the analysis of the civil servant data were reported in Metin

Heper, Chong Lim Kim, and S. T. Pai. "The Role of Bureaucracy and Regime Types: A Comparative Study of Turkish and Korean Civil Servants," *Administration and Society* 12 (March 1980): 137–57.

3. More details on sampling procedure and field work can be found in the constituents' and local notables' codebooks of the project, which can be obtained from the Comparative Legislative Research Center at the University of Iowa.

4. Field work in Kenya was conducted between March and June 1974, while the campaign leading to the general election of October 1974 was in progress. Since most MPs spent all of their time in their constituencies, it was extremely difficult to carry out MP interviews in Nairobi. As a result, the number of MPs that it was possible to interview in Kenya fell short of the intended total. Also, the fact that the election campaign was going on may have increased the citizens' awareness of their MPs and their activities.

5. Interviews were conducted with constituents and local notables in Kenya from March through June 1974; in Korea from September 1973 through February 1974; and in Turkey from July through September 1974.

6. The questions used in the survey instruments for constituents and for MPs can be obtained from the Comparative Legislative Research Center at the University of Iowa.

## 3. THE NATIONAL SETTINGS

1. For an extensive discussion of the relationship between clientelist politics, constituency service, and the electoral process, see Joel D. Barkan and John J. Okumu, "Semi-Competitive Elections, Clientelism, and Political Recruitment in a No-Party State: The Kenyan Experience," in *Elections Without Choice* (New York: Wiley, 1978), Richard Rose et al., eds. 88–108.

2. After Kenyatta was released from detention in 1961, he sought a merger of KANU and KADU, but was unsuccessful. He subsequently failed to bring about a measure of unity within KANU, and by 1966 concluded that it was better to have no party than to have an extensive organization torn by factional strife.

3. Several good reference materials exist, if one wishes to do a quick survey of the Japanese colonial rule and its nature in Korea: C. K. Eugene Kim and Han Kyo Kim, *Korea and the Politics of Imperialism: 1876–1910* (Berkeley: University of California Press, 1967); Gregory Henderson, *Korea: The Politics of the Vortex* (Cambridge: Harvard University Press, 1968); Chong Sik Lee, *Politics of Korean Nationalism* (Berkeley: University of California Press, 1968).

4. John Kie-Chaing Oh, *Korea: Democrary on Trial* (Ithaca: Cornell University Press, 1968), 18.

5. Chong Lim Kim and Byong-Kyu Woo, "Legislative Leadership and Democratic Development," in *Political Leadership in Korea*, Dae-Sook Suh and Chae-Jin Lee, eds. (Seattle: University of Washington Press, 1976), 41–66.

6. Ki-Shik Hahn, "Underlying Factors in Political Party Organization and Elections," in *Korean Politics in Transition*, Edward R Wright, ed. (Seattle: University of Washington Press, 1975), 87.

7. Robert A. Scalapino and Junnosuke Masumi, *Parties and Politics in Contemporary Japan* (Berkeley: University of California Press, 1962), 53.

8. See Chong Lim Kim and Seong-Tong Pai, *Legislative Process in Korea* (Seoul: Seoul University Press, 1981), 171–85.

9. Chong Lim Kim and Gerhard Loewenberg, "The Cultural Roots of a New Legislature: Public Perceptions of the Korean National Assembly," *Legislative Studies Quarterly* 1 (August 1976): 371–88.

10. For a description of representative behaviors of the Korean legislators, see Chong Lim Kim and Byung-Kyo Woo, "Political Representation in the Korean National Assembly," *Midwest Journal of Political Science* 16 (November 1972): 626–51; Chong Lim Kim and Seong-Tong Pai, "Constituency Service Among Korean National Assemblymen: A Study of Leadership Responsiveness," in *Political Participation in Korea: Democracy, Mobilization and Stability*, Chong Lim Kim, ed. (Santa Barbara: ABC-Clio Press, 1980), 181–204.

11. Following the assassination of President Park in 1979, the Yushin system was replaced by a new regime. The new regime, based on a constitution adopted nearly unanimously in the Fall of

1980, has increased the formal role of legislative oversight, a drastic departure from the previous *Yushin* system. Whether this will in fact lead to a stronger and more assertive legislature still remains to be seen.

12. For a more comprehensive discussion of the political history of the Republic, including developments leading to its establishment, see Ilter Turan, *Cumhuriyet Tarihimiz* (Istanbul: Caglayan Yayinevi, 1969). In English, Joseph S. Syzliowicz presents an excellent summary of recent political events in Turkey in "Elites and Modernization in Turkey," in *Political Elites and Political Development in the Middle East*, Frank Tachau, ed. (New York: Schenkman Publishers, 1975), 23–66. More comprehensive books on Turkey's politics are many and need no elaboration here.

## 4. THE MEMBERS OF THE LEGISLATURE

1. Unless otherwise noted, the data presented for Korean MPs in this chapter and subsequent chapters is for elected members only. Although one-third of the Korean National Assembly, prior to its dissolution in May 1980, was composed of MPs appointed by the president, we have chosen to present data only for the elected members because this group is most comparable to the legislators interviewed in Kenya and Turkey and because our primary concern is with the relationships between legislators and their constituents. Differences between elected and appointed MPs will be noted where they are significant. In respect to their demographic and social background characteristics, however, the elected and appointed members of the Korean National Assembly were basically the same. Appointed MPs were slightly older than elected MPs, while elected MPs were more likely to be the sons of fathers with higher occupational status than were appointed MPs. Neither of these variables were of any political significance, which is another reason for our decision not to present the data for the appointed MPs.

2. Robert Michels, *Political Parties* (New York: Dover Publishers, 1959).

3. This index, and the others presented in this chapter, are additive indices constructed from MPs' responses to a series of statements with which the respondents were asked to "strongly agree," "agree," "disagree," or "strongly disagree." The responses to each statement were scored from 1 to 4, depending on the intensity of the opinion expressed. Respondents who failed to express an opinion, or who replied "don't know," were scored as 0. Where necessary, the scores for responses to a given statement were assigned in reverse order, so that the score assigned was consistent with the order of the scores obtained for the other statements included in the index.

For the index on capitalism v. socialism, the respondents were asked to consider the following four statements: (1) "Projects designed to speed up developing should be spread equally throughout the country even if the overall rate of economic growth might suffer." (2) "The government should adopt policies designed to promote economic growth first, and should then concern itself with problems of economic inequality." (3) "The existence of social inequality is inevitable in a society like ours which is struggling to achieve rapid economic development." (4) "Any man who is willing to work hard enough has the opportunity to be a success in our society." When added together, the scores for the responses to these statements yielded raw scores of 1 to 16 for each respondent. These scores were then reduced to the four categories presented in table 4.7 by treating scores of 1 through 4 as equal to 1; 5 through 8 as equal to 2, 9 through 12 as equal to 3; and 13 through 16 as equal to 4.

4. For the index on authoritarianism v. liberalism, the respondents were asked to consider three statements: (1) "People should not be allowed to speak publicly that which is contrary to the opinion of the majority." (2) "When most of the people want to do something, the rest should not criticize." (3) "Society is better run by a few enlightened and experienced leaders than by the will of the masses." Responses to these statements yielded raw scores of 1 to 12 for each respondent. These scores were then reduced to the four categories presented in table 4.7 by treating scores of 1 through 3 as equal to 1; 4 through 6 as equal to 2; 7 through 9 as equal to 3; and 10 through 12 as equal to 4.

## 5. LEGISLATORS AND REPRESENTATION

1. The correlation between the ages of the MPs in our samples and the number of times they were elected to the legislature is 0.43, but surprisingly, the number of times MPs were elected is less strongly correlated with their propensity to be internals than is age. The simple $R$s were 0.23 for the

correlation between the ages of MPs and their roles, and 0.183 for the correlation between the number of times they had been elected and their roles. These figures in turn suggest that, given the importance of age, political experience might consist of more than election to parliament.

2. See John Walke et al., *The Legislative System* (New York: John Wiley, 1962); Malcolm E. Jewell, "Attitudinal Determinants of Legislative Behavior: Utility of Role Analysis," in *Legislatures in Developmental Perspective*, Allan Kornberg and Lloyd Musolf, eds. (Durham: Duke University Press, 1970); and all of the articles included in *Legislative Studies Quarterly* 1 (August 1976): 283–442.

## 6. CONSTITUENTS AND REPRESENTATION

1. Gabriel A. Almond and Sidney Verba, *The Civic Culture: Political Attitudes and Democracy in Five Nations* (Boston: Little, Brown and Co., 1965), 1–35.

2. The concept of political culture has also been applied to elite groups. See Robert D. Putnam, *The Beliefs of Politicians: Ideology, Conflict, and Democracy in Britain and Italy* (New Haven: Yale University Press, 1973).

3. The concept of legislative culture has been suggested in previous studies. See Gerhard Loewenberg and Chong Lim Kim, "Comparing the Representativeness of Parliaments," *Legislative Studies Quarterly* 3 (February 1978): 44; and Chong Lim Kim and Gerhard Loewenberg, "The Cultural Roots of a New Legislature: Public Perceptions of the Korean National Assembly," *Legislative Studies Quarterly* 1 (August 1976): 371–88.

4. Heinz Eulau et al., "The Role of the Representative: Some Empirical Observations on the Theory of Edmund Burke," *American Political Science Review* 53 (September 1959): 742–56.

5. The data matching involved a creation of a new file based on the data aggregated to the constituency level. In each district the individual attitude and behavioral data were summed and then divided by the number of respondents to obtain the mean scores. Since we drew upon three separate data files, one for the MPs, another for the constituents, and still another for the local notables, there was the need to bring together all these files from each country into a single file. With this step accomplished, we could proceed to directly match, compare, or correlate the data across nations as well as across groups.

6. The policy attitudes among the MPs were treated in some detail in chapter 4.

7. Almond and Verba, *The Civic Culture*, 17–26.

8. For the concept of purposive role, see John C. Wahlke et al., *The Legislative System: Explorations in Legislative Behavior* (New York: John Wiley & Sons, 1962), 245–66.

9. The cultural pattern in Korea has been heavily influenced by the Confucian precepts including a hierarchical organization of social relationships. In part because of this cultural heritage, Koreans tend to remain deeply deferential to authorities, seldom challenging the propriety of their leaders' behaviors. For a good discussion of this deeply ingrained attitude, see Yun Tae-rim, *Hankukin* (Seoul: Hyonamsa, 1978), 221–35.

10. Wahlke et al., *The Legislative System*, 237–76.

11. To classify MPs' role styles we used their responses to these four items: If you had to choose in your action between the following groups, which one would you choose? (1) between the leaders of your party and your own personal convictions, (2) between your constituents and your personal convictions, (3) between major interest groups and your own personal convictions, and (4) between your party faction and your personal convictions. When an MP chose his personal convictions over other groups three or more times, he was classified as having a trustee role orientation. Those who chose a specific group three or more times were classified as having a delegate orientation. The remaining MPs, who chose their personal convictions and other specific groups for an equal number of times, were placed into the "mixed" category.

12. Two sets of questions relating to MPs' qualifications were asked, one involving which personal qualities they regarded as most important and the other whether they thought their MPs in fact had such qualities. The percentages indicate the proportions of the respondents who regarded a given quality as important but found their MPs seriously lacking in it.

13. For specific items used to build the measures for the policy attitudes, see footnotes 3 and 4 to chapter 4. Because the identical questions were included in our surveys with the constitutents and local notables, the same procedures were followed to create the indices.

14. Wahlke et al., *The Legislative System*, 14–17.

15. Ibid., 15.

16. Role congruence was systematically used in one study to indicate the level of institutionalization of the legislative bodies. See Chong Lim Kim, "Consensus on Legislative Roles Among Japanese Prefectural Assemblymen," in *Legislatures in Comparative Perspective*, Allan Kornberg, ed. (New York: David McKay, 1972), 298–420.

17. In the questionnaire the constituency was paired with other groups three times. We counted the number of times an MP chose his constituency over other groups, which yielded the index scores ranging from a low of 0 to a high of 3. The higher scores indicate a greater emphasis on the constituency as a central focus of representation.

18. We have adapted these items from a study conducted in California. See Charles G. Bell and Charles M. Price, "Pre-Legislative Sources of Representational Role," *Midwest Journal of Political Science* 13 (May 1969): 258–61.

19. We counted the number of times a constituent or local notable indicated that the district should serve as a central focus for an MP's action. The resulting index has four values, from a low of 0 to a high of 3. The higher scores indicate a greater importance attributed to an MP's district focus.

20. The relatively weak correlations obtained in analysis could be attributed in part to the small *N*s employed and also, by the small variations in our measures. Our computations of correlations were based on twelve to fourteen cases in each country, and when the data were aggregated to the constituency level they yielded relatively small variations in the role perceptions between districts.

21. Gerhard Loewenberg and Chong Lim Kim, "Comparing the Representativeness of Parliaments," *Legislative Studies Quarterly* 3 (February 1978): 29.

22. There are a few exceptions. See Samuel C. Patterson, Ronald D. Hedlund, and G. Robert Boynton, *Representatives and the Represented* (New York: John Wiley & Sons, 1975); Warren E. Miller and Donald E. Stokes, "Constituency Influence in Congress," *American Political Science Review*, 57 (March 1963): 45–56; Charles F. Cnudde and Donald J. McCrone, "The Linkage Between Constituency Attitudes and Congressional Voting Behavior," *American Political Science Review* 6 (March 1966): 66–72; Richard F. Fenno, Jr., *Home Style: House Members in Their Districts* (Boston: Little, Brown, 1978); Chong Lim Kim and Young Whan Kihl, "The Linkages Between the Representative and the Represented: Roles, Behaviors, and Legislative Culture in South Korea," a paper delivered at the annual meeting of the Midwest Political Science Association, the Pick Congress Hotel, Chicago, April 20–22, 1978.

23. Because of our assumption of a close contact between local elites and members of their communities we have not treated other forms of linkages that are logically possible. In fact, there are four such forms: (1) an extensive contact between an MP and his constitutents, and between notables and constituents, (2) an extensive contact between an MP and his constituents, but weak contacts between him and local notables and also between notables and constituents, (3) extensive contacts between an MP and local notables and also, between him and his constituents, but a weak contact between notables and constituents, and (4) no contact among the three groups. These linkage forms may prove to be useful categories descriptive of situations elsewhere.

24. In an effort to place each constituency into a linkage category we have examined the contact data provided by all three groups simultaneously. For instance, when an MP indicated an extensive contact with his constituents and at the same time, if his constituents also indicated a close contact with him, then that relationship was regarded as a strong contact. A similar procedure was used to determine the degree of contact between an MP and his local notables. Because the overall level of such contacts varied significantly between our countries, we employed the country mean of contact scores to determine whether a given contact in a district was high or low. Thus, it should be noted that the cut-off points for a high or low contact were different in each country. The mean contact scores for each country and groups within it were: Kenya, 1.20 between MPs and constituents, 2.38 between MPs and local notables; Korea, 0.34 between MPs and constituents, 1.23 between MPs and local notables; Turkey, 0.62 between MPs and constituents, 2.15 between MPs and local notables.

25. Joel D. Barkan and John J. Okumu, "Semi-Competitive Elections, Clientelism, and Political Recruitment in a No-Party State: The Kenyan Experience," in *Elections Without Choice*, Richard Rose et al., eds. (New York: Wiley, 1978), 88–108.

26. Loewenberg and Kim, "Comparing the Representativeness of Parliaments," 42–46.

27. The results of analysis of variance showed no significant differences between the linkage forms. We have performed the analysis with the pooled data including all forty constituencies and also with the data divided into three different countries. In neither case were *F* values statistically significant.

## 7. GENERAL RESOURCE ALLOCATION

1. For a detailed analysis of the origins of bills and other legislative activities of the executive, see Chong Lim Kim and Byung-kyu Woo, "Legislative Leadership and Democratic Development," in *Political Leadership in Korea*, Dae-Sook Suh and Chae-Jin Lee, eds. (Seattle: University of Washington Press, 1976), 51–66.

2. For example, in May 1974, the government introduced a bill for the regulation of elections that was virtually the same as a bill which had been introduced by a backbencher, and which had been passed the month before.

3. For example, since 1974 select committees have been appointed to investigate rioting at the University of Nairobi; the assassination of J. M. Kariuki, an MP and popular critic of the government; corruption in the civil service; and the operation of land settlement schemes.

4. Joel D. Barkan and John Okumu, "Linkages Without Parties: Legislators and Constituents in Kenya," in *Political Parties and Linkage*, Kay Lawson, ed. (New Haven: Yale University Press, 1980), 289–324.

5. Metin Heper, Chong Lim Kim, and S. T. Pai, "The Role of Bureaucracy and Regime Types: A Comparative Study of Turkish and Korean Higher Civil Servants," *Administration and Society* 9 (August 1980): 137–57.

## 9. LEVELS AND SOURCES OF LEGISLATIVE SUPPORT

1. David Easton, *A Systems Analysis of Political Life* (New York: John Wiley, 1965).

2. Samuel C. Patterson, Ronald D. Hedlund, and G. Robert Boynton, *Representatives and Represented: Bases of Public Support for the American Legislatures* (New York: John Wiley, 1975), 40.

3. Ibid., 59–60.

4. Ibid., 59–62, 66–70.

5. David H. Smith and Alex Inkeles, "The OM Scale: A Comparative Socio-Psychological Measure of Individual Modernity," *Sociometry* 29 (December 1966): 353–77.

6. In an earlier analysis of the data collected in Korea we discovered evidence supportive of this point. See also Malcolm E. Jewell and Chong Lim Kim, "Sources of Support for the Legislature in a Developing Nation: The Case of Korea," *Comparative Political Studies* 8 (January 1976): 478–84.

7. Easton, *A Systems Analysis of Political Life*, 159.

8. The ambiguities and incompleteness of Easton's concept of support have been discussed in some detail in Chong Lim Kim, "Support for the Institution of Elections Among Legislative Candidates: An Empirical Test of Diffuse Support," *The Laboratory for Political Research Report Series*, No. 43 (Iowa City, Iowa: Department of Political Science, University of Iowa, 1971), 22–27.

9. Easton, *A Systems Analysis of Political Life*, 272–74.

10. Ibid., 273.

11. Jack Dennis, "Support for the Institution of Elections by the Mass Public," *American Political Science Review* 64 (September 1970): 819–35; Jack Dennis, "Support for the Party System by the Mass Public," *American Political Science Review* 60 (September 1966): 600–15; Chong Lim Kim, "The Nature of Elite Support for Elections," *American Politics Quarterly* 2 (April 1974): 205–19; G.R. Boynton, Samuel C. Patterson, and Ronald D. Hedlund, "The Structure of Public Support in Legislative Institutions," *Midwest Journal of Political Science* 12 (May 1968): 168–80; Samuel C. Patterson, John C. Wahlke, and G.R. Boynton, "Dimensions of Support in Legislative Systems," in *Legislatures in Comparative Perspective*, Allan Kornberg, ed. (New York: David McKay, 1972), 282–313; Gerhard Loewenberg, "The Influence of Parliamentary Behavior on Regime Stability," *Comparative Politics* 3 (January 1971): 177–200; Walter F. Murphy and Joseph Tanenhaus, "Public Opinion and the United States Supreme Court," *Law and Society Review* 2 (May 1968): 357–85; and Patterson, Hedlund, and Boynton, *Representatives and Represented*.

12. Loewenberg, "The Influence of Parliamentary Behavior on Regime Stability," 184.

13. See Malcolm E. Jewell, "Problems in Studying Support for Political Institutions" (unpublished paper, 1977); and Chong Lim Kim, "The Nature of Elite Support for Elections," *American Politics Quarterly* 2 (April 1974): 205–19.

14. See table 9.1 for the two items which we could not include in the Kenyan survey.

15. Boynton, Patterson, and Hedlund, "The Structure of Public Support," 169–73; Patterson,

Hedlund, and Boynton, *Representatives and Represented*, 56–66; and Jewell and Kim, "Sources of Support for the Legislature," 470–71.

16. Boynton, Patterson, and Hedlund, "The Structure of Public Support," 179.

17. The three items were (a) people like me don't have any say about what the government does; (b) government officials usually do not care a great deal about what people like me think; and (c) sometimes politics and government seem so complicated that a person like me can't really understand what's going on. A negative response was taken as an efficacious answer and was assigned a score of 1. The index scores range from a low efficacy of 0 to a high efficacy of 3.

18. The activism index was created from the five survey items, each pertaining to a different kind of political act. The index scores range from a low activism rating of 0 to a high activism rating of 5.

19. The difference in individual modernity scores between urban and rural residents was negligible in Korea, indicating little bifurcation in society. See Chong Lim Kim and Seong-Tong Pai, "Urban Migration, Acquisition of Modernity and Political Change," in *Korea: A Decade of Development*, Yunshik Chang, ed. (Seoul: Seoul National University, 1980), 241–70.

20. Alex Inkeles and David H. Smith, *Becoming Modern* (Cambridge: Harvard University Press, 1974).

21. The eleven modernity items employed to form an index were as follows: (a) Have you ever thought about some public issue, such as the cost of education, about which you really wanted to do something? (b) Do you think a man can be truly good without having any religion at all? (c) Which of the following kinds of news interest you most; world news, national news, local news, sports, religious events, or others? (d) How often do you read newspapers and magazines? (e) If you were to meet a person who lives in another country thousands of miles away, do you think you could understand his way of thinking? (f) Do you belong to social organizations such as unions, church groups, clubs, and cooperatives? (g) Do you belong to any political organizations? (h) What do you think is most important for the future of this society? (i) Scholars and scientists in the universities are studying such things as how a seed turns into a plant. Do you think such scientific studies bring benefits to people like you? (j) Some people say that it is necessary for a man and wife to limit the number of children to be born so that they can better take care of those they already have. Do you think it is a good idea to purposefully limit the number of children? (k) Suppose two young farm boys took time out from their work in the fields. They were trying to figure out a way to till the land faster. The father of one boy said, "That is a good thing to think about. Tell me how we might do it faster." The father of the other boy said, "We have always done it this way. There is no other better way. Talk about change will waste time, but will not help." Which father said the wiser words?

Except for a few minor differences, our modernity items are identical to what Inkeles and his group calls the OM–12 scale. We decided not to use two items which formed part of the Inkeles scale. The first, "If schooling were freely available, how much schooling do you think children of people like yourself should have?" was incorrectly translated in one version of the interview used in Kenya and therefore we had to discard it in the index construction. The second item "What should most qualify a man to hold high office?" was also dropped because it did not discriminate between the respondents in all three countries. Responses to these eleven items were summed to form an index with scores ranging from a low modernity of 0 to a high modernity of 11.

22. See chapter 2 for a brief description of how the elites, or local notables, were selected.

## 10. SALIENCE, SATISFACTION, AND SUPPORT

1. Malcolm E. Jewell and Samuel C. Patterson, *The Legislative Process in the United States*, 3rd ed. (New York: Random House, 1977), 302–305.

2. The index of legislative institutional salience was based on these four items: (1) The proportion of respondents who knew the approximate size of the legislature. (2) The proportion who were able to mention something that distinguished the legislature from other political institutions. (3) The proportion who were able to distinguish between the function of the MP and that of the civil servant. (4) The proportion who could remember when the country had no legislature (or, in the case of Kenya, when Africans could not run for the legislature).

The index of individual legislative salience was based on these three items: (1) The proportion who were able to name their legislator (in Korea and Turkey, those who could name at least one legislator). (2) The proportion who were able to make a judgment about whether their legislator was doing a good job in telling the government what people wanted (the job mentioned as most important by constituents in all three countries). (3) The proportion who were able to make a judgment about whether most legislators in the country were honest (the quality ranked as most important by constituents in all three countries).

The two indexes were constructed by summing the number of salient responses. The institutional salience index was based on four survey items with scores ranging from a low of 0 to a high of 4. Similarly, the individual MP salience index was constructed from responses to three items, with scores ranging from a low of 0 to a high of 3.

3. David Easton, *A Systems Analysis of Political Life* (New York: John Wiley, 1965), 343–50.

## 11. MULTIVARIATE ANALYSIS OF LEGISLATIVE SUPPORT

1. See Otis Dudley Duncan, "Path Analysis: Sociological Examples," *American Journal of Sociology* 72 (July 1966): 1–16; Kenneth C. Land, "Principles of Path Analysis," in *Sociological Methodology*, E. F. Borgatta, ed. (San Francisco: Jossey-Bass, 1969), 3–37; Hubert M. Blalock, ed., *Causal Models in Social Sciences* (Chicago: Aldine Prss, 1971).

2. In an effort to measure the level of individual modernity we have employed the OM–12 scale. See D. H. Smith and A. Inkeles, "The OM Scale: A Comparative Socio-Psychological Measure of Individual Modernity," *Sociometry* 29 (December 1966): 353–77.

3. For a detailed analysis of interdistrict variations, see Chong Lim Kim and Seong-Tong Pai, *Legislative Process in Korea* (Seoul: Seoul National University Press, 1981), 295–320.

4. See Malcolm E. Jewell and Chong Lim Kim, "Sources of Support for the Legislature of a Developing Nation: The Case of Korea," *Comparative Political Studies* 8 (January 1976): 478–84.

## 12. THE LEGISLATURE AND POLITICAL DEVELOPMENT

1. Adam Przeworski and Henry Teune, *The Logic of Comparative Social Inquiry* (New York: John Wiley, 1970), 74.

2. Ibid., 45.

3. Ibid., 53–56.

4. Ibid., 84.

5. Ibid., 68–72.

6. For a detailed analysis of the field work in one country, see Ilter Turan, "Survey Research in a Developing Country: Field Work in Turkey" (Iowa City: Comparative Legislative Research Center, University of Iowa, 1975).

7. Przeworski and Teune, *The Logic of Comparative Social Inquiry*, chs. 5 and 6.

8. Alex Inkeles and David H. Smith, *Becoming Modern* (Cambridge: Harvard University Press, 1974).

9. For the best example of such research, dealing with U. S. congressmen, see Richard F. Fenno, Jr., *Home Style: House Members in Their Districts* (Boston: Little, Brown, 1978).

10. See, for example, Richard Sisson and Lawrence L. Shrader, "Social Representation and Political Integration in an Indian State: The Legislative Dimension," in *Legislatures in Plural Societies*, Albert R. Eldridge, ed. (Durham: Duke University Press, 1977), ch. 2.

11. Heinz Eulau and Paul D. Karps, "The Puzzle of Representation: Specifying Components of Responsiveness," *Legislative Studies Quarterly* 2 (1977): 241.

12. Manindra K. Mohapatra, "The Ombudsmanic Role of Legislators in an Indian State," *Legislative Studies Quarterly* 1 (1976): 295–314.

13. Iqbal Narain and Shashi Lata Puri, "Legislators in an Indian State: A Study of Role Images and the Pattern of Constituency Linkages," *Legislative Studies Quarterly* 1 (1976): 315–30.

14. Shriram Maheshwari, "Constituency Linkage of National Legislators in India," *Legislative Studies Quarterly* 1 (1976): 331–54.

15. M. C. Kumbhat and Y. M. Marican, "Constituent Orientation Among Malaysian State Legislators," Michael Ong, "The Member of Parliament and His Constituency: The Malaysian Case," and Chan Heng Chee, "The Role of Parliamentary Politicians in Singapore," *Legislative Studies Quarterly* 1 (1976): 389–404, 405–22, 423–42.

16. Lloyd D. Musolf and J. Fred Springer, "Legislatures and Divided Societies: The Malaysian Parliament and Multi-Ethnicity," *Legislative Studies Quarterly* 2 (1977): 113–36.

17. George H. Gadbois, Malcolm E. Jewell, and Christine Sylvester, "The Representative Roles and Accountability of Legislators in Papua New Guinea" (paper prepared for presentation at the 1978 meeting of the Midwest Political Science Association. For similar findings from other countries see G. R. Boynton and Chong Lim Kim, eds., *Legislative Systems in Developing Countries* (Durham: Duke University Press, 1975).

18. See, for example, Robert E. Dowse, "The M.P. and His Surgery," in *The Backbencher and Parliament*, Dick Leonard and Valentine Herman, eds. (London: St. Martins, 1972), 46–61; Anthony Barker and Michael Ruch, *The Member of Parliament and His Information* (London: Allen Unwin, 1970).

19. Allan Kornberg and William Mishler, *Influence in Parliament: Canada* (Durham: Duke University Press, 1976), 83, 88–89.

20. Harold D. Clarke, "Determinants of Provincial Constituency Service Behavior: A Multivariate Analysis," *Legislative Studies Quarterly* 3 (1978): 601–18.

21. See, for example, Morris P. Fiorina, *Congress: Keystone of the Washington Establishment* (New Haven: Yale University Press, 1977); David Cover, "The Advantage of Incumbency in Congressional Elections" (unpublished Ph.D. dissertation, Yale University, 1976).

22. Gerhard Loewenberg, "Representative Linkages" (paper prepared for presentation at the Conference on "The Role of European Parliaments in Managing Social Conflict" (Stonybrook, New York: August 1978).

23. See, however, Robert J. Jackson, "Committees in the Philippine Congress," in *Committees in Legislatures*, John D. Lees and Malcolm Shaw, eds. (Durham: Duke University Press, 1979), ch. 5; and David L. Morrell, "Thailand's Legislature and Economic Development Decision," in *Legislatures in Development*, Joel Smith and Lloyd D. Musolf, eds. (Durham: Duke University Press, 1979), ch. 15.

24. Fenno, *Home Style: House Members in Their Districts.*

25. Ong, "The Member of Parliament and His Constituency: The Malaysian Case," *Legislative Studies Quarterly* 1 (1976): 405–22.

26. See, however, Loewenberg, "Representative Linkages." For a comparison of single and multimember districts in American state legislatures, see Malcolm E. Jewell, "Metropolitan Representation: State Legislative Districting in Urban Counties" (New York: National Municipal League, 1969).

# INDEX

65, 66, 217; and resource allocation, 12, 66, 217

Senate of the Republic (Turkey), 46, 48

Sessional Committee (Kenyan National Assembly), 31, 32, 126

Socialism: and economic development, 63, 64, 65; in Turkish politics, 43, 45, 64

Society for Revitalizing Reforms (Korea), 37, 38, 122, 123

Special interests. *See* Interest groups

Specific resource allocation: definition of, 11, 119, 130, 141; and economic and political development, 216–17; and representative linkages, 141, 211–12; role of civil servants in, 127–28; role of legislature in, 119, 126; role of legislators in, 12, 14, 76, 94, 127, 141–56, 215, 216–17. *See also* Resource allocation

Springer, J. Fred, 213

Sylvester, Christine, 213

Teune, Henry, 16, 207–8

Tribes, Kenyan. *See* Ethnic differences

Turkey: general resource allocation in, 128–39 passim, 215–16; geographic and socio-economic background of, 42–43; lack of sectional and ethnic differences in, 7, 21, 43; legislative electoral process and districts in, 17, 46, 49, 70, 75, 92, 123, 124, 155, 210–11; legislative-executive relations in, 7–8, 42, 46–48, 75–76, 77, 91, 120, 134, 174; legislative history of, 16–17, 40–42, 46, 91; legislative recruitment in, 59–60, 61–62, 211; legislative support in, 165–69, 171–72, 176, 181–98 passim; legislator-constituent relations in, 79–82, 84, 85, 143–44, 150–54, 201–2; legislators' views on economic development in, 64, 103–4, 133, 145–47, 212; linkage forms in, 113, 114; linkage role of legislators in political development of, 5, 219; membership, organization, and procedures in legislature of, 46–49, 61–62, 121, 125–26, 215–16; political parties in, 17, 41–42, 44–49, 57, 70, 71, 75, 81, 84, 85–86, 121, 123, 129, 132, 133; public expectations and evaluation of legislators in, 93–94, 96, 97, 98, 100, 101, 108, 177–91 passim, 194, 196, 198, 201–2, 215; public views on economic development in, 103–4, 145–47; purposive and behavioral roles of legislators in, 70–86 passim, 94, 96, 98, 100, 108, 137, 142–43, 215, 216; salience of legislature and legislators in, 91, 92, 93, 174–76, 177, 178, 181, 186, 188–91, 194, 196, 201–2, 214; social backgrounds of legislators in, 53–58, 211; specific resource allocation in, 142, 145–47, 148–49, 152–55; urbanization/rurality in, 7, 42–43, 56–57

Turkish Labor Party, 45

United Nations Temporary Commission on Korea (UNTCOK), 33

Urbanization/rurality, 29, 30, 35, 42–43, 56, 57, 58; and economic development, 6, 7, 63, 65–66; effects of on legislative salience, satisfaction, and support, 162, 168, 180, 201, 202; effects of on legislators' purposive and behavioral roles, 71, 76, 77, 110, 212, 219; and modernity, 170; and sectionalism, 6–7; and specific resource allocation, 149, 150, 153–54, 156

Verba, Sidney, 87–88, 91

Wahlke, John C., 104

*Yushin* Constitution (Korea), 37–38, 39–40, 120

## ABOUT THE AUTHORS

CHONG LIM KIM is Director of the Comparative Legislative Research Center and Professor of Political Science, University of Iowa.

JOEL D. BARKAN is Professor of Political Science, University of Iowa.

ILTER TURAN is Professor of Political Science, the Faculty of Political Science, University of Istanbul.

MALCOLM E. JEWELL is Professor of Political Science, University of Kentucky.